THE NAVAL WAR OF 1812

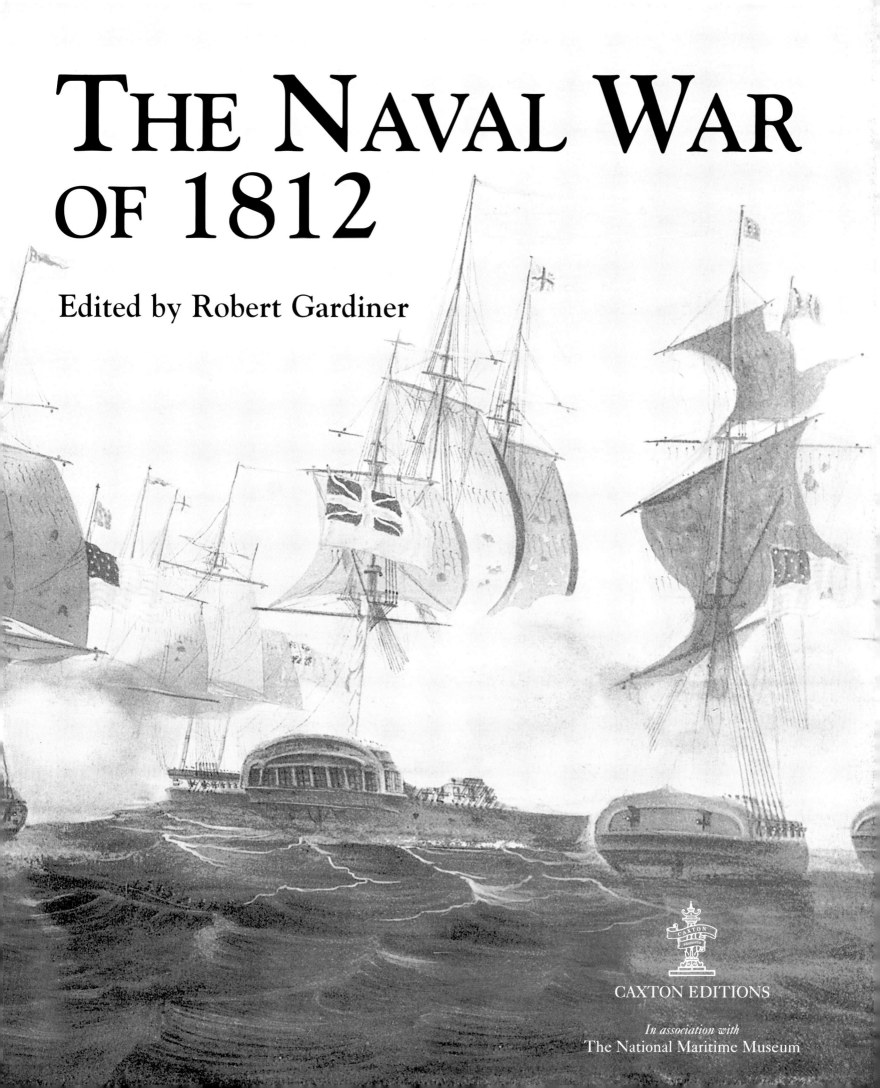

THE NAVAL WAR
OF 1812

Edited by Robert Gardiner

CAXTON EDITIONS

In association with
The National Maritime Museum

Contributors

Andrew Lambert
General Introduction

Robert Malcomson
Part II: War on the Great Lakes

Robert Gardiner

Part I: War on the high seas
Part III: The war on the coasts
     except:

Roger Morriss
Raiding in the Chesapeake in 1813
Burning Washington
Gordon's diversion on the Potomac
Baltimore reprieved

Stephen Chumbley
The New Orleans campaign

Julian Mannering
Notes on artists

FRONTISPIECE
A watercolour by George Thresher of Perry's victory
of September 1813 which gained control of Lake
Erie. Seapower was crucial to virtually every theatre
in this war, and it was only the intervention of the US
Navy in the campaign on the Canadian border that
saved the United States from disaster.
US Naval Acadamy Museum ref 76.27.1

Copyright © Chatham Publishing 1998

First published in Great Britain in 1998 by
Chatham Publishing, an imprint of Gerald
Duckworth & Co Ltd

This Edition Published 2001 by Caxton Editions
an imprint of The Caxton Publishing Group
ISBN 1 84067 3605

British Library cataloguing in Publication Data
A catalogue record for this book is available
from the British Library

Designed and typeset by Tony Hart, Isle of Wight
Printed and bound by C.T.P.S.

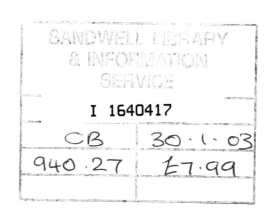

Contents

Thematic pages in italic

Preface

THE CHATHAM Pictorial Histories are intended to give the modern reader an impression of how the naval events of previous centuries were seen by those involved, or presented to the public by the visual media of the day – painters, engravers and printsellers. One of our concerns has been to seek out the less familiar, and in some cases the never previously published, so while we do use some finished paintings, we have preferred the artist's own sketchbooks where available; they reveal not only the lengths the painters went to get details correct, but often cover occurrences that are not otherwise represented, or where the art world has lost track of the finished work.

In the search for original and, if possible, eyewitness depictions, we have also dipped into some of the logs, journals and contemporary manuscripts. Naval officers, in particular, were encouraged to observe closely, and part of the training process involved making sketches of everything from coastal features to life on board. For this volume the search has extended to nearly twenty archives in three countries.

However, the series was specifically inspired by the Prints and Drawings collection of the National Maritime Museum at Greenwich, on the outskirts of London. Reckoned to comprise 66,000 images, it is a surprisingly under-used resource, despite the fact that an ongoing copying programme has made three-quarters of it available on microfilm. While this forms the core of the series, we have also had recourse to the Admiralty Collection of ship draughts - itself running to about 100,000 plans – as well as some reference to the charts collection in the Navigation Department and logs and personal journals kept by the Manuscripts Department. This last is a very substantial holding with no easy mode of access to any illustrations it may contain, so although some work has been done in this area, it must be said that there is probably far more to discover if only time were available for the task.

The series is intended first and foremost to illustrate the great events of maritime history, and we have made little attempt to pass artistic judgement on any of the images, which were chosen for content rather than style. The pictures are grouped, as far as practical, to show how events were presented at the time. Since this is not primarily a work of art history, for the technical credits we have relied on the Maritime Museum's extant indexing, the product of a massive and long-running documentation programme by many hands with some inevitable inconsistencies, depending on the state of knowledge at the time each item was catalogued. We have reproduced what information there is, only correcting obviously wrong attributions and dates, and quoting the negative number or unique reference number of each illustration for anyone wishing to obtain copies of these from the museum or archive concerned.

The Naval War of 1812 is the final volume of five titles covering the whole of the period of the great French wars from 1793 to 1815. The series follows the order of the original events, and each covers its period completely. However, the thematic spreads are cumulative in their coverage, because we are keen to illustrate many general aspects of the weapons and warfare of the period which stand outside the chronological structure. Therefore, we devised a single programme of such topics and simply positioned each at an appropriate point in the series. The best example is provided by the many features on individual ship types and their roles, which through this five-volume set add up to a complete analysis of the function of the Royal Navy's order of battle. This, we believe, avoids predictability and gives every volume variety and additional interest.

Acknowledgements

In terms of picture research this has been the most difficult volume of the series for the simple reason that the illustrations have come from a large number of sources spread across three countries. In the early stages I was heavily dependent on advice from Bob Malcomson about Canadian archives, and on help from Major Grant Walker in chasing up some of those in the United States. It was also a learning experience, and I enjoyed an enlightening correspondence with Claudia Jew of The Mariners' Museum, Newport News about Irwin Bevan.

Obtaining the photoprints would have been impossible without the courtesy and efficiency of individuals in many institutions, and I am particularly indebted to the following in the USA: Sigrid R Trumpy, Curator of the Beverley R Robinson Collection at Annapolis; also at Annapolis, Jim Cheevors, Curator of oil paintings at the US Naval Academy Museum; Jennifer Davis Heaps, Maps and Plans Group, US National Archives and Records Administration, College Park, Maryland; Charlotte Houtz and Eveline S Overmiller, Library of Congress, Washington; Jennifer M Lloyd, Photographic Section, Naval Historical Center, Washington; Jean Rees of the Peabody Essex Museum, Salem; Arlene Shy of the William L Clements Library, University of Michigan; Peter Harrington, Curator of the Anne S K Brown Military Collection, Brown University Library, Providence, Rhode Island; and also the Smithsonian Institution, Washington, and the Erie County Society.

A similar vote of thanks must be extended in Canada to: Jennifer Spaans, Reference Officer, National Archives of Canada; Tania Henley, Special Collections, Metropolitan Toronto Reference Library; Raymonde Cadorette and Kate O'Rourke of the Archives of Ontario; Melissa Thompson, Registration Coordinator, Royal Ontario Museum; and Benoit Cameron, Massey Library, Royal Military College, Kingston.

In Britain I am grateful to the Merseyside Maritime Museum, Liverpool for permission to use an illustration from the Samuel Walters journal. Despite the foregoing, however, by far the largest single source of illustration was still the National Maritime Museum, and my thanks in proportion are due to David Taylor of the Picture Library for his role as the great facilitator.

Robert Gardiner
London, September 1998

Sources

Introduction
R Brown, *The Republic in Peril, 1812* (New York 1964)
P Coletta, *American Secretaries of the Navy* (Annapolis 1980)
W S Dudley (ed), *The Naval War of 1812: A Documentary History*, Vols I & II (Washington, DC 1985 & 1992)
J C Fredriksen (ed), *Free Trade and Sailors' Rights: A Bibliography of the War of 1812* (Westport, Connecticut 1985)
D E Graves, *The Battle of Lundy's Lane: On the Niagara in 1814* (Baltimore 1983)
J M Hitsman, *The Incredible War of 1812* (Toronto 1965)
W James, *Naval History of Great Britain*, 6 vols (London 1826)
B Jenkins, *Henry Goulburn 1784-1856: A Political Biography* (Quebec 1996)
A T Mahan, *The Influence of Sea Power Upon the War of 1812*, 2 vols (Boston 1905)
R Morriss, *Cockburn and the British Navy in Transition: Admiral Sir George Cockburn 1772-1853* (Exeter 1997)
C A Mckee, *Gentlemanly and Honourable Profession: the Creation of the US Naval Officer Corps, 1794-1815* (Annapolis 1991)
P Padfield, *Broke and the Shannon* (London 1968)
T Roosevelt, *Naval History of the War of 1812* (New York 1882)
J C A Stagg, *Mr Madison's War: Politics, Diplomacy and Warfare in the early American Republic 1783-1830* (Princeton 1983)
C L Symonds, *Navalists and Anti-Navalists: The Naval Policy of the United States, 1785-1827* (Newark, New Jersey 1980).

The slide into war
K Jack Bauer, *A Maritime History of the United States* (Columbia, South Carolina 1988)
W S Dudley (ed), *The Naval War of 1812*, Vol I
George Selement, 'Impressment and the American Merchant Marine 1782-1812: an American View', *The Mariner's Mirror* 59 (Nov 1973)

Part I War on the high seas
W S Dudley (ed), *The Naval War of 1812*, Vols I & II
J C Fredriksen (ed), *War of 1812 Eyewitness Accounts: An Annotated Bibliography* (Westport, Connecticut 1997)
A T Mahan, *The Influence of Sea Power Upon the War of 1812*
B R Mitchell, *European Historical Statistics 1750-1975* (London 1975)
James Duncan Phillips, *Salem and the Indies* (Boston 1947)

The United States Navy in 1812
American State Papers: Class VI: Naval Affairs, Vol I (Washington, DC 1834)
K Jack Bauer & Stephen S Roberts, *Register of Ships of the US Navy 1775-1990: Major Combatants* (Westport, Connecticut 1991)
Howard Chapelle, *The History of the American Sailing Navy* (New York 1959)
W S Dudley (ed), *The Naval War of 1812*, Vols I & II
William M Fowler, 'America's Super-Frigates', *The Mariner's Mirror* 59 (Feb 1973)

Spencer C Tucker, *The Jeffersonian Gunboat Navy* (Columbia, South Carolina 1993)

Lucky escapes
W S Dudley (ed), *The Naval War of 1812*, Vol I
W James, *Naval History of Great Britain*, Vol VI

First blood
W S Dudley (ed), *The Naval War of 1812*, Vol I
E S Maclay, *A History of American Privateers* (London 1900)
A T Mahan, *The Influence of Sea Power Upon the War of 1812*, Vol I

Constitution **versus** *Guerriere*
W S Dudley (ed), *The Naval War of 1812*, Vol I
Benson J Lossing, *Pictorial Field Book of the War of 1812* (New York 1869)
A T Mahan, *The Influence of Sea Power Upon the War of 1812*, Vol I
Tyrone G Martin, *A Most Fortunate Ship* (2nd ed, Annapolis 1996)

Frolic **versus** *Wasp*
W S Dudley (ed), *The Naval War of 1812*, Vol I
Robert McHenry (ed), *Webster's American Military Biographies* (New York 1978)
Charles Loftus, *My Youth by Land and Sea*, Vol I (London 1876)

United States **versus** *Macedonian*
Anon [Samuel Leech], 'We Must Fight Her', *US Naval Institute Proceedings* 99 (1973)
A T Mahan, *The Influence of Sea Power Upon the War of 1812*, Vol I
Samuel Leech, *Thirty Years from Home* (Boston 1843)
James Tertius de Kay, *Chronicles of the Frigate Macedonian 1809-1922* (New York & London 1995)

Constitution **versus** *Java*
W S Dudley (ed), *The Naval War of 1812*, Vol I
A T Mahan, *The Influence of Sea Power Upon the War of 1812*, Vol I
Tyrone G Martin, *A Most Fortunate Ship*

Hornet
Alan Conrad Aimone, 'The Cruise of the US Sloop Hornet in 1815', *The Mariner's Mirror* 61 (Nov 1975)
Harding Craig, Jr, 'Notes on the Action between Hornet and Peacock', *The American Neptune* 11 (Jan 1951)
W S Dudley (ed), *The Naval War of 1812*, Vols I & II

Shannon **versus** *Chesapeake*
J G Brighton, *Admiral Sir P V B Broke: A Memoir* (London 1866)
P Padfield, *Broke and the Shannon*

Brigs at war, 1813
W S Dudley (ed), *The Naval War of 1812*, Vol II

American privateers
Howard Chapelle, *The Baltimore Clipper: Its Origin and Development* (1930, reprinted New York 1969)
E S Maclay, *A History of American Privateers*
J R Garitee, *The Republic's Private Navy: The American Privateering Business as Practised by Baltimore during the War of 1812* (Middletown, Connecticut 1977)

War as business: privateers in action
Privateers v small cruisers
George Coggeshall's *History of American Privateers* (New York 1856)
E S Maclay, *A History of American Privateers*
J R Garitee, *The Republic's Private Navy*

Irwin Bevan's War of 1812
Notes from the Mariner's Museum, by courtesy of Claudia A Jew
W S Dudley (ed), *The Naval War of 1812*, Vol II
E S Maclay, *A History of American Privateers*
J R Garitee, *The Republic's Private Navy*

The destruction of American trade
K Jack Bauer, *A Maritime History of the United States*
James Duncan Phillips, *Salem and the Indies*

Ships of the Royal Navy: schooners
David Lyon, *The Sailing Navy List* (London 1993)

Cruise of the *Essex*
W S Dudley (ed), *The Naval War of 1812*, Vol II
Parker H Kemble, 'The USS Essex versus HMS Phoebe', *US Naval Institute Proceedings* 57 (1931)
A T Mahan, *The Influence of Sea Power Upon the War of 1812*, Vol II
Naval Chronicle XXXII (1814).
Richard Woodman, *The Victory of Seapower* (London & Annapolis 1998)

Sloops of war – the new generation
Lt William Bowers, *Naval Adventures During Thirty-Five Years Service*, 2 vols (London 1833)
Deposition of Benjamin Waine, Acting Pilot of the Frolic, 14 May 1814, printed in *New York Public Library Bulletin* 7 (August 1903)
Robert McHenry (ed), *Webster's American Military Biographies*
A T Mahan, *The Influence of Sea Power Upon the War of 1812*, Vol II

Ships of the Royal Navy: brig sloops
Lt William Bowers, *Naval Adventures During Thirty-Five Years Service*
David Lyon, *The Sailing Navy List*

Warrington and the *Peacock*
Lady Bourchier (ed), *Memoir of the Life of Admiral Sir Edward Codrington*, Vol I (London 1873)
A T Mahan, *The Influence of Sea Power Upon the War of 1812*, Vol II
Commander R W Mindte, 'Another Navy Rodgers', *American Neptune* 19 (July 1959)

Constitution's **last victory**
Tyrone G Martin, *A Most Fortunate Ship*

Part II War on the Great Lakes
Howard Chapelle, *The History of the American Sailing Navy*
E A Cruikshank, *The Documentary History of the Campaign on the Niagara Frontier in 1814*, Vol 2 (Welland 1897)
_____, 'The Contest for the Command of Lake Erie in 1812-1813', *Transactions of the Royal Society of Canada* 6 (1899)
_____, 'An Episode of the War of 1812: The Story of the Schooner *Nancy*', *Ontario History* 9 (1910)
_____, 'The Contest for Control of Lake Ontario in 1812 and 1813', *Transactions of the Royal Society of Canada* 10 (1916)
_____, 'The Contest for Control of Lake Ontario in 1814', *Ontario History* 21 (1924)
W S Dudley (ed), *The Naval War of 1812*, Vols I & II
A S Everest, *The War of 1812 in the Champlain Valley* (Syracuse, New York 1981)
Paul L Ford (ed), *The Works of Thomas Jefferson*, Vol 2 (New York 1905)
David Wingfield, 'Four Years on the Lakes of Canada. . .', National Archives of Canada, MG 24, F 18

Lake Ontario, 1813
E A Cruikshank, 'The Contest for Control of Lake Ontario in 1812 and 1813'
William Dudley (ed), *The Naval War of 1812*, Vol II
Robert Malcomson, *Lords of the Lake: The Naval War on Lake Ontario, 1812-1814* (Toronto 1998)
_____ (ed), *Sailors of 1812: Memoirs and Letters of Naval Officers on Lake Ontario* (Youngstown 1997)
David Wingfield, 'Four Years on the Lakes of Canada . . .'

British shipbuilding on the Lakes
Howard Chapelle, *The History of the American Sailing Navy*
Robert Malcomson, 'HMS *St Lawrence*: The Freshwater First-Rate', *The Mariner's Mirror* 83 (Nov 1997)
Jonathan Moore, *Preserve Our Wrecks (Kingston): Photo Project Final Report* (Kingston 1997)
R A Preston, 'The Fate of Kingston's Warships', *Ontario History* 44 (1952)

Perry on Lake Erie
W S Dudley, (ed) *The Naval War of 1812*, Vol II
Robert and Thomas Malcomson, *HMS Detroit: The Battle for Lake Erie* (Annapolis 1991)
W J Welsh and D C Skaggs, *War on the Great Lakes: Essays Commemorating the 175th Anniversary of the Battle of Lake Erie* (London 1991)

The shipbuilders' war and the attack on Oswego
E A Cruikshank, 'The Contest for Control of Lake Ontario in 1814'
Robert Malcomson, *Lords of the Lake*

Ships-in-frame: the fir frigates
Extracts of House of Lords, Accounts and Papers, Vol 75, 13 February 1815, p12, Report No 9, PRO

Thomas Malcomson, 'HMS *Psyche*: A Frigate in Frame', *Seaways' Ships in Scale* 4 (1993)

The Battle of Plattsburgh, 11 September 1814
K J Crisman, *The Eagle: An American Brig on Lake Champlain during the War of 1812* (Annapolis 1987)
A S Everest, *The War of 1812 in the Champlain Valley*

American shipbuilding on the Lakes
Howard Chapelle, *The History of the American Sailing Navy*
J F Cooper, *Ned Myers: or A Life Before the Mast* (Philadelphia 1843; reprinted Annapolis 1989)
K J Crisman, *The Jefferson: The History and Archaeology of an American Brig from the War of 1812* (Ann Arbor, Michigan 1989)
Daniel and William Dobbins, 'The Dobbins Papers', *Buffalo Historical Society Publications* Vol 8 (1905)
Richard F Palmer, 'James Fenimore Cooper and the Navy Brig *Oneida*', *Inland Seas* 40 (1984)
Max Rosenburg, *The Building of Perry's Fleet on Lake Erie: 1812-1813* (Harrisburg, Pennsylvania 1987)

Mackinac and the struggle for the Upper Lakes
Andrew Bulger, *An Autobiographical Sketch of Captain Andrew Bulger* (Bangalore 1865)
E A Cruikshank, 'An Episode of the War of 1812: The Story of the Schooner *Nancy*'
Brian L Dunnigan, *The British Army at Mackinac: 1812-1815* (Mackinac, Michigan 1980)
J D Haeger, *John Jacob Astor: Business and Finance in the Early Republic* (Detroit 1991)

Part III The war on the coasts
Robert J Barrett, 'Naval Recollections of the late American War', *United Services Journal* (London, April & May 1841)
K Jack Bauer, *A Maritime History of the United States*
Abraham Crawford, *Reminiscences of a Naval Officer* (London 1851)
W S Dudley (ed), *The Naval War of 1812*, Vols I & II
James Duncan Phillips, *Salem and the Indies*

Ships of the Royal Navy: 80-gun ships
Captain Frederick Hoffman, *A Sailor of King George* (London 1901)

The blockade
W S Dudley (ed), *The Naval War of 1812*, Vols I & II
Joseph A Goldenberg, 'Blue Lights and Infernal Machines: The British Blockade of New London', *The Mariner's Mirror* 61 (Nov 1975)

Raiding in the Chesapeake in 1813
Burning Washington
Gordon's diversion on the Potomac
Baltimore reprieved
R Morriss, *Cockburn and the British Navy in Transition*

Steam, torpedoes and rockets
Robert Fulton, *Torpedo War, and Submarine Explosions* (New York 1810)
Joseph A Goldenberg, 'Blue Lights and Infernal Machines: The British Blockade of New London'
Wallace S Hutcheon, Jr, *Robert Fulton: Pioneer of Undersea Warfare* (Annapolis 1981)
Alex Roland, *Underwater Warfare in the Age of Sail* (Bloomington, Indiana 1978)

W B Rowbotham, 'Robert Fulton's Turtle Boat', *US Naval Institute Proceedings* 62 (1936)
Frank H Winter, *The First Golden Age of Rocketry* (Washington & London 1990)

Ships of the Royal Navy: big frigates
R Gardiner, *The Heavy Frigate*, Vol 1 (London 1994), and research for Vol 2

Capture of the President
J G Brighton, *Admiral Sir P V B Broke*
A T Mahan, *The Influence of Sea Power Upon the War of 1812*, Vol II

The occupation of Maine
W James, *Military Occurrences of the Late War between Great Britain and the United States of America*, Vol II (London 1818)
A T Mahan, *The Influence of Sea Power Upon the War of 1812*, Vol II

The southern theatre
W S Dudley (ed), *The Naval War of 1812*, Vols I & II

The New Orleans campaign
Lady Bourchier (ed), *Memoirs of the Life of Admiral Sir Edward Codrington*, Vol I
William Laird Clowes, *The Royal Navy*, Vol VI (reprinted London 1997)
Tim Pickles, *New Orleans 1815*, Osprey Campaigns Series No 28 (London 1993)

Prisoners of war
F Abell, *Prisoners of War in Britain, 1756-1814* (London 1914)
W S Dudley (ed), *The Naval War of 1812*, Vols I & II
Brian Lavery, *Nelson's Navy* (London 1989)

POSTSCRIPT: 1815 - The Hundred Days
W James, *Naval History of Great Britain*, Vol VI
A T Mahan, *The Influence of Sea Power Upon the War of 1812*, Vol 2
James Pack, *The man who burned the White House: Admiral Sir George Cockburn 1772-1853* (Annapolis 1987)

Notes on Artists
E H H Archibald, *Dictionary of Sea Painters* (Woodbridge, England 1980)
E Bénézit, *Dictionnaire critique et documentaire de Peintres, Sculpteurs, Dessinateurs et Graveurs* (Paris 1976)
James F Carr, *Mantle Fielding's Dictionary of American Painters, Sculptors and Engravers* (New York 1965)
Maurice Harold Grant, *A Dictionary of British Etchers* (London 1952)
George C Grose and David H Wallace, *The New York Historical Society's Dictionary of Artists in America 1564-1860* (Newhaven and London 1957)
Ian Mackensie, *British Prints: Dictionary and Price Guide* (Woodbridge, England, 1987)
Lister Raymond, *Prints and Printmaking* (London 1984)
Ronald Vere Tooley, *Tooley's Dictionary of Mapmakers* (New York and Amsterdam 1979)
Jane Turner (ed), *The Dictionary of Art* (London 1996)
Ellis Waterhouse, *The Dictionary of 18th Century Painters in Oils and Crayons* (Woodbridge, England 1980)
Arnold Wilson, *A Dictionary of British Marine Painters* (Leigh-on-Sea, England 1967)

INTRODUCTION

THE WAR of 1812 was a by product of the Napoleonic War of 1803 to 1814. Its origins lay in the increasingly oppressive measures adopted by France and Britain to undermine the economies of their rivals, and the problems these created for the largest, and most dynamic, neutral maritime trading nation. The fractured state of American domestic politics also played a significant part in forming the crisis, and greatly affected the conduct of the war.

After the outbreak of the Revolutionary War in 1793 American shippers had developed a major interest in transporting the produce of French, Dutch and Spanish colonies back to Europe, circumventing the British blockade. Between 1794 and 1807 this trade increased thirty-fold, providing the springboard for the development of American shipping. It also undercut the exports of the British West Indian Islands, which fell by 50 per cent between 1802 and 1806. The subsequent collapse of sugar prices severely damaged the British West Indian economy, which brought a powerful group of Members of Parliament to lobby the Government for aid. The British Government was also under pressure to improve the economic condition of Canada. The American advantage was built on cheap ships, which reflected the cost of timber at the shipyard. Here the United States had a great advantage over Britain, which imported much of its timber from the Baltic, and the American merchant marine began to undercut the British as deep-sea carriers. This formed a fundamental element in the economic crisis of 1806-07 that threatened the very survival of Britain, and encouraged Napoleon to persist with his Continental System.

The British response was wide-ranging, and highly effective. The Admiralty Courts reintroduced the 'Rule of 1756' which denied neutral carriers access to the lucrative colonial trade, even if the ships had stopped at an American port. The West Indian planters then demanded, and secured, a blockade of the remaining French sugar islands, which were later captured, to exclude the Americans. This was followed up by a wide-ranging campaign against American shipping on every ocean. In this context the attack on the USS *Chesapeake* by HMS *Leopard* can be seen as merely one element in a programme to coerce the United States. Two months later the man who ordered the attack, Vice-Admiral Sir George Berkeley, commanding on the North America Station, proposed a preventive strike on New York to destroy American shipping and fishing vessels and demand an enormous war indemnity. Instead the Ministers relieved Berkeley, disavowed the attack on the *Chesapeake* and, in November, introduced the Orders in Council. While the Orders in Council were a response to Napoleon's Continental System, they were equally effective in destroying the basis of American maritime prosperity. For Britain, fighting for her survival, they were necessary measures; for the United States, seeking to profit from the war, they were a threat to her new-found affluence.

In essence the issues of the war were maritime. Britain, the dominant seapower, sought to use her sea control for strategic ends, relying on naval power and legal instruments to impose her strength. The instruments included the age old right to impress British subjects for service aboard His Majesty's warships. The rigorous, and not particularly careful, application of this right on board American merchant ships on the high seas resulted in the impressment of some thousands of American citizens, men whose language and culture had yet to diverge sufficiently from that of their motherland to make their allegiance obvious. The question was further blurred by native-born Englishmen who secured genuine American citizenship, although there was also a flourishing trade in bogus naturalisation papers.

The American response to the British attack on their maritime economy was largely handled by James Madison, first as Secretary of State under Thomas Jefferson, and after 1809, as President. Madison's actions were dominated by a concern for the sanctity of the republican system of government, and the survival of the Republican party. For the Government to accept the British imposition would be a national humiliation, and almost certainly fatal to the party. Madison considered the continuation of British economic pressure would inflict severe financial harm on all Americans, not just merchants and shipowners. He believed that the most powerful weapon in the American diplomatic arsenal was to deny Britain access to the raw materials of North America, especially 'naval stores'.

Although Anglo-American relations worsened steadily after the return to war in Europe in 1803, it was not until 1806 that any American action was taken. The Non-Importation Law of April 1806 was a weak measure of limited coercive potential. In December 1807, following the Orders in Council and the Berlin Decree, a Trade Embargo was adopted, cutting off all commerce with the belligerents, to remain in force until the coercive legislation of the British or French was repealed. However, the Republican government was unable to make the measure effective, because the northern states, which were predominantly Federalist, engaged in large scale smuggling across the vast, effectively uncontrolled land, river and sea borders with Canada and Newfoundland. In early 1809 Congress replaced the Embargo with the Non-Intercourse Act, which Madison considered useless, although he did try to trade its repeal for the retraction of the Orders in Council. When American coercive diplomacy was ignored, Madison dismissed the British minister, but his efforts were undermined by opposition within his own party, and Napoleon's decision in early 1810 to seize American ships in French ports. In October 1810 the French promised they would repeal the Berlin and Milan Decrees as they affected the Americans, a claim which Madison accepted without waiting for proof. In fact, Napoleon was playing on Republican hopes to increase pressure on the British: he had no intention of carrying the repeal into effect.

The European war and problems of access to Baltic timber and naval stores led the British to promote the development of Canadian timber resources, and by 1807 Canada was supplying more timber than the Baltic. Much of the material was actually smuggled into Canada from America. At the same time Canadian shipbuilding was encouraged, to build mer-

'Map of the Seat of War in North America', a good example of contemporary American cartography: Plate 1 from A Military and Topographical Atlas of the United States, *published by John Mellish, Philadelphia, 1815.* Chatham collection

chant ships as cheaply as the Americans, increasing the number of seamen and deep-sea fishermen. This dramatic rise in Canadian activity threatened Madison's trump card, by making Britain independent of American raw materials. If he was going to coerce Britain now he would have to conquer Canada and impose a full scale embargo. The increasing economic value of Canadian shipping, notably that which replaced the Americans in supplying the West Indies with lumber, fish and grain, brought many more British warships onto the American coast, and another example of impressment from an American ship lead to a clash between the large frigate USS *President* and the British ship sloop *Little Belt* on 16 May 1811. In September the Orders in Council were further refined to exclude American produce from the West Indian Islands. In July Madison

had recalled Congress early, and began preparations for war. In November Madison requested 10,000 more regular troops, 50,000 volunteers and naval increases. These were intended to be coercive, rather than real, but the effect was ruined by domestic opposition, the failure to recruit troops and the ineffective reporting of the British minister in Washington.

The Republican administrations had failed to develop effective naval policies, with various factions supporting the large scale construction of coast defence gunboats, severe economy, or the building of further frigates; the end result was confusion. Even allowing for the limited funds provided, the United States Navy was inadequately equipped with ships, men and dockyards. There were no significant warships on order or under construction at the outbreak of the war, and some of those laid up

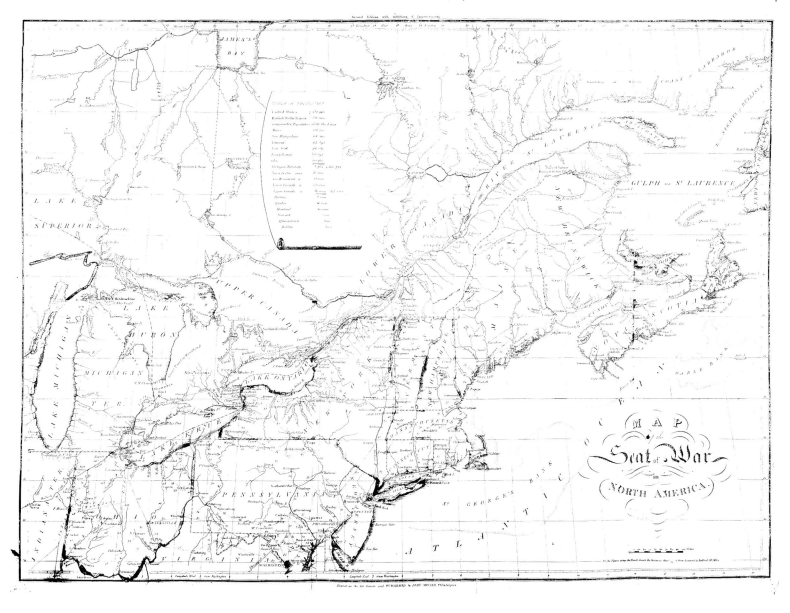

out of commission were already beyond economic repair. This limited instrument was about to take on the greatest navy the world had ever seen. Few, on either side, expected it would achieve much.

In 1812 the Royal Navy was essentially a power projection force. Although it still deployed powerful battlefleets off Brest, Toulon and the Scheldt, the reality of war at sea was the incessant application of naval power against the Napoleonic Empire. These operations ranged from the full scale amphibious expeditions that captured Copenhagen in 1807, and attempted to take Antwerp in 1809, through the support of Wellington's Peninsular Army, to the sustained campaigns against offshore islands, coastal shipping, signalling stations and harbours that formed the day to day staple of life for frigates and other cruisers on detached service. While the French battlefleets were growing steadily towards a hundred large battleships, they never put to sea in any numbers. The threat they posed was aimed more at the British economy, forcing Britain to build and man ever more ships, rather than any realistic attempt to contest the command of the sea. The French simply did not have the seamen and maritime resources to compete at sea, even if they could have concentrated their scattered fleets in one or two ports. After 1805 there had been little glory, promotion or prize money to win at sea, so the more dynamic, ambitious British officers were drawn inshore. The skills they had acquired in the European, Caribbean and East Indian theatres were equally applicable to the long, largely undefended coastline of the United States.

Although Madison must have been aware of the threat posed by the Royal Navy, he was convinced that Britain was in no position to ignore American demands. With Napoleon's invasion of Russia generally expected to result in the complete exclusion of British economic activity from Europe, there could be no better time to strike. Even so, he did not expect to have to fight. However, the British proved extremely obdurate, Prime Minster Spencer Perceval considering the Orders in Council one of the foundations of British strategy, and until his assassination on 11 May 1812, the Government showed no interest in their repeal. Finally, after sending an ultimatum to London which was rejected, Madison called for a declaration of war. He gave Congress a list of four major grievances: the impressment of American sailors, the use of illegal blockades, the Orders in Council, and the fomenting of Indian warfare on the northwest frontier. This last did at least give some small measure of justification for an invasion of Canada. That the expansionists were anxious to add Canada and Spanish Florida to the States of the Union was rather more significant, bringing in a politically powerful group of 'War Hawks' from the western states to support the administration and direct the strategy of the war. War was declared on 18 June 1812. Although the new British ministry of Lord Liverpool had repealed the Orders on the 17th, they did not change the basic tenets of British economic war policy; it remained unique, based on a highly aggressive view of belligerent rights at sea.

The severe miss-match between American strategy and American resources at the outbreak of war provides powerful evidence that Madison had expected the British to accept his demands, or at least make some politically worthwhile concessions. He selected the aged and corpulent Henry Dearborn to be Commander-in-Chief, symbolising a slow and ineffective build up of military strength. This was disastrous, because the invasion of Canada – the only measure available that could hope to secure his war aims, the removal of the hostile economic measures – required American armies ready to cross the frontier in strength before the British could respond. Instead, the few units raised were in no condition to conquer the country. Most were short of officers, men, equipment and even a common doctrine. Perhaps Madison shared the opinion of his predecessor, Jefferson, who considered the conquest of Canada would only be 'a matter of marching'. While Canada was still divided, by language and administration, and sparsely populated, it was not ready to join the United States. Many of the English-speaking population were ex-American loyalists, while the staunchly Catholic French-Canadians were no more enthusiastic for the republican allies of the Revolution. This national feeling would be reflected in the wartime performance of the locally raised regiments and militia which, together with the small garrison of British regulars, defeated the American attack.

The War of 1812 overlapped and interlinked with the continuing US expansion into the territory of the Native Americans. The radical Shawnee religious leader known as 'the Prophet' and his half brother Tecumseh were actively seeking a united Indian front against American encroachment. When General William Henry Harrison moved his small army toward the Prophet's town he was attacked at Tippecanoe on 6 November 1811. The American victory, and the subsequent destruction of the Prophet's town drove Tecumseh into alliance with the British. The link between the Indians and the British gave many in the American west a particular interest in the invasion of Canada; while they claimed the conquest would end the danger of British-supported Indian incursions, their real interests lay in securing further land.

When he received news of the outbreak of war General Isaac Brock, Governor of Upper Canada, ordered his forces on Lake Huron to capture the American position at Fort Michilimackinac, at the narrows that connected Lake Huron with Lake Michigan. The operation was a complete, bloodless, success. The fort surrendered on 17 July, giving the British possession of the entire region. Madison's strategy was based on the ideas of General Dearborn and General William Hull, then commanding at Detroit. They suggested a two-pronged attack on Upper and Lower Canada. Madison pushed Hull to advance into Canada, but the aged Revolutionary War hero had been rendered mentally infirm by a stroke. After a brief foray into Canada Hull pulled back to Detroit. Here, after suffering a brief artillery bombardment, he surrendered his army of 2500 men to General Brock and his 1300 Anglo-Canadian troops. Brock's master-stroke was to intimate that he might not be able to control his Indian auxiliaries after a battle. Brock had secured the support of Tecumseh and his followers by the dynamic seizure of Michilimackinac. For the rest of the season the Northwest frontier witnessed one American disaster after another as small forces were humiliated or driven back by the British, Canadian and Indian units.

The main thrust of the American attack was aimed at Montreal, to be followed by a siege of Quebec. Success here would, Madison believed, be enough to secure his war aims. He relied on numbers and enthusiasm, convinced that the British and Canadian forces were less effective than those in Upper Canada. However, his plans were crippled by local politics and the inability of the Government to control the individual states. Most states that bordered on Canada actually opposed the war, reflecting their close economic ties with Britain and Canada, and voted for Federalist governors and congressmen. This seriously weakened the American effort throughout the war. In New England the predominantly Federalist anti-war views of the majority ensured that the militia was not called out, while plans to invade New Brunswick were impossible for lack of men.

The administrative and logistical pivot of the American attack on Canada lay at Albany, in the north of New York State. This was the political heartland of the Clinton family, leaders of Republican opposition to Madison and his war. Initially Dearborn signed an armistice with the Governor of Lower Canada, General Henry Prevost, but this was repudiated by the administration. Brock then paraded Hull's captured army before the American forces on the Niagara frontier, which did nothing to improve their morale. When the Americans finally attacked over the Niagara River, at Queenston Heights on 13 October, most of the militia men refused to cross the frontier, and the regulars, driven back by the outnumbered British, surrendered. The few units that escaped the debacle disintegrated before the season had ended. Unfortunately for the British, Brock, their dynamic and inspirational commander, had been killed. His loss would be severely felt throughout the rest of the war. By blunting the first two American advances into Canada, Brock and his mixed forces created a sense of Canadian identity that would give this war a particular importance when the country came of age. The victory was almost immediately turned into a Canadian national myth. Dearborn finally crossed the frontier at the head of Lake Champlain in November, but quickly returned after an inconclusive skirmish, having achieved nothing.

The British response to the American attack was dominated by Prevost's view that Quebec was the key to the safety of Canada. While waiting for reinforcements from Britain, he favoured remaining on the defensive, and even signing an armistice, to avoid exciting the Americans. The American declaration of war

on 18 June had taken the ministers in London by surprise. With the country weary of the French wars, and of war taxes, they had no desire for another enemy, and had been doing their best, within the wider picture of the struggle with France, to conciliate the Americans. Their information was that Madison's government was weak and divided, and therefore would not go to war. Only the conclusion was wrong. They were convinced that when news of the repeal of the Orders in Council arrived the war would be stopped, and were horrified to find that impressment had now become a major issue. This finally convinced them that Madison, a typical Francophile Republican, was in league with Napoleon, and bent on the conquest of Canada and Florida. Brock's victories gave the ministers time to respond with diversionary naval attacks on the American coast. The successful defence of Canada in 1812 convinced many waverers that it would be possible to hold the country, increasing the support for the war effort.

By contrast to the land war, which had been expected to deliver a decisive success, the Americans anticipated little at sea. Republican ideology suggested that the activity of privateers fitted out by the merchant community would inflict great damage on British trade, a factor that would have weighed heavily with Madison. When the war began two American frigate squadrons were cruising in the north Atlantic to cover homeward-bound merchant ships. The squadrons were then broken up to attack British trade, but the American captains, with Presidential support, sought the glory of capturing British warships. In this they succeeded beyond all expectation. On 19 August General Hull's nephew Isaac Hull, commanding the USS *Constitution* captured the British frigate *Guerriere* after a 40-minute action 700 miles east of Boston. The American ship mounted 24-pounder guns to the 18-pounders of the smaller and more lightly built British ship, and had a crew at least one-quarter larger. Because the *Guerriere* was severely damaged, and a long way from home she was burnt. On 25 October the frigate *United States*, Captain Stephen Decatur, captured HMS *Macedonian* after a long gunnery duel in the mid-Atlantic, in which a similar disparity of force applied. The prize was taken into the American navy.

Finally on 29 November the *Constitution*, now commanded by William Bainbridge, took HMS *Java* off the coast of Brazil. Despite the usual preponderance in favour of the American frigate, the *Java* put up a good fight, and only surrendered after losing 122 killed and wounded, including her captain. Being concerned to avoid any serious damage so far from home, Bainbridge fought a cautious battle which thus lasted nearly four hours. His prize was destroyed.

Other single-ship actions in 1812, between smaller vessels, produced similar results. In most cases overmatched British vessels were taken. This was hardly surprising: the British were fighting a world war with France, the vast majority of their ships were in European waters, and the unprecedented expansion of the Royal Navy had produced a dilution in both the size and quality of many crews. The under-strength 'third reserve' team cruising off the hitherto peaceful American coast was not the best that Britain had to offer. However, the true value of the American victories was political. They demonstrated that the new nation could win, and were immediately seized upon by the administration's supporters. At the same time they depressed the British Government and people far more than any military defeat or loss of territory, for the prestige of the Royal Navy was the bedrock of British power, the security of the state and the guarantee of her economic prosperity. Despite the individual American successes the sheer size of the British fleet on the North American station ensured that by the end of 1812 the British blockaded the remaining American warships in harbour, and controlled the coastline of the Chesapeake and Delaware Bays. They left New York and the New England states open to trade. This was done both to exploit divided American opinion, and to continue the supply of grain to Wellington's army in Spain. It also weakened the American privateering effort, which was led by Baltimore, rather than Boston.

Madison had hoped to capture much of Canada in 1812, as a prelude to a complete conquest that would secure his war aims and reunite the Republican Party behind his leadership. By November his plans were in ruins. Napoleon's invasion of Russia had failed, undermining one of the key bases of the

American strategy. His defeat would give the British unlimited access to Russian Baltic supplies, greatly strengthening their position against American economic coercion. Internally the failure of the first campaign led many State Governors to look for local, defensive, solutions that necessarily drew men and resources away from the field armies. The repeal of the Orders in Council shortly after the outbreak of war had divided the Republicans. Despite this, and the pathetic military campaigns of 1812, Madison was re-elected to the Presidency in December 1812. However, many states in the war zone were won by his Clintonian/Federalist opponents. This political weakness, and the dominance of local concerns, ensured that Congress refused to introduce the trade embargo he requested, primarily to deny the British army in Canada access to American food. Unable to secure peace by commercial embargo Madison had little option but to try another military campaign, using the winter to enlarge the army. He would need additional men to meet the inevitable British attacks on the American coast. However, financial weakness restricted military recruitment to around 35,000 troops. The New Secretary for War, General John Armstrong, advised that attacks on York (modern Toronto), Kingston and the Niagara frontier were the only realistic options in 1813. His planning was given particular urgency by the forthcoming Gubernatorial elections in New York State at the end of April. After the British reinforced Kingston the only target within his capability in the time available was York. The deflection of strategy, from the more difficult, but critical naval dockyard at Kingston, the loss of which would have destroyed the British position below Montreal at a stroke, to the strategically insignificant provincial capital of York, was a heavy price to pay for a domestic political advantage.

The Secretary of the Navy, Paul Hamilton, remained committed to further operations on the broad oceans, reflecting the views of career officers, rather than shifting resources to the development of naval power on the Lakes, to support the land war. His demands for funds to build 74s and more frigates, together with his profligacy and drunkeness led to his being replaced at the end of the year by William Jones, who was more attuned to the strategic

needs of the Lakes, and found extra funds to encourage seamen to serve there, while putting off the construction of 74s that could not be completed in time to serve in the war. He preferred smaller vessels, especially sloops, that could be built quickly and carry the war to the British in their own waters.

Early in 1813 Madison saw a window of opportunity in an offer of mediation from Tsar Alexander I, which he hoped might influence the British to accept a more liberal view of belligerent rights at sea. Consequently he sent a delegation to St Petersburg, but this did little more than balance the waning power of France, leaving him with no option but to continue the war for Canada. The land frontier, and the Great Lakes that were the key to strategic mobility in the area, would remain the core of the war. Powerful navies were created on Lake Erie and Lake Ontario. In March 1813 Secretary Armstrong ordered General Harrison to secure command of Lake Erie, by supporting Captain Oliver Hazard Perry's efforts to build a fleet of warships at Presque Isle, and collect transports at Cleveland for his army. The size of Harrison's force alarmed General Procter, and anxious for his supply lines he pressed the young Captain Barclay, commanding the British force on Lake Erie, to give battle to Perry's superior force. The struggle in the far west took a decisive turn when Perry captured the British ships after a savage action at Put-in Bay on 10 September 1813. His success was quickly followed up on land, and within two weeks he had carried Harrison's 7000-man army across the Lake, forcing Procter to evacuate Detroit. Harrison pursued Procter and effectively wiped out his 900-man force at the Battle of the Thames on 5 October. In the fighting Tecumseh was killed. This battle settled the control of the Detroit area for the rest of the war, and destroyed the last vestiges of Indian power.

On Lake Ontario Dearborn's forces, carried by Commodore Isaac Chauncey's fleet, captured York on 27 April, burning the public buildings. The army then re-embarked, crossed the Lake and landed on the Niagara peninsula, capturing Fort George in late May, and advancing westward along the Niagara frontier. On the night of 6 June a much smaller British forced attacked the American camp at Stoney Creek. In a confused action the

Americans drove off the British, but both the American Generals were captured in the process, which negated their tactical success. With their Lake communications cut by Commodore Sir James Yeo's squadron, the Americans retreated. On the 24th 600 Americans were surrounded by Indians and forced to surrender at Beaver Dams. This latest disaster led to Dearborn's enforced retirement. Once again the American army would wither away by the end of the season under the pressure of low morale, poor logistics and ill-health. York had been a key political victory for the New York elections, but the subsequent failure on the Niagara frontier left upstate New York exposed to British raids.

For the rest of the war the two fleets on Lake Ontario spent their time building and skirmishing, neither side being prepared to fight when inferior in numbers. The astonishing shipbuilding efforts at Sackets Harbor and Kingston progressed rapidly from sloops to frigates, and culminated with the commissioning of HMS *St Lawrence*, a 100-gun three-decker in late 1814, which gave the British undisputed command of the lake. At the end of the war she had sisters on the stocks at Kingston, and two American rivals in the same state at Sackets Harbor. Although these Lake ships were smaller than their salt-water cousins, since they needed no drinking water and few stores for their short cruises, they were still colossal vessels to build in what was little more than a wilderness.

The American army fared no better to the east. A two-pronged advance against Montreal came to nothing. In October 1813 General Wade Hampton's 4000 men moved northwest from Lake Champlain and crossed the frontier along the Chateauguay River, heading for the St Lawrence. They were driven back by a far smaller, wholly Canadian, force of embodied and sedentary militia at the Battle of Chateauguay on 26 October. Hampton then retired across the frontier and took up winter quarters. In November General Wilkinson led nearly 8000 men from Sackets Harbor down the St Lawrence towards Montreal, but was resolutely pursued by a small British force. When Wilkinson turned to engage the 800-strong British, Canadian and Indian force at Crysler's Farm on the 12th, his troops were beaten off. The following day, when he heard that

Hampton would not be linking up with him, Wilkinson crossed back into American territory and went into winter quarters. Another season had passed without any worthwhile achievement by the American army, and this only served to bolster the morale of the Canadian and British forces. In late December British troops crossed the frontier to capture Fort Niagara and sack the villages of Buffalo and Black Rock.

At sea the British assumed complete control, reinforcing the Commander-in-Chief of the North America and West Indies Station, Admiral Sir John Borlase Warren, with additional ships, and ensuring that those on station were used with more skill. On 1 June 1813 HMS *Shannon*, Captain Philip Broke, captured the USS *Chesapeake*, Captain James Lawrence, off Boston in a frigate action of unequalled intensity. It has been described as the finest example of a single-ship action in the history of war at sea under sail. Both ships carried 18-pounder guns. Lawrence, a successful sloop commander, had just taken over the *Chesapeake*, but she had a veteran crew of nearly 400 men. By contrast Broke had commanded the *Shannon* for seven years, which he had devoted to the perfection of naval gunnery, and the pursuit of honour. His smaller crew had been trained to hit the mark, and fire rapidly. The battle took only eleven minutes. In those eleven minutes 148 Americans and 83 Englishmen were killed or wounded, a higher toll than the *Victory* suffered at Trafalgar in six hours! The heavy casualties aboard the *Shannon* demonstrated just how good the American crew were; their own losses, together with the annihilation of their officers, explained why the ship was taken. Building on the effective command of the sea, secured by powerful forces based at Halifax and Bermuda, Admiral Warren detached Rear-Admiral Sir George Cockburn to conduct an amphibious raiding campaign in the Chesapeake Bay region between March and June 1813. Although successful, notably in destroying an important cannon foundry, these punitive operations were limited by the paucity of troops. By contrast the introduction of convoys rapidly reduced the threat posed by American warships and privateers.

In July 1813 the United States found itself engaged on another front, with the outbreak of the Creek War. The Indians of the Mississippi/Florida region, inspired by Tecumseh, were resisting American encroachment, but General Andrew Jackson, commander of the Tennessee Militia, attacked the Indians, with the ultimate object of securing Spanish Florida. The ruthless, driven, dynamic Jackson was unique among American military officers in having a clear idea of what he wanted to achieve, and would stop at nothing to realise his plans. On 27 March 1814 he finally broke Creek resistance at Horseshoe Bend, releasing forces for the defence of New Orleans.

Elsewhere the war was less promising. The decisive defeat of Napoleon at the Battle of Leipzig suggested that the British would be under no obligation to negotiate, as they demonstrated by rejecting the Russian offer of mediation. Instead Foreign Secretary Lord Castlereagh offered direct talks in London or Gothenburg. Madison's acceptance of negotiations led many to expect the war would soon end, and weakened the war effort. To maintain pressure on the British Madison finally secured an embargo on trade with the enemy in late 1813, but it had little effect on the vast business that fed the British armies in Canada and Spain. Secretary Armstrong called for an army of 55,000 men and a larger naval effort to take command of the Lakes. However, the country was desperately short of money, and found it very difficult to collect revenues, especially in areas that were opposed to the war. The Secretary of the Navy recommended lifting the embargo, so that the state could at least raise revenue from a trade that could not be stopped, switching to the defensive on the Canadian frontier and taking the war to Britain at sea. On 30 March, with Napoleon facing total defeat, Madison lifted the embargo, opening trade with neutral European states in the hope that they could exert some influence on Britain. In late June the administration hoped that the end of the war in Europe would see the end of impressment, and that the British would be prepared to negotiate on the basis that it was no longer practised. When they heard from their former colleague Albert Gallatin that the British were thinking of a 'harsh' war aims programme, including ending fishing rights and territorial seizures, they elected to negotiate without mentioning impressment. Half a world away the frigate USS *Essex*, Captain David Porter, spent 1813 destroy-

ing the British South Pacific whaling fleet, but eventually HMS *Phoebe* caught up with her off the Chilean port of Valparaiso. *Phoebe*'s captain, relying on his superior long-range gunnery, knocked the *Essex* to pieces in a one-sided battle on 28 February 1814. Not one of Porter's prizes made it to an American port.

The war in Europe ended in April 1814, allowing the British Government to devote greater resources to the American theatre, especially troops from Wellington's army. Since British war aims remained, as they had always been, to persuade the Americans to stop the war, and hopefully secure some useful border rectifications, the question was how to apply the new forces to maximum effect. The strategy was to rely on coastal raids and a major offensive down the Lake Champlain route to force the Americans to pull back from Canada and make peace. Prevost was promised up to 10,000 more troops and directed to seize control of the Lakes and advance into the United States, while General Sherbrooke took part of Maine, to improve communications between Halifax and Quebec. The new naval Commander-in-Chief, Admiral Sir Alexander Cochrane, had formed a powerful hatred of Americans during the War of Independence, and now hoped to turn his local knowledge and strategic ideas into a war-winning campaign. In early May he proclaimed a complete blockade of the American coast, as the prelude to further offensive operations. This prompted Secretary of the Navy William Jones to order the construction of Robert Fulton's pioneer steam battery, *Fulton the First*, for the defence of New York Sound; later another was begun at Baltimore, and a third projected for Philadelphia, but only the first was completed, and that too late for the war.

The only realistic American response was another campaign on the Niagara frontier. They now had some 27,000 regular troops across the country, together with militia, opposed to 12,000 British in Canada, and a slight naval advantage on the Lakes. However, any hope of an effective strategy was ruined by Cabinet quarrels over priorities at Niagara and Washington. During the spring the second in command, General Winfield Scott, drilled the Niagara army into an effective force that could perform manoeuvres on the field under fire. General Jacob Brown expected that with the support of Chauncey's fleet he could drive the British off Lake Ontario. Without waiting for Chauncey's concurrence he crossed the frontier on 1 July, captured Fort Erie on the 3rd and defeated the British at Chippewa on the 5th. However, Chauncey had no intention of subordinating his campaign to the army, and he had not been instructed to support Brown by the Government. Recognising the critical importance of Lake Ontario to American defences, and that the existence of his fleet alone denied the British easy communications, he considered the British fleet to be his true objective. With no naval support Brown had to fall back, and his army was badly mauled by Lieutenant General Gordon Drummond's army at the Battle of Lundy's Lane on 25 July. With Brown and Scott badly wounded the American army pulled back and the offensive on the Niagara front was halted for the rest of war. The one redeeming feature of the campaign was the much improved performance of the American regular army. The failure of the campaign reflected the lack of a clear command chain: neither Brown nor Chauncey was supreme, and there was no defined system of co-ordination. Within the government Navy Secretary Jones took a narrowly 'naval' view of the question, supporting Chauncey. Further problems were created when much of General Izard's army from Lake Champlain was ordered up to Lake Ontario, leaving the major north-south route into America undefended.

Between May and December Cockburn resumed work in the Chesapeake Bay area, under the new Commander-in-Chief. He exploited the opportunity to offer freedom to any slaves who would desert their owners and join the British. This had a powerful effect in the Southern states, where the slave population greatly outnumbered their masters. By early August Madison had finally recognised that America was facing a war for survival, and that the coastal attacks might well include operations against Washington. He responded by creating the new 10th Military District, covering Washington, Baltimore and Annapolis, commanded by General William Winder, a political appointee with no obvious military talent. Secretary Armstrong did not share Madison's concern for the capital, and provided few troops or fixed defences. In mid-August Cockburn wiped out Commodore Barney's

gunboat flotilla in the Patuxent River, just as the British troops arrived from Spain. Guided by Cockburn, General Sir Robert Ross landed his army in the Patuxent and marched on Washington. Winder was uncertain of their target until too late, belatedly assembling 7000 men at Bladensburg on the 24th to meet 4500 British troops. When the British advance guard attacked the American militia promptly ran away before Ross could reach the battlefield. This left Commodore Barney and his naval gunners to cover the 'Bladensburg races', the precipitate retreat of the army. That night Ross and Cockburn entered Washington, ate President Madison's celebration dinner and set fire to the public buildings in retaliation for York. The scorching of the Presidential mansion required it to be whitewashed, and subsequently renamed 'The White House'. The Americans had already burnt Washington Navy Yard, destroying three old frigates, a new frigate and a sloop. Ross evacuated the city on the 26th. The blow to American confidence in the ability of their government to run the war was tremendous, and although Madison was back in Washington on the 27th, the whole coast was open to the British. On the 28th a small British squadron, two frigates, with bomb and rocket vessels, captured Alexandria in Virginia, seized the shipping lying there and retreated down the River Potomac. In September the British attacked Baltimore, which was strongly held by local forces, but which had rejected all instructions from the Government. During the initial reconnaissance Ross, this time too far ahead of his troops, was killed. Despite a prolonged naval bombardment of Fort McHenry on the 11th and 12th, the army was unable to penetrate the American defences and withdrew. The spectacle of rockets and bombs fired from the fleet, their fuses burning brightly, arching through the night sky, inspired Francis Scott Key to pen 'The Star Spangled Banner'.

However, before the Baltimore attack the biggest British operation of the war had been brought to an ignominious end. General Prevost, the cautious Governor General of Lower Canada, and defender of the St Lawrence frontier, was ordered to advance across Lake Champlain with 11,000 regulars, many of them veterans from Spain. Before he attacked the heavily outnumbered American defenders at

With a personal dislike of Americans and orders that allowed his prejudices full rein, Admiral Sir Alexander Cochrane was a more formidable opponent than his predecessor, Admiral Warren had been. Engraved portrait for Brenton's Naval History. *1825.* NMM neg B742

Plattsburgh on the western shore of the lake he ordered his naval force to attack the American ships. On 11 September the British squadron was decisively defeated by Commodore Thomas Macdonough's American squadron. After a vicious close-range action in light winds, the American ships were able to haul round on their cables to present their undamaged broadside to the immobilised British. Prevost, who had no enthusiasm for the offensive, retreated into Canada. He was recalled in disgrace, but his failure persuaded the British to accept the status quo in the peace negotiations at Ghent.

Between September and January 1815 Madison reconstructed his Cabinet: Armstrong resigned as Secretary for War, being replaced by James Monroe, while Jones stood down as Navy Secretary, with Benjamin Crowninshield taking over. Jones argued that the Navy could not provide any more men for the Lakes without completely stripping the ocean-going forces and local naval defences. Monroe sought additional troops for a 'decisive' attack on Canada, but the Senate crippled his measures, leaving him to develop a plan for 15,000 regulars and 40,000 volunteers under Jacob Brown to cross the St Lawrence, but these plans were forestalled by peace. More immediately, he had to move troops to guard against the possibility that the Federalist Hartford Convention of December-January might result in an attempt to secede from the Union, or negotiate a separate peace. With the British occupying part of Maine in early September and extending the blockade to their harbours, the frightened New Englanders sought government protection and redress for their grievances. In the event the Convention was something of an anti-climax.

Peace was signed at Ghent on Christmas Eve 1814, effectively on the basis of the *status quo ante*, with no reference to American war aims. It was quickly ratified in London and Washington. However, before news of the Peace could reach the war zone the British attacked New Orleans. This time their General, Wellington's brother-in-law Sir Edward Pakenham, was as rash as Prevost had been cautious. Rather than wait to secure control of the Mississippi River, or turn the flank of Andrew Jackson's strong position on the east bank of the river, Pakenham led a frontal assault on 8 January 1815. He was killed, one of 2036 British casualties. Pakenham was given a hero's burial near to Nelson in St Paul's Cathedral. His army re-embarked and moved along the coast to capture Mobile.

At sea the last major action of the war was the capture of the USS *President*, Captain Stephen Decatur, on 15 January 1815. Decatur put to sea from New York in a gale and grounded heavily on the bar. He was pursued by a British frigate squadron, of which HMS *Endymion*, Captain Henry Hope, a rare British 24-pounder frigate, was the fastest. Hope ran up to the quarter of the American ship and kept up a heavy fire, trying to cripple her so that the rest of the squadron could get into action. He knew his ship was too lightly built, and too short handed, to fight the American heavyweight alone, but he forced Decatur to turn and engage. While the *President* engaged *Endymion*, *Tenedos* and *Pomone* closed in, with the powerful *rasée Majestic* in support. Decatur surrendered. As the largest American prize of the war, one of the three 'super-frigates', *President* was taken to Britain, carefully measured and a replica built to retain the name on the list of the Royal Navy. The first deployment of the new HMS *President* was to the American station in the early 1830s, flying the flag of Sir George Cockburn, the man who burnt Washington. It hardly needs to be observed that this was a period of Anglo-American tension. In old age the ship became the headquarters of the London Division of the Royal Naval Reserve, and the name is still carried by the shore base that ultimately replaced her.

At the heart of the maritime war, and the subsequent historical analysis, lay the contrasting strategies of blockade and privateering. The British blockade of the American coast, initially restricted to the area south of New York, was startlingly effective. The American merchant marine was decimated. All told, the Royal Navy took 1400 American prizes; in addition, several hundred ships were taken by British and Canadian privateers. The pressure of the British blockade was applied to the New England states in 1814, and led several to consider leaving the Union. In 1813 only one-third of all American sea-going merchant ships left port, and in 1814 the figure had fallen to one-twelfth. Coastal shipping was equally badly affected, and although more ships tried to operate, the only result was higher losses. Not surprisingly, merchant shipbuilding effectively ceased.

United States Commercial Activity: (in millions)

	1811	1814
Exports	$61.3	$6.9
Imports	$53.4	$13.0
Customs revenues	$13.3	$6.0
Overseas shipping (tons)	948,000	60,000
Cost of the war	£158,000,000	

The large scale stoppage of economic activity depressed the Customs revenues that the American Government relied on to fund the war, despite their rates being doubled, while causing sharp, inflationary, price rises that further weakened their spending power. The only alternative to coastal shipping, the uneconomic, slow and labour intensive system of land transport, hitherto little developed in the well-watered American coastal states, was brought into service. The experience of the blockade, and of the cost of land carriage, prompted the post-war policies of creating a blockade-breaking fleet of very heavily armed battleships, and the construction of inland canals and canalisation of rivers. Additional canals were built to ease communications with the Great Lakes, for the delivery of shipbuilding stores and munitions.

Mahan used his study of the war to argue that the United States needed a navy capable of preventing such a blockade. Even though the United States did not have any battleships during the war, the Royal Navy still deployed twenty of their own capital ships to watch the main American ports and support their cruisers. The economic effect of the war, which created artificial demand for a variety of hitherto imported products, followed by the rapid return to the prewar suppliers, crippled American industry for a generation, while the postwar boom was import-driven, and resulted in a severe slump. The disruption and damage of the war set back the development of the American merchant shipping industry for some years, which helped to maintain British competitiveness until the advent of steam began to change the nature of commercial shipping activity.

It was a testimony to the effectiveness of the British blockade that, with no alternative use for their capital, ships and seamen, the mid-Atlantic states turned to large scale privateering. During the war American privateers captured nearly 1350 British merchant ships, while national warships took a further 254 warships and merchant vessels. However, less than one-third of all prizes got back to American ports. The Royal Navy recaptured at least 750 prizes, while others were handed back by pro-British neutrals or lost at sea. The introduction of effective convoys by early 1813 cleared the seas of easy captures. For the British government this reduced the danger to a politically acceptable level, even if the merchant communities of Liverpool and Glasgow complained bitterly about the increased risk, and rising insurance rates.

Once the British and Canadians demonstrated they would resist the invasion of Canada, this was a war America could not win. Only the sterling performance of her small navy, the impact of large scale privateering and the belated improvement in the American army, enabled Madison to escape the disaster he had brought upon himself by failing to match American warlike preparations to the ambition of his high-risk diplomacy. Simply by surviving the Americans had improved the credibility of the country, and the republican form of government. On the other hand, by settling for the *status quo* they allowed the British to preserve their interpretation of belligerent rights at sea, the core of their strategy, for another half century. The early success of the United States Navy proved crucial to the long term existence of the service. The exaggerated pursuit of 'honour' by the small officer corps had gone down well with a nation starved of glory. After the war the service was given a major boost, rather than being demobilised, although attempts to turn it into a battlefleet sea-control navy were premature. After 1812 the British took the Americans seriously as a naval power, an honour they afforded to very few nations. The threat of American cruisers and privateers was still taken seriously in the 1860s.

The two nations took similar lessons from the war. The sheer size of the theatre made it difficult to sustain an appropriate level of local strength. Consequently improved, and secure, water communications became a priority. The construction of the Rideau canal facilitated the easy movement of heavy materials to the Lakes, while linked British fortress programmes at Kingston, Quebec, Montreal, the Niagara front and Halifax promised to bring the full weight of British naval power to bear more quickly, and more effectively than had been the case in the last war. American canals, Lake forts and a vast coastal fortress programme demonstrated all too well how effective naval power had been in defeating American war aims, and carrying British sea-power onto the American littoral. Commercial friction over restrictions of American access to West Indian trade remained a sore point, but it was the struggle for influence in the newly independent states of Latin America that caused a crisis in 1826-27. This was resolved after the death of George Canning and the retirement of John Quincy Adams, but it was the occasion for an early outburst of activity on another important front.

Historiography

Civil wars apart, the War of 1812 was the first in which two literate populations, who used the same language, found themselves on opposite sides. In consequence it was the occasion for a large amount of polemical literature, beginning long before the war, and carrying on long afterwards. One version of the war, the one which concentrated on the three frigate victo-

ries and the battle of New Orleans, was used by American politicians to support a claim that they had 'won' the war. This was a powerful domestic propaganda tool, and was frequently revived for international service, notably in the 1826-27 crisis. While imprisoned in America during the war William James, an Admiralty Court Officer based in Jamaica, was so incensed by the audacity of the American argument that he began to collect the 'facts', and in 1816 published a detailed rebuttal, *An Inquiry into the Merits of the Principal Naval Actions between Great Britain and the United States* in which he pointed out the great disparity in force, of guns and crew, between the British and American ships in the actions of 1812. He followed this with the much enlarged edition *A Full and Correct Account of the Chief Naval Occurrences of the late war between Great Britain and the United States of America* in 1817. His larger *Naval History of Great Britain* had the same polemical purpose and he sent the second edition to Prime Minister George Canning in 1826 specifically to assist him in repelling American

bluster based on what he saw as a false version of history. The production of partisan accounts of the war helped to sustain Anglo-American hostility long after the causes and aims of the war itself had been forgotten. The American historian Henry Adams rounded off nearly a century of anti-British writing, in which the Americans 'won' the 'Second War for Independence', in his powerful nine-volume *History of the United States, 1801-1815* of 1889-1901. Subsequently the most ambitious accounts of the war at sea were written by Americans. Theodore Roosevelt sprang to prominence by rebutting many of James's claims in his *Naval History of the War of 1812* in 1882, while Alfred Thayer Mahan's *The Influence of Sea Power Upon the War of 1812* of 1905 was used to make the case for an American ocean-going battlefleet. British interest in the war quickly waned, and while Canadian historians have examined the land and Lake wars the overall strategic picture from the London perspective has yet to be drawn.

Long after the Treaty of Ghent the American view of the War of 1812 was used for the purposes of national propaganda. This print of 1831 shows President Andrew Jackson, hero of New Orleans, flourishing the treaty of 31 July 1831 at the French king Louis Philippe, whose government had refused to ratify the agreement to compensate America for French depredations during the Napoleonic period. The roll of honour propped against Jackson's full treasury lists the naval victories of 1812, while the ships backing him include Constitution *and* New Orleans. *Behind Louis Philippe are empty coffers, a divided nation, and the ever-present spectre of Napoleon. The caption makes a series of comparisons between the flourishing state of the republic and the debilitated European monarchies.   Berverley R Robinson collection ref BRR88.10*

1

The slide into war

SINCE the outbreak of the European wars that followed the French Revolution, the infant United States had sought to remain aloof from the conflict while benefiting from neutral trade. Before independence American-built ships already made up one-third of the huge British merchant marine, and since its advantage in construction costs continued after 1783 the new United States soon had the second largest commercial fleet in the world (1). Exports that in 1792 stood at around $20 million had risen to over $100 million by 1807, and imports followed a similar curve at somewhat higher figures. The need to protect this expanding carrying trade from the predatory attentions of the Barbary states of North Africa quickly led to the establishment of the US Navy in 1794, despite political opposition to the formation of any permanent military force.

The position of a neutral trader during a major maritime war combines the opportunity for increased profit with the danger of interdiction by either side. However, at this time there was no universally accepted international law relating to the status of neutrals and their cargoes on the high seas, and the belligerents tended to search and sometimes make prizes of neutrals on the flimsiest of pretexts. At first the United States suffered most from French depredations, particularly from privateers, which led directly to the undeclared 'Quasi-War' of 1797-1801. This resulted in the commissioning of the first US Navy warships, the establishment of a Navy Department in 1798, and the first victories at sea. Despite its historical misnomer, it was a serious shooting war, and provided the new Navy Department with experience of organising squadron deployments, and the nascent navy with the taste of victory.

After the collapse of the short-lived Peace of Amiens in 1803, trading conditions for the Americans deteriorated further. While neutrals were usually allowed to import goods from one belligerent without the molestation of another, they were liable to seizure if they were

2

merely substituting for the enemy's own commerce, such as carrying goods from one enemy port to another. A widespread abuse of the principle had grown up among American merchants, whereby goods were temporarily landed in the United States, and instantly reloaded for re-export. The British had ignored this practice until 1805, when a landmark decision in the case of the US ship *Essex* gave warning that this would no longer be tolerated. Alarmed by the growth of the US merchant marine, mercantilist interests in Britain forced the government to reverse the relaxations of the Navigation Acts that had been granted to the Americans. Thereafter the number of captures made under this doctrine of Continuous Voyage rose dramatically.

To make matters worse, the Anglo-French economic war intensified when in the Berlin Decrees of 1806 Napoleon declared the whole of Britain blockaded and prohibited British goods from any port under his dominion. Britain responded with the Orders in Council, announced in January and November 1807, which did much the same for the Napoleonic Empire, allowing only ships which had cleared British customs to proceed to the remaining open ports of Europe. In December Napoleon issued the Milan Decrees, tightening the provisions of his so-called Continental System, which now effectively removed the protection of neutrality from anyone in British trade. Already a pawn in the Great Power struggle – in all 528 US flag merchantmen were seized by the British between 1803 and 1807, and 206 by the French before the Berlin Decrees – America had responded with the Non-Importation Act of April 1806. This was designed to prohibit the trade in selected British manufactures which America could obtain from elsewhere or produce for herself. It was an ineffective measure, and an attempt at a new treaty between the United States and Britain also foundered on British intransigence. Britain saw herself as embroiled in a life-or-death struggle with the French empire in which seapower was her one advantage; she would not voluntarily surrender the maritime weapons that power conferred.

This was to be underlined to the Americans in June 1807 through the notorious *Chesapeake-Leopard* affair (2). The Royal Navy was always short of men in wartime, and employed impressment both on shore and at sea; with so many reluctant men in most crews, desertion was rife, and the well-paid American merchant service was an especially attractive alternative. Individual British captains were sometimes indiscriminate and high-handed in their recruiting, and zealous in their pursuit of deserters. Americans suffered more than most from this policy, since they had many well-manned merchant ships at sea which the commercial war gave every excuse to stop and search. Even the American

Secretary of the Treasury, Albert Gallatin, estimated that there were at least 5000 British seamen employed in the US merchant marine in 1803 (but a recent American study put the figure at 20,000); although by no means all were Royal Navy deserters, in British eyes they were nevertheless liable to serve their country. With the benefit of historical knowledge, it is now clear that many genuine Americans were illegally pressed – one estimate puts the number at almost 10,000 between 1790 and 1812 – but it is equally true that American ships often harboured British deserters. It was by no means obvious whether a seaman was British or American – and in any case the two nations disagreed on what constituted naturalisation – but there was also a brisk trade in fake papers pedalled by unscrupulous American consuls.

3

The American government protested long and loud, but the British gave a graphic demonstration of their attitude when seamen from the squadron off the Chesapeake deserted and signed-on aboard a number of American ships, including the frigate USS *Chesapeake*. The local authorities refused to return the men, but when the *Chesapeake* sailed on 22 June, she was intercepted by the small two-decker *Leopard* of 50 guns. Humphreys (3), *Leopard*'s captain, had orders from Vice-Admiral Sir George Berkeley to search the frigate and retrieve any deserters, and when negotiations failed, *Leopard* fired on the surprised American until she hauled down her colours. Flying the pendant of Commodore James Barron (4), *Chesapeake* was on her way to the Mediterranean, and was totally unprepared for combat; she was only able to fire one gun *pour l'honneur du pavillon* before surrendering. A British boarding party then mustered the crew and took off four deserters, but declined to treat the ship as a prize of war.

Even Barron admitted that the men were deserters, but the humiliation of a US warship off its own coast was an outrage that America neither forgave nor forgot. Three men were killed, sixteen wounded and the *Chesapeake* badly damaged. Barron himself was found guilty of 'neglect' and suspended without pay for five years; despite his most earnest entreaties he was not employed again during the War of 1812. Passions ran high over his treatment, dividing the US Navy's officer corps and resulting in many duels, the most notorious being Barron's own killing of Stephen Decatur in 1820. However, the American government's reaction to the incident was more considered, Jefferson seeking further economic measures to pressure Britain, although he did ban British warships from American waters from July. For its part, the British government repudiated the action and removed Berkeley from the North America station, but it did not signal any major change of policy.

Jefferson believed that America could deploy three

4

economic strengths against Britain: her value as a consumer of manufactures, her importance as a producer of raw materials and agriculture, and the position of the second largest merchant marine as a global carrier. By withdrawing these from the world market, the British war effort would be unsustainable, and Britain would have to accede to American demands without the necessity of war. From such logic was born the Embargo Act of December 1807, whereby all American commerce with foreign nations was prohibited, and even incoming neutrals could not transport US cargoes outward. It failed to convince the British, but rapidly destroyed American trade and threatened the prosperity of much of the nation, and treasury receipts fell off dramatically. An estimated 55,000 seamen were thrown out of employment, and about 100,000 in related industries. The Embargo quickly became unpopular, especially in mercantile New England, and despite various attempts to eliminate loopholes, was widely evaded. To the merchant community it seemed both disproportionate and counterproductive, as pointed out in a satirical broadside of the time.

Lest Britain should take
A few men by mistake,
    Who under false colors may dare go:
We're manning their fleet
With our Tars, who retreat
    From poverty, sloth and Embargo

What a fuss we have made,
About rights and free trade
    And swore we'd not let our own share go,
Now we can't for our souls
Bring a Hake from the shoals
    'Tis a breach of the twentieth Embargo

Ironically, both the US Navy and the Revenue Service found themselves in the same position as the pre-Revolutionary Royal Navy, attempting to execute laws which the majority of the populace refused to acknowledge. More damaging in the long run was the transfer of Navy emphasis from the big ships (which were laid up, some never to sail again) to the Jeffersonian gunboats needed to enforce the Embargo.

5

6

1. An Italian engraving by Roselli of
an American merchantman reflects
how common the sight of the Stars
and Stripes was in the Mediterranean
in the years before the Embargo.
NMM ref PAG8197

2. Vignette of the *Chesapeake* and
Leopard affair, from a portrait of J C
Calhoun, stipple engraving by W
Joseph Edwards after an original by
Brady, no date.
NMM ref PAD3587

3. 'Captn Salisbury Pryce Humphreys,
RN', stipple engraving by R Page,
published by Joyce Gold, 30
November 1812.
NMM ref PAD3422

4. Commodore James Barron,
engraving by J W Steel after an
original painting by Neagle, no date.
*Beverley R Robinson collection ref
BRR51.7.732.21*

5. 'The Little Belt Sloop of War, Captn
Bingham nobly supporting the Honor
of the British Flag against the
President United States Frigate, May
15th 1811', coloured aquatint
engraved by William Elmes after his
own original, published by Edward
Orme, 25 October 1811.
NMM ref PAH8097

6. 'This print elucidating the extreme
disproportion of force . . . and
representing the situation of both
ships in the morning after the Action
of the 16 May 1811', coloured aquatint
engraved by J Haskell after an original
by J Cartwright, published by J
Hassell, 1 December 1811.
NMM neg C668

7. 'The capture of the Gipsey
schooner New York on the 30th of
April 1812, by HM Ships Hermes and
Belle Poule in the middle of the
Atlantic . . .', coloured aquatint
engraved by Charle Rosenberg after
an original by William John Huggins,
published by the artist, no date.
NMM ref PAG9064

The Embargo itself was replaced in March 1809 by a Non-Intercourse Act, which once again allowed trade with all countries, except Britain and France. The new Madison administration was prepared to reopen commerce with either of the belligerents if the other would mend its ways. France appeared to offer the repeal of the offending Decrees, although in practice it did not, but the resulting ban on trade with Britain once again drove up Anglo-American tensions. The government decided on a policy of more active protection for American commerce, especially in its own coastal waters, and from 1810 the US Navy began to recommission some sea-going warships. With a conscious reference to the *Chesapeake* affair, US officers, while enjoined to preserve strict neutrality, were instructed 'to maintain and support at every risk & cost, the dignity of our Flag; And, that offering yourself no unjust aggression, you are to submit to none . . .'

In May 1811 Commodore John Rodgers and the *President* were sent off New York to investigate a report that British or French cruisers were interfering with shipping in American waters. On the 14th the big frigate sighted and pursued what was evidently a warship, but could not catch up until after darkness had fallen. The stranger refused to identify herself, a shot was fired (both sides claimed it was the other) and a short, sharp battle of about half an hour ensued, before the antagonists drifted apart (5). When daylight dawned it revealed a badly battered British sloop, the *Lille Belt* (a Danish prize, sometimes called the *Little Belt* in Royal Navy service); she had 11 dead and 21 wounded, whereas casualties in the American frigate were confined to one wounded boy (6). Rodgers expressed his regrets to Commander Bingham of the sloop and to his government, but he was completely exonerated by a court of enquiry. Like most of his

generation of naval officers, Rodgers was very sensitive on matters of honour and was slightly embarrassed by the disparity of force, spending some time trying to prove how a flush-decked corvette could look like a frigate, but most of the country did not care: it was revenge of a sort for the *Chesapeake*.

Britain, far more concerned with great issues on the Continent, was not inclined to make much of the affair, but equally was not about to concede on any American demands. Ships continued to be seized and seamen impressed (7), and gradually the mood of the United States shifted towards war. Although the Federalist states of New England were fervently opposed to a conflict with Britain, their influence was more than offset by southern and western 'War Hawks' who blamed the British for encouraging Indian raids and saw the easy conquest of Canada as an attractive war aim. After a final attempt at sabre-rattling failed to persuade the British to compromise, war was declared on 18 June 1812. By then Britain had actually rescinded the Orders in Council, but the die was cast.

7

Part I

WAR ON THE HIGH SEAS

DESPITE THE long prologue to the war, when it came the American Government had taken few positive steps to prepare its armed forces, strongly suggesting that President Madison expected his combination of diplomacy and economic coercion to achieve his aims. Of the two services, the US Navy was the better equipped to fight a war. Unlike the army, with a tiny professional cadre of only 6000 men, the navy did not rely on a citizen militia, but comprised career officers and experienced seamen. A significant number of the officers had seen action in the 'Quasi-War' with France and against Tripoli, while there was no shortage of skilled seamen in a maritime country where embargoes and restrictions had laid up so many merchant ships.

Warships were in short supply, however. To the fourteen sea-going ships in commission in January 1812, only two refitted frigates were added during the course of the year. They were opposed to a navy with nearly 600 active ships and more than 300 others refitting, under construction, or in harbour service. Furthermore, it had been at war almost continuously for twenty years and had won a string of victories unmatched in the age of sail over every maritime power of any significance. Not surprisingly, US naval officers admired the Royal Navy, and as much as they were irked by the British assumption of natural superiority, they organised and ran their ships along similar lines. The question for the American administration, therefore, was what might be achieved at sea against such an opponent?

Expectations in many quarters were very low, the land campaign in Canada being the centre of Madison's hopes. In February 1812 there had even been a debate about whether it might be safer not to employ the navy at all in the coming conflict. This pessimistic view was not shared by American naval officers, who knew that prospects at sea were neither as simple nor as gloomy as landbound politicians seemed to think. The US Navy possessed some

real advantages: the big spar-decked frigates were a secret weapon that would give them tactical superiority; the very paucity of numbers in the fleet made them an elite, each ship being afforded a large, highly trained and well-motivated crew; and the officer corps, proud and self-confident, was not at all daunted by the task.

Being professionals, they knew that their enemy was not as formidable as might appear; the Royal Navy, for all its reputation, had weaknesses. Two decades of war and a huge expansion of the fleet had drained the natural pool of British seamen, to the point where on a man-per-ton basis Royal Navy crews were the smallest of all maritime powers. Desperation led British officers to press seamen without much regard for nationality, so many were poorly motivated. The quality of many crews had also been diluted by various emergency measures which had resulted in the indigent, incompetent and criminal, as well as the very young, being carried off to sea in large numbers. Rated 'landmen' (for which the US Navy needed no equivalent), they were often kept in order only by the most draconian discipline.

British seapower was based on numbers of ships and as a result individual designs were as small as possible for the role envisaged. This did not make them bad ships, although their officers often compared them unfavourably with the larger equivalents they faced in battle, but it placed greater onus on the skill and training of their personnel. After the destruction of the Franco-Spanish battlefleet at Trafalgar in 1805, the nature of the war shifted to a conflict of economic attrition. Commercial blockade required ever more ships, and the Admiralty responded, as its twentieth-century descendants did, by building large numbers of standard ships. They were often based on existing successful designs – like the 38-gun frigates of the *Macedonian*'s class, or the *Cruizer* class brig sloops – but they were chosen for mass-manufacture for the very reason that they were not

the largest and most costly of their type. The US took a diametrically opposite approach: it could only justify very few ships, but each would be larger and more powerful than the generality of their class.

Even the numbers were not as overwhelming as Steel's Navy List suggested. The Royal Navy had massive commitments around the world, and since the focus of the war was in Europe, only a small proportion of the total force was in American waters. There were four individual commands closest to the coasts of the United States: the North America station based at Halifax (and Bermuda in winter); a smaller Newfoundland squadron operating from St John's; the Leeward Islands station using Antigua and Barbados; and the Jamaica station with its headquarters in Port Royal. Each had a small or old two-decker as a station flagship, between two and four 18-pounder-armed frigates, a few smaller frigates, between eight and ten sloops, and perhaps a similar number of smaller gunbrigs and schooners. In the Caribbean the last French stronghold, Guadeloupe, had fallen in 1810 and although small-scale commerce-raiding continued, it was effectively a strategic backwater. Much the same was true of the more northerly stations, whose active work consisted primarily of enforcing the Orders in Council and, the reverse of the coin, the protection of British trade. None of these commands included a battle squadron and even in cruiser terms they were not high priorities for the best ships, men or supplies – Halifax, for example, suffered shortages of dockyard workers and stores that never caught up with the expansion of the station as the war intensified.

When a weak power is forced into maritime war with a far stronger one (especially where that stronger one is also the largest shipowner in the world), there can be only one strategy: an attack on trade. The question of how this might be made most efficacious was put to the senior commodores, John Rodgers and

Stephen Decatur, by Secretary of the Navy Hamilton just before the outbreak of war. For the *querre de course* to have any effect on the outcome of the war, Rodgers believed it would be necessary to take or destroy whole convoys, for which he advocated the employment of strong raiding squadrons. There were historical precedents, the most spectacular being the capture of almost all of the hugely valuable Smyrna convoy in 1693 or the Spanish assault on a Channel convoy in August 1780, from which only eight of sixty-three vessels escaped. Both of these had a seismic impact on British commercial life, but, significantly, both successes were achieved by battlefleets. British convoys were now more numerous, and individually of less value in relation to a massively expanded volume of trade; even so, the most important might well include a battleship escort. However powerful Rodgers' frigates, he would not be able to risk attacking a line of battle ship, even as a diversion while his smaller ships tackled the merchantmen, because of the high risk of damage that could prevent the attacking frigate from escaping.

Decatur preferred the notion of individual cruising or at most pairs of vessels operating together. Outside convoys, targets could include stragglers, fast 'runners' licensed to sail alone, and coastal traffic that was not convoyed. But in order to influence the outcome of the war, it would be necessary to achieve a high rate of capture. In the event both men were wrong. Rodgers never found, let alone captured a whole convoy, and while US Navy warships may have taken more merchant ships pro rata than privateers it was the latter that provided most of the prizes from the British mercantile marine.

The course of the war on the high seas

The war which was declared on 18 June, as fought on the high seas, might be considered in three phases, each equating with a calendar year: in 1812 the strategic advantages lay, temporarily, with America, and it was here that the most spectacular single-ship actions were won; in 1813 the British war effort swung into gear, reinforcements were sent to Halifax, and a newly-instituted coastal blockade made it more difficult for American warships to get to sea; by 1814, if raiders could get away at all, it

was necessary to operate in distant waters to have much chance of success, and much of the trade war devolved on privateers.

The first phase could be said to have begun on 4 April 1812, when Madison approved a 90-day embargo designed to get the majority of American merchant ships safely home before the declaration of war. With prior warning of the outbreak of hostilities, the US Navy had an opportunity to destroy some of the scattered British forces before they were aware of the war and had a chance to concentrate. This Rodgers was keen to attempt, and sailed with a strong squadron from New York on 21 June. The government's intention was that he and Decatur should command separate divisions and operate separately in defence of returning American trade; but some ships like *Constitution* and *Essex* had not yet joined, and Rodgers and Decatur were already at sea in company before these orders arrived.

Rodgers' immediate target was a large convoy rumoured to be en route from the West Indies, which he set off to find with the *President, United States, Congress, Hornet* and *Argus*. They found no convoy, but Rodgers had the first opportunity to reduce local British forces in detail when they discovered and chased the frigate *Belvidera* on the 23rd. She escaped, taking the first notice of hostilities with her to Halifax. As a first reaction, Philip Broke, Commodore of the station's cruisers, formed a squadron comprising *Africa*, 64 and the frigates *Shannon* (flag), *Belvidera, Aeolus* and later *Guerriere* to afford extra protection to the home-going Jamaica fleet being sought by Rodgers. This squadron in turn discovered the *Constitution* about a month later attempting to join Rodgers, and chased her for three days; she too escaped, but Captain Isaac Hull decided on a separate cruise off the Grand Banks. The danger having passed, Broke dispersed his squadron, and one of these, *Guerriere* on her way to refit at Halifax, then encountered the *Constitution*, giving the US Navy the first of a string of single-ship victories.

Rodgers finally returned to Boston on 31 August, having crossed the Atlantic but taken only seven merchantmen; it was not a particularly long cruise by the standards of the day but the outbreak of scurvy on board indicates a certain lack of experience of oceanic cruising. When Captain David Porter finally took the *Essex* to sea on 9 July, he too cruised alone,

Admiral Sir John Borlase Warren, the first British naval commander sent to take over the North America station lacked both the drive and the instructions to prosecute the war with vigour. Engraving and etching by James Fittler after an original by Mark Oates, published by J & J Boydell, 1799.
NMM ref PAG9416

escaping from the *Shannon*, and taking eight merchant vessel and the sloop *Alert*, only a converted collier but formally the first British warship to be captured during the war.

In terms of their effect on the enemy, the individual successes of *Constitution* and *Essex* seemed to cast doubt on the wisdom of Rodgers' large-squadron approach, so a compromise was agreed for the next operations. September was spent refitting, the plan for the autumn being to send out three squadrons each comprising a '44', a smaller frigate and a sloop. However, one ship from each squadron was not available for various reasons, and the divisions eventually sailed as two-ship units. Rodgers was missing the sloop *Wasp* when he sailed from Boston with *President* and *Congress* on 8 October; initially he had Decatur's *United States* and brig *Argus* in company (*Chesapeake* which should have joined the latter was still refitting), but they separated on the 11th. Rodgers then made another long cruise, ranging right across the Atlantic to the Azores, but was even less successful than on his first sortie, taking only two merchant ships. From this Rodgers drew the inference that the volume of British trade was vastly overstated, whereas in fact it merely reflected the effectiveness of a vigorously enforced convoy system.

Decatur was more fortunate. Following his

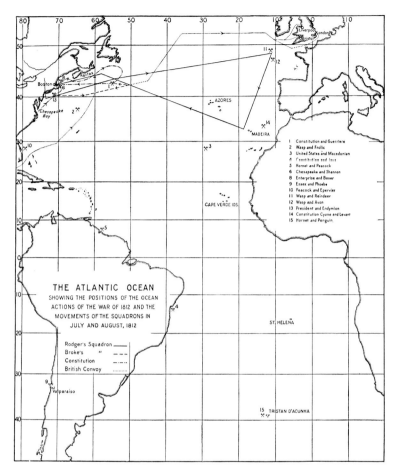

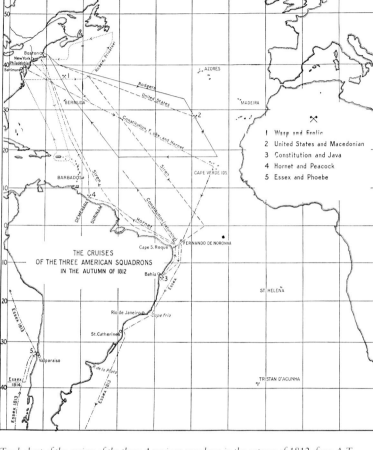

Positions of the ocean actions of the war of 1812, and the movements of the squadrons in July and August 1812, from A T Mahan, Sea Power in its Relation to the War of 1812, *Vol I.* Chatham collection

Track chart of the cruises of the three American squadrons in the autumn of 1812, from A T Mahan, Sea Power in its Relation to the War of 1812, *Vol I.* Chatham collection

preference for individual action, he sent the *Argus* to operate off South America and through the Caribbean, where she safely completed a 96-day deployment, despite at one point being chased by a strong British squadron. Decatur took his flagship across the Atlantic, where he won his famous victory over the *Macedonian* in the open ocean. Despite operating in the same waters as Rodgers, their respective fortunes could not have been more different; and to underline the workings of chance, Decatur lay-to for nearly two weeks refitting his prize, without encountering another ship.

If Rodgers felt abused by Dame Fortune he can only have been further upset by the news of his 'missing' sloop. The *Wasp* sailed from the Delaware on a separate cruise and captured the brig sloop *Frolic*, intimating that American sloops might be just as superior to their opposite numbers as the big frigates were proving to be. The euphoria, however, must have been

tempered by news of the immediate loss of both vessels to the 74-gun *Poictiers*: individual skill and gallantry might win battles but it could not win a war against overwhelming seapower.

The third squadron was to comprise *Constitution, Hornet* and *Essex* (although the last was still in the Delaware) and in the absence of Isaac Hull on family business, it was commanded by William Bainbridge. His division of *Constitution* and *Hornet* also stretched across the Atlantic to the Cape Verdes before heading for Brazil. Here they encountered the British sloop *Bonne Citoyenne*, which was carrying valuable specie and when a challenge to single combat with the *Hornet* was not taken up, she was blockaded in the port of Bahia. Standing offshore to encourage an engagement between the sloops, Bainbridge soon found himself in a battle of his own. The action on 29 December between the *Java* and the *Constitution* was the most hard-fought, and the last, of the Ameri-

can frigate victories; *Java* was so shattered she had to be scuttled and Bainbridge thought it was wise to break off his cruise to bring his damaged flagship home. *Hornet*, however, was not done, and having evaded the 74-gun *Montagu*, went on to destroy the brig sloop *Peacock*.

Nearly 130 years later when America entered the Second World War, German U-boat commanders were allowed such freedom with US coastal shipping that they dubbed those months 'The Happy Time'. The same phrase might have been used by US naval officers about 1812. The initial British response was restrained, and largely confined to the tightening of convoy rules, since it was believed that the abolition of the hated Orders in Council might be enough to persuade America to give up the war. The US Navy had achieved a series of single-ship victories that stunned a service used to considering itself invincible, while losing only a few minor warships — the schooners *Nautilus* and *Vixen* and the sloop *Hornet* — and all to far more powerful forces. It was a sharp contrast to the dismal showing of the military on the Canadian border, and with a new respect for naval power, in December Congress voted for the first major shipbuilding programme for more than a decade.

Once Britain finally accepted that America was serious about the war, the Admiralty was stirred into action. The European alliance against Napoleon remained the top priority, but as the French advance ground to a halt on the vast steppes of Russia, the Royal Navy was able to commit more resources to the American war. The western hemisphere stations were amalgamated under a new commander-in-chief, Admiral Sir John Borlase Warren, and the second phase of the war could be said to date from 27 September 1812 when he took up his post. The British moved to adopt the classic strategy of the dominant seapower, namely coastal blockade. The term actually covers two aims, related but separate in their strategic goals, namely the prevention of raiders (warships or privateers) getting to sea or returning to port, and the wider economic blockade intended to suppress all trade. General reprisals were authorised on 13 October 1812, followed on 27 November by an Admiralty order for the commercial blockade of the Delaware and Chesapeake. As required under international law, this was notified to neutrals on 26 December, but winter weather prevented the institution of the actual blockade until 4 February 1813. It was further extended by order of 30 March to New York, Charleston, Port Royal, Savannah, and the Mississippi, and by order of 16 November to everywhere south of Narragansett Bay.

Warren's forces were clearly inadequate for such a task and at the end of December he requested substantial reinforcements, emphasising his particular concern about the American spar-decked frigates. Despite a welter of criticism in Britain, the Admiralty had acted with commendable swiftness on this issue, and before they had news of either the *Macedonian* or the *Java*, they had ordered a new class of 24-pounder frigates (on the lines of the *Endymion*, the only instantly available prototype) and as an interim measure three small fast-sailing 74s were cut down to the kind of *rasée* that had inspired the American frigates in the first place. Built rapidly of fir, and 300 tons smaller than

Constitution, the frigates were not a real answer, but the *rasées*, which retained their 32-pounder main batteries, were far more powerful than the American frigates and were available by the middle of 1813. Later, two purpose-designed spar-decked frigates, *Leander* and *Newcastle*, were laid down, and they were also in service by the end of the year.

Operational conditions for the US Navy in 1813, therefore, had deteriorated sharply. It became more difficult to get to sea, and even more dangerous to try to make port again; once at sea targets became rarer, thanks to the tighter convoy regulations; and even the chance of a morale-boosting frigate victory was reduced from July when the Admiralty forbade any single 18-pounder frigate to engage one of the American '44's. Worried that the increased forces ranged against them might mean the destruction of a whole squadron, the Secretary of the Navy decided to deploy US ships singly. Ships that did get to sea included the *President* and *Congress*, which escaped from Boston at the end of April. *President* captured a dozen prizes, including the naval schooner *Highflyer*, and returned to Newport in September. *Congress* was less successful, making only four captures in the course of a very long cruise before slipping into Portsmouth, New Hampshire in December; her hull proved so decayed that she was laid up for the rest of the war.

A more typical experience was that of Decatur's squadron, comprising *United States, Macedonian* and *Hornet*, whose dash for open water ended with their being chased into New London in June. Only *Hornet* ever got to sea again before the end of the war. However, one pointer to a brighter future was the cruise of the brig *Argus*, which sailed in June from New York on what became the single most damaging commerce-raiding operation of the war. Old hands like Rodgers understood that Britain deployed her main naval strength on the coasts of her enemies, leaving her own local waters less heavily patrolled. Furthermore, convoys tended to break up as individual ships peeled off for their own destinations, leaving plenty of opportunities for a raider. That this was right in principle was proved by the great success of the *Argus*, although the lesson may have been temporarily obscured by her loss to HMS *Pelican*.

Taking prizes was one question, but getting

them to a friendly port was quite another. A raider might rely on its speed to evade the enemy, but a merchant ship with a weak prize crew was unlikely to escape even the dullest-sailing warship. As the numbers of British cruisers increased the US Navy had to accept that reality, and by the end of 1813 it was instructing the captains of the *Siren, Enterprise* and *Rattlesnake* to burn all prizes, since there was so little chance of their reaching a US port. Not only were the prize crews being captured, but the weakened raiders were in danger of falling prey to British warships: they were told that the US Navy 'needs no sacrifices by unequal conflict'.

The great success story of 1813 was the exploits of the *Essex*, which on Porter's sole initiative had rounded the Horn and reached Valparaiso in March. Since the Napoleonic deposing of the Spanish ruling house, the political situation in Spain's Latin American colonies had become complicated, with divided loyalties and the stirrings of independence movements in some provinces. Porter was able to exploit these divisions to obtain stores and maintenance support for his very successful assault on the British whaling industry in the area. Over the next few months he captured twelve whalers, representing about sixty per cent of the vessels in the South Seas trade. It was a substantial blow, although a number were recaptured and not one of the prizes ever reached the United States.

Omitting the *Hornet*'s cruise, which began the previous year, 1813 probably showed a net loss for the US Navy. Admittedly, the *Enterprise* took the *Boxer* in a pretty even fight, but that hardly balanced the capture of the *Chesapeake* in June and the *Argus* in August. Even before the end of the year the growing strength of British forces on the American coasts must have made it obvious that success would have to be sought in more distant waters. The frigate *Essex* was already blazing a trail in the Pacific, and the US Navy had the perfect long-range commerce-raiding tool in the shape of the new *Frolic* and *Erie* class sloops about to enter service.

Nevertheless, the third phase of the sea war beginning in 1814 offered only darker prospects for the US Navy, especially after the abdication of Napoleon in May, when the Royal Navy was able to direct its full attention to the American war. The more aggressive British stance, which had seen the beginnings of coastal raiding in 1813, was reinforced by the appointment in January 1814 of a new commander-in-chief, Sir Alexander Cochrane. Strongly prejudiced against all things American, he could be expected to pursue the new British offensive strategy with relentless vigour. With a serious threat of invasion from Canada, the crews of long-blockaded frigates were transferred to the Great Lakes, and when the *Essex* was captured in March, the presence of the US Navy on the high seas was confined to a few sloops.

Wasp made a successful foray in the middle of the year, taking the war to the enemy in the waters around Great Britain, but she then disappeared at sea in October. *Peacock* was also able to cruise against trade in the Caribbean, winning another of the US Navy's many victorious encounters with British brigs, but her sister *Frolic* was taken by a British frigate. The only American frigate to make a contribution was the *Constitution*, which finally escaped from Boston in December. Off Madeira in February 1815 she won her cleverest battle, taking both the *Cyane* and *Levant*, and escaping from a far superior force. The final blue-water naval operation of the war was an ambitious plan to attack British shipping in the East Indies in squadron force, but its ships were not able to escape from New York until the January gales of 1815. Even then the *President* was captured after a running fight with the blockading squadron, but *Hornet, Peacock* and their store vessels were able to rendezvous in the south Atlantic. All these sloops did less damage to British trade than might have been expected, but found consolation in a sequence of morale-raising victories over British brigs: *Epervier, Reindeer, Avon* and *Penguin*.

With the limited means at its disposal, the US Navy had fought a creditable campaign at sea. In aggregate effect, its attack on trade was probably less important than the efforts of the far more numerous privateers, but by inflicting an unprecedented sequence of defeats on the Royal Navy it helped to persuade a war-weary Britain that there was little to be gained by continuing the war.

The single-ship actions

From the years of the war itself much of the attention of the press, the public and historians has concentrated on the single-ship actions,

especially between the frigates. Like the air combat of the First World War, they reflected a romantic notion of the most chivalrous aspects of war, and certainly in America their importance was greatly exaggerated for political ends. For the Royal Navy, unfamiliar with defeat whatever the odds, it was necessary to explain to an outraged public and Parliament what had gone wrong. For years after the real fighting ceased, protagonists for both sides traded charges of lies, deceit and extreme chauvinism. Like most polemical argument, the heat of the debate created more smoke than light, and even today it is difficult to form a view of some battles that agree with the descriptions given by those on different sides.

At the root of the problem are the official reports by the officers involved, which only the naïve would treat as objective evidence. The defeated captain faced a court martial and had to put the best face on his performance. Obviously, it was in his interest to maximise the power of his opponent and make the most of the damage inflicted; he might also use a substantial 'butcher's bill' among his own crew to prove that he had not surrendered until there was no alternative. However, he was often ill placed to know how his enemy had fared – American frigates were usually carefully repaired and returned to fighting trim before taking the surrender of their foes – so exaggerated estimates of casualties were common. Nor was it easy to define 'wounded': in the Royal Navy every man who visited the surgeon was listed since they could then claim 'smart money', but US practice seems to have confined the term to those unable to do duty.

In many ways the victorious captain had even more reason for giving his report a similar spin. His career depended on how his achievement was judged, but there was also a significant financial advantage if the prize was purchased for the navy. Most Royal Navy officers wrote glowing advertising copy about their prizes, but unless they were on a distant station where the commander-in-chief would make the decision, the judgement rested on an impartial Navy Board survey. The temptation to exaggeration was greater in the US Navy where the whole value of the prize was only allocated to the crew if the prize was judged of equal or superior force to the capturing ship; otherwise they received only half. An unhappy

precedent had been set during the 'Quasi-War' by Truxton's attempts to prove that the 12-pounder frigate *L'Insurgente* was somehow superior to his 24-pounder-armed *Constellation* and in this conflict Decatur ended up in a similarly disreputable argument about the *Macedonian*.

The principal tactic used by the officers of both services was to exploit the inherent ambiguities of the rating system. At one time warships had carried precisely the number of guns alongside their name in the navy list, with few and generally minor exceptions – a 36-gun frigate had thirty-six guns, and a 44 had forty-four. However, the introduction of the carronade around 1780 confused the issue, because at first they were both additional and not counted in the established force of ships (possibly because they were regarded as temporary like swivel guns). The next step was to replace some long guns with the far more powerful carronades, but the formal rating remained the same, because the old classification was an accepted convention – the main features of, say a 36, had not altered despite the fact that it might now carry only thirty long guns plus twelve carronades. Frigates usually showed the greatest variation between nominal and real armament, and being the first to introduce the new weapon, the British were most guilty of ignoring their existence: many of the frigate victories of the 1790s gained by British '32's over French '40's were actually won by more powerful ships. It was widely understood by professionals that ships usually carried far more guns than their rating, but it might have bemused outsiders. Master Commandant Ludlow, for example, complained about the USS *John Adams*: 'in her present state she will be considered by the public, and particularly by any vessel she may have to contend with, as a 32-gun frigate, when she mounts but 32 guns' – in other words, it is misleading that she only mounts her rated armament.

The rating '44' applied to the American spar-decked ships was probably meant to convey the notion of a frigate of the first class, that figure being the largest regularly applied to frigate-type vessels – anything larger, like a 50, was understood to be a small two-decker. But if it was not originally intended to mislead, in practice there was a huge difference between rated and real force, and this was exploited to great propaganda effect during the war. The reports of victorious American captains were scrupulous to enumerate every gun – including the little boat carronade – carried by their opponents. While never overtly misrepresenting their own force, they were not above glossing silently over the disparity in numbers or ignoring the smaller calibre of their opposition's guns. Soon the press and printmakers were announcing that American '44's had beaten British ships with '49' guns. For the British the defeats were hard enough to swallow, but the claim that it was achieved by inferior force was an outrage. The rabidly anti-American tone of the historian William James is one product of this feeling of injustice, but on a more significant level it drove the Admiralty to revise the rating system to indicate real gun-power the moment the war was over, so that similar American propaganda victories could never occur in the future.

Another fruitful area for misrepresentation was in the tonnage of vessels. British and American methods of measurement differed in detail, the latter usually producing a higher figure. For example, the *Epervier* was rated at 382 tons in the Royal Navy but 447 in the US service. Looking at prize ships gives reasonably consistent results:

Ship		Length	Breadth	Tonnage
American prizes				
Macedonian	USN	156ft 2in	40ft 0in	1325
	RN	154ft 0in	39ft 5in	1082
Cyane	USN	120ft 4in	31ft 6in	643
	RN	118ft 0in	32ft 0in	537
British prizes				
President	USN	175ft 0in	44ft 2in	1571
	RN	173ft 3in	44ft 4in	1533
Chesapeake	USN	153ft 10in	40ft 11in	1244
	RN	151ft 0in	40ft 11in	1135
Wasp	USN	105ft 7in	30ft 11in	450
	RN	105ft 10½in	30ft 10in	434

However, given the similarities in dimensions, the big differences in tonnage for *Macedonian* and *Cyane* are suspicious, and suggest some administrative conniving to make the prizes look bigger than they were (either to produce more prize money for the captors, or to avoid official embarrassment about their over-valuation). However, there are two British exceptions also: USS *Frolic* measured 509 tons in the US Navy but 539 as HMS *Florida*, while *Essex* was listed as 850 tons in the US Navy and 867 in British service.

In the individual sections on the single-ship actions that follow, in general the figures adopted are those stated by each side, a degree of scepticism being reserved for any claim made about the size, force, complement or casualties of the opposing ship. Every officer might be expected to know the details of his own ship, but for the opponent he was, at best, making an honest estimate, and at worst exaggerating for any one of the reasons enumerated above.

Privateering

Much of the burden of the war on trade was carried by American privateers. With opportunities for the legitimate occupation of shipping almost extinguished by the British blockade and the prevalence of enemy cruisers at sea, the American merchant marine turned to privateering with gusto. It was the only possible employment of expensive capital assets, and was entered into with the same entrepreneurial judgement of risk versus reward that has made the American economy the largest of the present century. Yet there has always been a tendency to romanticise what was essentially a business. It perhaps began with George Coggeshall, who had been a privateer in his youth and tended to glamorise the activities of his contemporaries, although the attitude can

be detected earlier in the press treatment of privateers and blockade-runners as local heroes during the war itself.

Even among modern historians this leads to a predisposition to exaggerate the qualities of the ships and the achievements of the men. In general, merchant ships were slow, lightly armed and crewed by the minimum number a profit-oriented owner could get away with. Capturing them with a speedy, well-armed and massively crewed privateer was not an heroic act – but, for the lucky ones, it was good business. Contrary to popular opinion, however, the successful privateer was in the minority. It has been calculated that of 526 vessels known to have received the 'letter-of-marque and reprisal' commissions that made them a privateer, only 207 ever took a prize, three out of every five returning empty handed. Not that all bearers of a commission were genuine privateers: most were primarily traders whose principal profit came from the cargo successfully run through the blockade, the letter-of-marque merely giving them legal right to pick up enemy merchant ships should the opportunity arise. The privateer proper cruised for no other purpose, and was heavily manned in order to send in prizes.

Since he ignored this distinction, Mahan's argument that US warships made a higher rate

Mere statistics could not so well convey the difference in size between the American '44's and the standard British 38-gun frigate, so William James published these comparative deck plans, based on the President *and a* Macedonian *class ship. The difference was not just dimensions, but the broad gangways of the American ship – which made the quarterdeck and forecastle into a continuous 'spar deck' – also allowed the mounting of additional guns in the waist (although the US frigates had given up carrying continuous upper deck batteries by the time of the war). Plate 2 from James's* A Full and Correct Account of the Chief Naval Occurrences of the late war . . . *published in May 1817.* NMM neg D9542

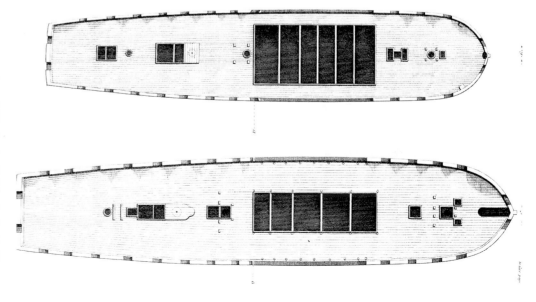

of capture than privateers is probably spurious. Warships took 165 merchant ships and privateers a further 1344, but at least a half of these were recaptured and others were employed as cartels (to return prisoners), ransomed to their owners or simply sunk or burned as it became too dangerous to bring them into a friendly port. There were great success stories, perhaps the foremost being the Salem privateer *America*, which captured 41 vessels, 33 of which were ordered to the US, and only 6 retaken on their way home.

As for the navy, conditions for privateers were most favourable at the beginning of the war. In the first six months of the conflict Salem privateers took 87 prizes, 58 of which arrived, despite the fact that the first generation of privateers were not purpose-built but simply existing merchantmen refitted. It was only later, as the blockade became tighter and the possible need to fight off small cruisers became more pressing, that larger and more powerful vessels were built specially for the commerce war – the biggest Baltimore schooners reached 300 tons. This phenomenon was also true of the earlier French *guerre de course*, but American merchantmen had a design advantage, having been developed when trade restrictions and enemy interference had made the speedy carriage of small quantities of high-value goods a very profitable business. Unlike the boxy bulk carriers of the European merchant marines, sharp-lined American brigs and schooners made good improvised privateers.

Even with the development of dedicated privateers, the business became ever more dangerous. This can be seen in the declining numbers commissioned at a major port like Salem: 20 privateers in 1812, 14 in 1813 and 6 in 1814, and of these only about 13 escaped capture or destruction. In total 148 known carriers of letters-of-marque were captured, representing 28 per cent; when others lost by other forms of enemy action are added the percentage must be higher. Since different parts of the coast were blockaded with varying degrees of rigour throughout the war, some ports may have suffered more than others. Baltimore, whose famous clipper schooners were supposedly uncatchable, actually lost 19 privateers and 36 other letters-of-marque representing 45 per cent of all private commissions.

Even more damaging was the loss of prize crews. Privateers might be fast sailers, but their victims were usually not, and in total some two-thirds of all prize crews were captured before they could reach port. Friendly ports were available outside the US, but these were gradually reduced: prizes were banned from sale in French ports from July 1814 by the new Bourbon administration, for example. The situation became so bad in the latter half of the war that privateers simply took what was valuable from most prizes and scuttled or set fire to them. There had been the option of ransoming the ship, since many a master was also the owner, but in the US government's eyes the privateering war was designed not to enrich its citizens but to destroy the enemy's commerce, so it prohibited the practice in January 1814. Knowing that Britain was permanently short of seamen, the US government also offered a bounty for each prisoner brought in. This stood at $20 per man in 1812, but even allowing for a privateer captain's natural reluctance to fill his ship with potentially dangerous prisoners, the increasingly adverse nature of the trade war can be seen in the raising of the bounty to $25 in 1813 and $100 in 1814.

Although small in comparison with the American effort, the British privateering counter-campaign is often forgotten. In practice the most active of the vessels involved were actually Canadian, operating out of the Maritime Provinces. Privateers like the famous *Liverpool Packet* were far smaller than their ocean-going cousins, and much of the warfare was directed at the crucial coastal traffic of New England. The Americans responded in kind, and since many of the Canadians were Loyalists forced north after the Revolution, the conflict was carried on with the vehemence characteristic of civil war.

A weakness of all historical writing about the privateering of this war is the failure to evaluate its effect on the enemy. For individuals privateering was a method of eking out a living in hard times, and it is important to know exactly how this was done, but if it is represented as a national strategy it is more important to analyse just how much pressure it exerted on British decision-making. It is not enough to quote the memorials of merchants or insurers whose personal business was under threat – such protests had always occurred whenever there was a surge of French privateering – but

the damage needs objective quantification. This is a task for a future economic historian, but there are a few crude indicators that suggest that the impact of the trade war has been exaggerated.

To begin with, the size of the British merchant marine was hardly dented by the losses, and continued to grow at the same steady rate that had applied throughout the war with France:

British shipping growth

	Ships	Tonnage
1811	20,478	2,247,000
1812	20,637	2,263,000
1813	20,951	2,349,000
1814	21,450	2,414,000
1815	21,869	2,478,000

Nor was the volume of trade appreciably affected. Figures for 1813 have been lost, but again the trend is steadily upwards:

British trade – aggregate current value (£m)

	Imports	Domestic exports	Re-exports
1811	51	33	7
1812	56	42	9
1813	[n/a]		
1814	81	46	25
1815	71	52	17

Furthermore, the global picture was reflected at local level. The West Indies, which were said to 'swarm' with American privateers, enjoyed the same upward tendency in both exports and imports, a particular surge being recorded in 1814 at the height of the trade war.

With so little visible impact on British shipping and trade it is extremely unlikely that the *guerre de course* could ever have become a war-winning weapon. On the other hand, whether the *perception* of its effect had an influence on ending the war is a moot point. What seems more certain is that without the contribution of the US Navy the provisions of the peace treaty would have been far more onerous. The string of victories on the high seas persuaded a war-weary Britain that there would be no quick knock-out blow, while the Navy's crucial intervention at Plattsburg destroyed British hopes of a decisive invasion from Canada.

1

1. 'US frigate *Constitution* of 44 guns',
engraving, line and tint, engraved by
William Lynn after an original by Abel
Bowen, published by William Lynn,
Boston, no date but probably about
1813-15. This is probably the best guide
to the ship's appearance during the
war, without a continuous battery on
the the spar deck, and a break in the
barricading at the waist as in more
conventional frigates.
NMM neg 522

2. 'La fregate des Etats-unis
d'Amerique, le President venant
d'appareiller, avec des ris dans les
Huniers. Plate 13 in Collection de
Toutes les especes de batimens . . .
2eme Livraision', engraving by
Baugean after his own original,
published by Jean, 1826
NMM ref PAD7389

The United States Navy in 1812

2

THE AMERICAN navy of 1812 was a young service, tracing its foundation to an act of March
1794 authorising the construction of its first vessels to counter the depredations of the Barbary powers of
North Africa (see, in this series, *Nelson against Napoleon*,
pages 146-150 for further details). Its subsequent development had been, at best, sporadic: the 'Quasi-War' with
France, and the clash with Tripoli, had lead to expansion
in 1798-1800 and to a lesser extent from 1803 to 1805, but
no frigate had been launched since 1800. Furthermore,
basically pacifist administrations since 1801 had been very
reluctant to spend money on a navy, and what limited
resources that were available were utilised on a programme of gunboat construction for coast defence.
Although there were a number of Navy Yards, the facilities were basic. For example, the US Navy still did not
possess a single dock, major repairs involving the costly
and time-consuming business of heaving down, with its
consequent risk of straining the ship's frame. Most of the
sea-going vessels were laid up for long periods, and some
were allowed to rot so comprehensively that they

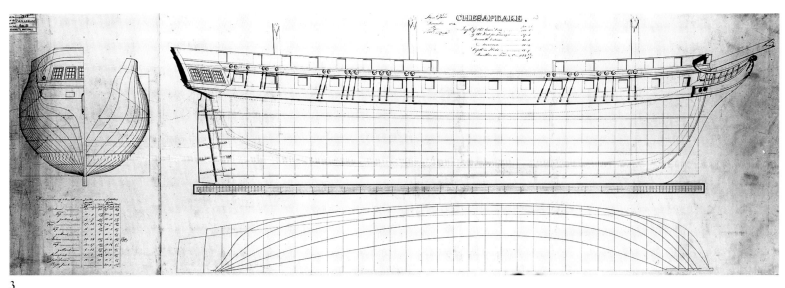

3

3. Sheer draught of the *Chesapeake*, as captured; dated Plymouth December 1814.
NMM ref DR7343

4. 'Fregate des Etats-unis d'Amerique faisant secher ses hamacs. Plate 2 in Collection de Toutes les especes de batimens . . . 2eme Livraision', engraving by Baugean after his own original, published by Jean, 1826. One of the small frigates, possibly the *Boston*.
NMM ref PAD7378

4

proved impossible to repair economically. Others were repaired with inferior and unseasoned timber, and this caused further problems later.

As a result of politically inspired neglect, at the beginning of 1812 the US Navy had only fourteen vessels ready for sea service: the three 44-gun frigates *United States, Constitution, President*; the smaller frigates *Congress, Essex* and *John Adams*; the ship sloops *Hornet* and *Wasp*; brig sloops *Argus, Syren* and *Nautilus*; and the smaller brigs *Enterprise* and *Viper*. There was also the brig *Oneida* on Lake Ontario, and, scattered around the creeks and harbours of the eastern seaboard, some 165 gunboats, 62 of which were in commission. Laid up in Ordinary (reserve) were the frigates *Constellation, Chesapeake, Adams, New York* and *Boston*, and in June 1812 it was decided to repair the first three, *Constellation* being ready for service by October and *Chesapeake* a month later; *Adams* needed more substantial work and was reduced to a corvette, not completing until the middle of 1813.

The officer corps was small, at around 500, but was well trained and experienced in actual combat, many having fought in the conflict with France and the Tripolitan war. The service itself was too young to have developed accepted precedents, and officers were inclined to dispute promotions and quarrel on points of personal honour, resulting in some fatal duels. On the whole, however, such disputes were confined to the shore, and the aggression of these men was turned to good effect in the war to come. The bombast and egotism apparent in the correspondence of officers like Rodgers and Porter, reflected a high level of self-confidence and genuine fighting spirit.

In personnel terms the US Navy of 1812 included some 5230 seamen, only 2346 of which were assigned to cruisers, the remainder serving in fortifications, navy yards or on the Great Lakes. The Marine Corps had a nominal strength of 1000, although only about half that number were actually signed up. By way of comparison, the navy it was about to take on had voted funds to support 113,600 seamen and 31,400 marines in 1812, and had 548 cruising warships in commission, 102 being line of battle ships.

However small its numbers, the US Navy had a distinct qualitative advantage. The long wars with France had forced the Royal Navy to build large numbers of ships, the pressure for sheer numbers resulting in designs which were regarded as the smallest equal to their various roles. It had expanded beyond a size it could conveniently man, even with impressment – indeed, its requirements exceeded pre-war estimates of the whole seafaring population of Great Britain – and as a consequence its ships were thinly, and in many cases poorly, manned. For America the reverse was true: her navy required only about five per cent of the country's professional seamen, and in consequence was all-volunteer, and its ships were designed to be superior individually to any European equivalent.

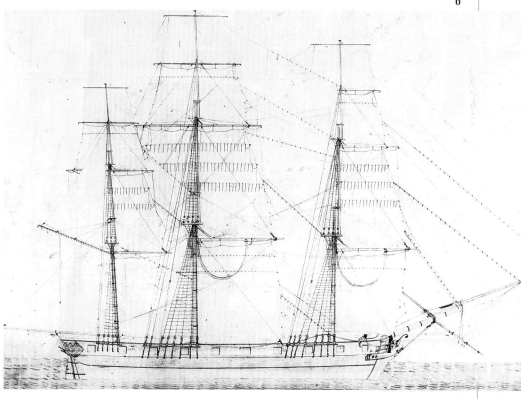

5. 'American corvette', brown wash by John William Huggins, no date. Probably represents the *John Adams* as cut down, with shortened quarterdeck and no armament on the upperworks.
NMM ref PAH5248

6. Original draught of the sloop *Wasp* as converted to ship rig.
US National Archives ref RG19, 109-8-2D

The best and most famous example of this design philosophy was the *Constitution* class of large frigates (1). According to Joshua Humphreys, who was responsible for the concept, they were inspired by the French *rasées* of 1794, 'they having cut down several of their seventy-fours to make heavy frigates'. They were not the first frigates to carry a main armament of 24-pounders, but were original in having a continuous upper deck — instead of separate quarterdeck and forecastle — allowing them to mount a second complete battery on this so-called spar deck. When they were first completed, they came in for some criticism from their officers, who variously complained of their sailing qualities, lack of stowage, poor stability and the hogging stresses caused by such a heavy weight of metal. The officers were themselves responsible for fitting out the ships, so in most cases the remedies were in their own hands, and by 1812 there were no more complaints.

With the scantlings of 74s, they were predecessors of the German 'pocket battleships': as Humphreys himself predicted in 1794, 'From the construction of those ships, it is expected the commanders of them will have it in

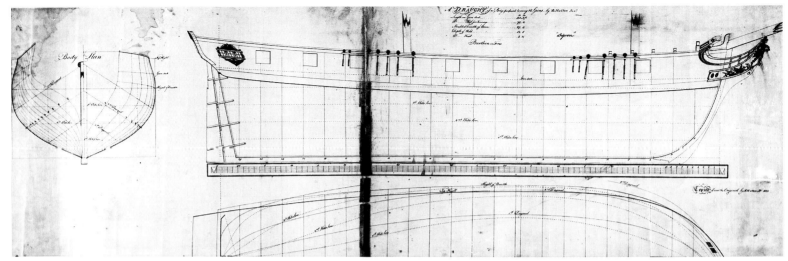

7

their power to engage, or not, any ship they may think proper; and no ship, under sixty-four, now afloat, but what must submit to them.' They were not identical in qualities, the received wisdom of the service making *President* the best (2). Bainbridge thought her 'one of the finest ships in the world' and offered Rodgers $5000 to change ship with him when he had *Constitution* (Rodgers refused). *United States* was the least regarded. Her sailing qualities earned her the nick-name 'the Wagon', and even after she had captured the *Macedonian*, she was out-sailed by her jury-rigged prize.

The frigates armed with 18-pounders were more conventional, although they were still large by European standards. *Chesapeake*, originally intended to carry 24-pounders, was considered 'over-built' by her British captors (3), and her sailing qualities insufficient to warrant copying her hull lines (the sincere form of flattery applied by the British to many of their finest prizes). With the exception of the *Essex*, the smaller frigates contributed little to the war. *Congress* made some long cruises but to no great effect, and was laid up from the middle of 1813; *Chesapeake* was captured; *Constellation* never eluded

the blockade at all; and *New York* and *Boston* (4), not thought worth the cost of repair, were burned when the British occupied Washington in August 1814. Unlike their larger cousins, these ships had no advantage in fire-power or sailing over their British counterparts, and it is significant that *Essex* was most successful in waters where she was unlikely to meet a British frigate. Captain Porter had little confidence in his ship's sailing abilities or her short-range carronades, so when he came up against HMS *Phoebe*, he could neither fight effectively nor run away.

There were also two very small 'frigates', the confusingly similar *Adams* and *John Adams*, of the kind the British described as post ships (the smallest rate commanded by a post captain). With a full quarterdeck and forecastle, they were high for their length, the substantial topsides tending to make them leewardly. With a small-calibre main armament, they were generally regarded as obsolescent, although the Royal Navy had recently revived the type as a convoy escort (like the *Cyane* later taken by the *Constitution*). The American ships were no better, and the captain of *John Adams* was especially critical: 'She cannot pass for more than a tolerable sailing merchant ship,

7. Original draught of the brig *Syren*. *US National Archives ref RG19, 40-10-2A*

8. Original draught of the schooner *Vixen*. *US National Archives ref RG19, 109-4-15*

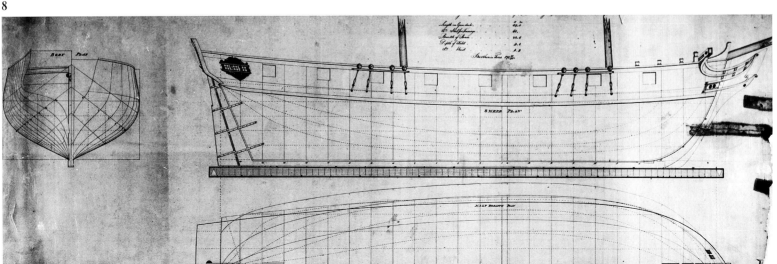

and so crank [unstable] that a ship of 20 guns ought to take her, in what would generally be called a topgallant breeze for ships of war.' He thought she was fit only as a corvette, and like *Adams* she was eventually cut down to this rate (5). *Adams* underwent the more radical transformation, being reduced to a flush ship and having an extra 15 feet inserted, and did some useful work before having to be burnt to avoid capture in the Penobscot in September 1814. The other retained the after part of the quarterdeck with the topgallant forecastle, but with no armament on the upper works: she then carried twenty 12-pounders and two 18s, all long guns.

Newest and most effective of the sloops were the 18-gun *Hornet* and *Wasp*, originally designed as brigs but in a prescient move, converted to ship rig by 1812 (6). They were somewhat larger than their likely British opponents, but it was the ship rig that gave them the real advantage over the brig sloops of the *Cruizer* class they were to meet during the war. With only two masts the balance of a brig rig was easily upset by damage aloft, whereas a ship could retain manoeuvrability with far more injury to her rigging.

Brigs, of course, required smaller crews, and even the well-manned US Navy found them useful. The two largest were the 16-gun *Argus* and *Syren*, and while 'not extraordinary in size or design' (according to the *doyen* of sailing ship historians, Howard Chapelle), both were fast sailers, the latter being slightly sharper in hull form. Of the remainder of the brigs, *Enterprise* and *Vixen* (8) were purpose built, the others being purchased. All had been altered from other rigs, the *Viper* having been a cutter and the rest schooners – and all were said to have lost out in sailing qualities by the conversion, which raises the question of why the US Navy did it. Schooners will always have an advantage to windward over any square rig, but even with square topsails a schooner is less efficient before it. There was also the matter of fighting qualities: in a genuine warship, the ability to back square canvas gave them a manoeuvring advantage in battle, and although not as resistant as a ship, a brig had a greater variety of canvas than a schooner, which made the rig less vulnerable to a single disabling hit. Not surprisingly, after a war in which its small craft spent much of their time trying to escape superior forces, the US Navy revived its interest in schooners from 1815.

The remainder of the US fleet comprised flotillas of gunboats. These were built in 1802-6 to a variety of designs, ranging between about 50 and 70 feet in length, and usually armed with one or two large guns (18- or 24-pounders) on slides or pivot mountings (9). Intended to defend harbours, river estuaries and coastal traffic, they could be rowed or sailed, although some were optimised for one or the other. Under sail, an incredible diversity of

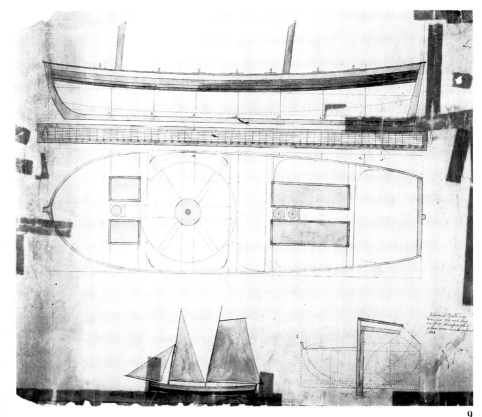

9

fore-and-aft rigs were used, with one or two masts, gaff, gunter or lateen sails, and occasionally square topsails. Although vulnerable to boarding by the boat crews of larger warships, they had a few successes during the war, but they were often replaced by smaller fast-rowing gun-barges for riverine fighting. These gunboats also absorbed much of the Navy's limited manpower, and many were decommissioned in order to transfer their crews to more active employment.

9. A draught of the Gunboats *Nos 29-37* drawn by Commissioner Coffin at the request of Edward Preble about 1804.
US National Archives ref RG19, 80-7-19A

10. Supposedly the three-decker *Pennsylvania*, but actually a two-decked *rasée*; the number and disposition of the gunports suggest the *Independence* in later life. Coloured lithograph published by F Sala & Co, no date.
NMM ref PAF8076

10

Seagoing Ships of the US Navy in 1812

Name, rate	Launched	Length	Tonnage	Wartime Armament
United States, 44	1797	175ft 0in	1575	30x24pdr; 2x24pdr, 22x42pdr carr
Constitution, 44	1797	175ft 0in	1575	30x24pdr; 1x18pdr, 24x32pdr carr
President, 44	1800	175ft 0in	1575	30x24pdr; 2x24pdr, 1x18pdr, 22x42pdr carr
Constellation, 38	1797	163ft 3in	1265	28x18pdr; 2x32pdr, 18x32pdr carr
Congress, 38	1799	163ft 3in	1265	24x18pdr; 20x32pdr carr
Chesapeake, 38	1799	133ft 10in	1244	28x18pdr, 20x32pdr carr
Essex, 32	1799	140ft 0in	850	26x32pdr carr; 6x18pdr, 10x32pdr carr
John Adams, 28	1799	139ft 0in	544	2x18pdr, 20x12pdr
Hornet, 18	1805	106ft 9in	441	2x12pdr, 18x32pdr carr
Wasp, 18	1806	105ft 7in	450	2x12pdr, 18x32pdr carr
Argus, 16	1803	94ft 6in	299	2x12pdr, 18x24pdr carr
Syren, 16	1803	93ft 4in	250	2x12pdr, 16x24pdr carr
Nautilus, 14	1803	87ft 6in	c150	2x9pdr, 12x18pdr carr
Vixen, 14	1803	84ft 7in	170	2x9pdr, 12x18pdr carr
Enterprise, 12	1799	84ft 7in	165	2x9pdr, 14x18pdr carr
Viper, 12	1809	73ft 0in	148	2x6pdr, 12x12pdr carr

Armament quotes the main battery first; then the upperworks (spar deck or forecastle/quarterdeck). Carr = carronade.

Despite the months of contemplating war, Madison's government made no preparations for expanding the Navy. At the end of 1811 the Secretary of the Navy had reported that twelve 74s and twenty frigates was minimum force needed to protect the American coast properly in the event of conflict with either of the main European belligerents. However, it took the naval actions of 1812 to spur the administration into action, the first major building programme for more than a decade being voted by Congress on 23 December 1812. It provided for six more 44-gun frigates, enlarged from the *Constitution* concept, and four '74's, which were intended to be proportionately more powerful than their European equivalents. Wartime conditions meant that none of these ships saw service in the conflict; indeed, it was unrealistic to expect the British to allow such powerful ships to get to sea, or even to be completed, if they could possibly stop them. The *Independence* (10), the most advanced 74, was closely blockaded in Boston right at the end of the war.

Far more useful to the immediate war effort was the programme of six big ship sloops approved in March 1813. In effect, these flush-decked vessels were to become the corvette equivalent of the 44s – they were fast and weatherly, so could escape most larger predators, but could outfight any of the standard British sloop classes. Of the two basic designs, *Argus, Erie* and *Ontario* (11) had the sharper hull form, but they were wayward as built and needed much modification. The real success story was the other class, for although the *Frolic* was soon captured, *Wasp* and *Peacock* became highly effective commerce destroyers in the last year of the war.

11. 'The USs Sloop of War *Ontario* Dedicated to Lieut. Bigelow, Mahon, the 1st of Febry 1822', watercolour by A Carlotta. Built in 1813-14, the sloop was blockaded during the war and unable to get to sea.
Peabody Essex Museum, Salem, MA neg 11765

Lucky escapes

THE OPENING moves of the sea war were notable for a remarkable series of escapes from superior forces by the frigates of both sides, which, if nothing else, proved that fine seamanship was not the monopoly of either navy.

On the outbreak of war Commodore Rodgers (1) sailed from New York with a powerful squadron comprising the two 44s *President* and *United States*, the 38-gun *Congress* and the sloops *Hornet* and *Argus*. Two days out on 23 June, some 100 miles southwest of the Nantucket Shoals, he encountered the British 36-gun frigate *Belvidera*. In light winds *President* ranged up on her weather quarter and opened fire with her bow chase guns in an attempt to disable *Belvidera* aloft (2). Rodgers enjoyed the initial advantage of surprise, since the outbreak of war could not be known to his target, but the British Captain Byron was an experienced and wily officer: as her later reported, 'Although ignorant of the war, we were of course prepared, and about five minutes afterwards opened ours with two carronades 32-pounders and two long eighteens from the stern.' *President* sailed better in light winds than the British ship, and having reached point-blank range on her quarter it should have been the end of *Belvidera*. However, Rodgers' flagship suffered a

burst chase gun which killed or wounded sixteen, but it was the subsequent yawing (3) to attempt broadside firing that lost *President* the initiative, and eventually she gave over the chase. Both ships were damaged aloft, although not seriously, and considering they were for a time within grape shot range, the *President*'s broadside firing was poor. It did not augur well, and indeed the rest of Rodgers' cruise was a disappointment to him.

Sailing from Annapolis on 5 July, *Constitution*, under Isaac Hull, was due to join Rodgers' force, and in a mirror-image of the previous incident, ran into a strong British squadron off the Jersey coast under Captain Philip Broke of the *Shannon*, 38. It also included the *Africa*, 64, the *Aeolus*, 32 and, thirsting for revenge, the *Belvidera*; further off were the *Guerriere*, 38 and the captured US brig *Nautilus*. Again the wind was very light, and on 18 July began an epic three-day struggle to escape capture. The *Constitution* had the advantage of being fresh from port, and was stored only for a short cruise, so the hull was both light and clean. At first both sides resorted to boats to tow their becalmed commands, but being in soundings they eventually turned to the backbreaking expedient of kedging – carrying small anchors ahead in the boats, and then heaving in on the capstan. The British had the

1. 'Commodore Rodgers', engraved by John R Smith after an original by Henry Williams, no date.
Beverley R Robinson collection ref BRR51.7.732.41

2. 'Escape of *Belvidera*, 23 June 1812', oil painting in the style of William John Huggins (1781-1845).
NMM ref BHC0598

3. 'Escape of the *Belvidere* [sic] Commanded by the Late Adm Rd Byron CB from the American Squadron', lithograph produced and published by C Hullmandel after an original by Lt F Edwards.
US Naval Academy Museum

4. 'Chase of the USS *Constitution* off the Jersey Coast, 17-19 July 1812', oil painting by Philip Inch, 1834.
US Naval Academy Museum

5. David Porter's diagram of the escape of the *Essex* off Georges Bank, 4 September 1812.
US National Archives and Records Administration

6. '*Galatea* with *Congress* and *President*, 31 October 1812', watercolour by Irwin Bevan (1852-1940), no date.
Beverley R Robinson collection ref BRR51.7.494.9

3

advantage of numbers and the ships further off sent their boats to assist the nearest frigate, the *Shannon*. Every tiny adjustment was made, like furling all the sails to reduce windage, to gain a few yards, but even eight or ten boats could not close the gap (4).

Very light breezes arose from time to time, and occasionally the pursuers crept close enough to exchange a few shots, but by the 19th in gradually rising winds the *Constitution* was gaining. On the 20th Captain Hull set his crew to wet the sails, to retain more wind, and by the

4

middle of the morning the American frigate was so far ahead that the British squadron gave up the chase and returned to their blockade station off New York. Hull was relieved but knew he could no longer keep his rendezvous with Rodgers, and so decided to head for Boston, and eventually to a meeting with the *Guerriere*.

Captain David Porter of the *Essex* also reported an escape from a superior force on 4 September. What he thought were two warships were actually the *Shannon* and a captured American merchant ship, but he neatly cut across the bows of the British frigate and escaped to windward in the dark. Porter was so pleased with himself that he enclosed a drawing of his exploit in his official letter (5). He was certainly fortunate to get away from Broke's crack ship, but he did not mention abandoning the American merchantman he was escorting in order to achieve it. *Shannon* then seized and burned this vessel, the *Minerva*.

Rodgers' second cruise also contained a number of missed opportunities: he chased and lost the *Nymphe*, 38, in October, and later fell in with the *Galatea*, 32, which was escorting two South Sea whalers, the *Argo* and *Berkeley*. Despite having two ships, *President* and *Congress*, both of which were individually superior to *Galatea*, Rodgers settled for taking the *Argo*, one of only two ships he captured during the whole of his cruise (6). The other, however, was the packet *Swallow* carrying boxes of gold and silver to the estimated value of $150,000-$200,000.

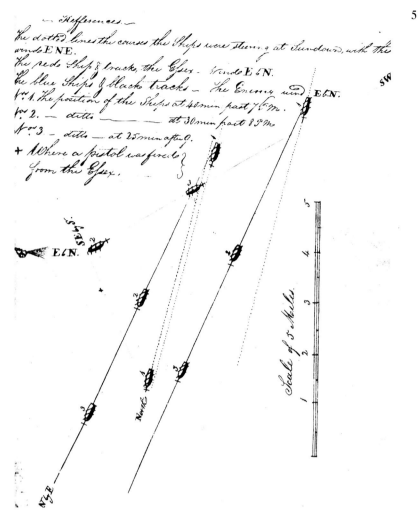

5

6

1

First blood

IT TOOK some months for news of the declaration of war to reach the thousands of British ships, naval and mercantile, that were at sea. American privateers were quick to take advantage of this situation, and in the case of the *Dash*, premature. Sailing out of Chesapeake Bay on her first cruise, she noticed the British naval schooner *Whiting* at anchor in Hampton Roads, with her boat rowing for shore. Living up to her name, *Dash* promptly took the boat, ran alongside the schooner and overawed the remaining crew of twelve into surrender (1). The British were certainly unaware of the outbreak of war, but unfortunately for Captain Carroway of the privateer the *Whiting* was carrying official dispatches for the US government, who instructed him to release his prize. Since the crew had thrown the dispatches overboard as soon as they were threatened, the British vessel had no further business to conduct and was ordered out of US waters. Unfortunately, her bad luck with privateers was not over: on the return voyage she was captured by the French brig *Diligent*.

The first legal capture of a British warship fell to USS *Essex*, although Captain Porter hardly felt it an honour. His prize, the sloop of war *Alert*, was taken on 13 August off the Grand Banks after a 'trifling skirmish' of eight minutes (2). Even Porter, the great self-promoter, could make little of his crew's easy victory, and his report 'regretted that so much zeal and activity could not have been displayed on an occasion that would have done them more honor.' Although the term 'sloop of war' summons up ideas of a sleek fighting ship, *Alert* was a converted collier, purchased by the Royal Navy as a crisis measure during the invasion scare of 1804. Rather like the armed merchant cruisers of later world wars, she had been armed with a scratch collection of available weapons – in her case 18-pounder carronades – and assigned to convoy protection.

When asked for his opinion of the ship, Porter thought her sailing qualities too poor to make a cruiser. She was very high-sided, which must have made her leewardly, but the 8 feet of height on the berth deck could be turned to advantage if she was converted into a block ship (floating battery). The local commander at New York wanted to use her as a receiving ship, the spacious accommodation contributing 'very much to the comfort and health of the recruits, for which she is well calculated.' However, she was ordered to be commissioned, although she never cruised as a warship during the hostilities.

2

3

The US Navy also had its early losses, the first being the brig *Nautilus*, which was less than a day out from New York when on the morning of 16 July she ran into Broke's blockading squadron. This comprised the same ships which two days later were to pursue the *Constitution*, but this time they were more successful. Strong winds and a heavy swell gave the advantage to the hunters, and as *Shannon* ranged up on the brig's quarter, Lieutenant William Crane had no option but to haul down his colours. He recorded 'polite and gentlemanly' treatment from Broke, but he and his crew were the first of many American seamen dispatched as prisoners of war to Halifax.

Further south, another brig, USS *Vixen*, fell easy victim to a British frigate on 22 November. Despite the best exertions of the American crew, the brig could not escape, and was forced to surrender to the 32-gun *Southampton* (3). Commanded by James Lucas Yeo, who was to become better known in America as Chauncey's opponent on Lake Ontario, the frigate was the oldest in the Royal Navy, having been built in 1757. However, her long service was about to come to an abrupt end, when five days later she ran on an uncharted reef off the Bahamas. *Vixen* was also wrecked, but both crews were rescued and taken to Jamaica.

Constitution **versus** *Guerriere*

WHEN SHE originally sailed from Annapolis in July *Constitution* had been victualled only for the short voyage to New York, but his encounter with Broke's squadron forced Isaac Hull (1) to take his ship into Boston instead for provisions. Not finding any specific orders waiting for him, and fearing being blockaded by a superior force, he quickly put to sea, planning to meet up with the rest of Rodgers' force at sea or, failing that, to cruise against shipping off the Canadian coast. Information from prizes warned him of the proximity of a British squadron, which Hull assumed to be Broke's, and he decided to switch his cruising ground further south. On 18 August he was told by the American privateer *Decatur* of a British warship she had spotted the previous day, and Hull set off to investigate.

At about 2pm on the 19th *Constitution* sighted a ship to the east standing westwards, and crowded on sail to close with the stranger. Two hours later she was identified as a large frigate, which with great confidence had backed her main topsail and lay in wait for the American ship to come down. She was HMS *Guerriere*, an ex-French ship taken by the *Blanche* in 1806 and now commanded by James Richard Dacres (2), a highly competent if not out-

standing officer. Rated at 38 guns, she was not a particularly large frigate even by European standards, carrying a main battery of thirty 18-pounders (although two were bow-chasers that could not be fired on the broadside). The ship was in a poor material state, being en route to Halifax for a refit - the weak state of her masts was later quoted in extenuation of her loss, and it is certainly true that she had covered only 200 miles in the previous twelve days.

Hull approached with circumspection, reducing to fighting sail and double reefing his topsails while clearing for action (3). *Guerriere* ran up two battle ensigns and two jacks, and fired a broadside, which largely fell short, before wearing round to offer the other, portside, battery. Hull then had his own ensign and two jacks hoisted, while yawing the ship to avoid being raked (4). In fact, Dacres wasted his opening broadsides, firing too early to inflict any damage, possibly because he was more intent on outmanoeuvring *Constitution* and taking the weather gage, the favoured British position. Hull was too skilful to allow this and in an acknowledgement of failure the *Guerriere* bore up at about 6pm; Hull quickly responded by setting the main topgallant, and *Constitution* ranged up on

her opponent's port side within pistol shot.

The action then became a slugging match, where the greater American firepower quickly took its toll. The British ship was well drilled, firing three broadsides for every two American, but was not accurate enough to redress the balance in weight of metal. After about a quarter of an hour *Guerriere*'s mizzen mast went by the board (5), and *Constitution* forged ahead, turning across her bow in a perfect raking position. The British ship attempted to shadow the move, but with the wreck of the mizzen trailing over the quarter she would not answer the helm. After enduring this deadly close-range fire for about twenty minutes, Dacres decided boarding was his last option, but as the boarders were assembling, the main mast fell forwards taking the fore mast and jib-boom with it. This dramatic moment, when the defeat of the British frigate became inevitable, was very popular with the artists (6), although often depicted with more drama than accuracy (7).

Although not badly damaged, *Constitution* hauled off to repair her rigging, and after about half an hour returned to find out whether her opponent had surrendered or not. By this time it was dark and Hull could not see if she still had any colours flying, and had to send a boat to find out. As Dacres' own report admits, 'The ship lying in the

trough of the sea and rolling her main deck guns under water and all attempts to get her before the wind being fruitless, when calling my few remaining officers togeth-er, they were all of opinion that any further resistance would be a needless waste of lives, I order'd, though reluctantly, the colours to be struck.' Reality of course is rarely as neat as the official report. According to Lieutenant Read, *Constitution*'s boarding officer, on arriv-ing on the *Guerriere*'s deck he said, 'Commodore Hull's compliments, and wishes to know if you have struck your flag?' Dacres, surveying the carnage about him, dryly retorted, 'Well, I don't know; our mizzen mast is gone, our main mast is gone, and, upon the whole, you may say we *have* struck our flag.' What sound like aristo-cratic detachment may well have been shock. Few British frigate captains during two decades of war had found themselves in Dacres' position, and none had pre-viously surrendered to a ship of the infant United States Navy; it would not have been much consolation to know he would not be the last.

Although Dacres was sympathetically treated by Hull, the ordeal was by no means over. Like all French-built ships, *Guerriere* was lightly constructed and had not stood up at all well to the close-range hammering she had received. Hull reported, 'At daylight we found the

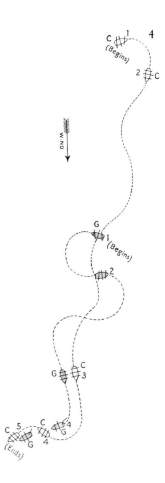

5

1. 'Capt Isaac Hull of the United States Navy', mezzotint by Edwin after a painting by Gilbert Stuart, no date.
Beverley R Robinson collection ref BRR51.7.732.22

2. 'Captain James Richard Dacres, RN', engraving from Benson J Lossing, *Pictorial Field Book of the War of 1812* (New York 1869).
Chatham collection

3. *Constitution*, reefing topsails, sails down on *Guerriere*, which waits with backed main topsail, watercolour by W A K Martin (1817-1867), no date.
Beverley R Robinson collection ref BRR80.26.12

4. Track chart of the engagement, from A T Mahan, *Sea Power in its Relation to the War of 1812*, Vol I.
Chatham collection

5. *Constitution* and *Guerriere*, 19 August 1812', one of a series of oil paintings by Michèle-Félice Corné (1752-1832), no date.
US Naval Academy Museum

6

7

enemy's ship a perfect wreck, having many shot holes between wind and water, and above six feet of the plank below the bends [wales] taken out by our round shot, and her upperwork shattered to pieces, that I determined to take out the sick and wounded as fast as possible, and set her on fire, as it would be impossible to get her into port.' In the afternoon of the 20th the wreck was fired (8), and shortly afterwards the main magazine blew up, sending the old warrior rapidly to the bottom.

Because Hull had decided to repair damages at the end of the action rather than pound the helpless *Guerriere*, the 'butcher's bill' was not as great as in some later battles, but was heavy enough to prove that she had not been surrendered prematurely. There were 15 dead and 63 wounded, the majority according to Dacres being sustained from grape and musketry when *Constitution* lay off the British frigate's bow; he also admitted that his opponent's losses were 'trifling' in comparison (7 killed and 7 wounded in the official return).

Hull's arrival at Boston on 30 August was greeted with massive celebrations. Not only was his victory the first good news of the summer, contrasting starkly with the humiliations to US land forces on the Canadian front, but it was also the first intimation that the all-powerful Royal Navy was not necessarily invincible. Nobody cared to remember the fifty per cent advantage in size, firepower and manning of the American ship, and in the final analysis it did not matter: in whatever chivalric light a naval officer might like to see himself, warships were instruments of national policy, not the weapons of a medieval knight. For propaganda purposes, a fair fight might be useful, but in a struggle for survival the country needed victories under any circumstances.

For the losers, it was necessary to enquire into the reasons for defeat. Like any captain losing his ship, Dacres underwent a court martial, in which he blamed the poor material condition of his ship, and claimed that he would happily face *Constitution* again with a well-found ship of the same force as the *Guerriere*. The skill with which Hull had handled his ship, even allowing for the advantages of size and weight of metal, rendered this hollow bravado, but Dacres was acquitted, the official verdict blaming the defective state of *Guerriere*'s masts. This was making the best of a bad job, but there was some evidence to support the position: much of Dacres' behaviour before the engagement — the very slow progress, and wearing rather than tacking — suggests a captain keen not to strain his masts. Furthermore, the Navy Board had submitted a complete survey of the material state of the every ship in the Royal Navy in January 1812 in order to estimate their remaining lifespan. The entry for *Guerriere* says 'six months': it was uncannily accurate about the timing, if not the reason.

9

6. 'This Representation of the US Frigate Constitution Isaac Hull Esqr. Commander, capturing His Britannic Majesty's frigate Guerriere, James R Dacres Esqr. Commodore . . . Fought August 19 1812', stipple engraving by C Tiebout after an original by Thomas Birch, published by James Webster, 19 August 1813.
NMM neg 334

7. A watercolour miniature (3½in diam) by Ambroise Louis Garneray (1783-1857), no date. Sometimes catalogued as '*Wasp* and *Frolic*', it clearly depicts the climactic moment of the *Guerriere* action, when her main mast went over the side.
Beverley R Robinson collection ref BRR80.26.14

8. 'Brilliant Naval Victory with the U. States Frigate Constitution of 44 Guns, Capn Hull, & the English Frigate Guerriere of 38 guns Capn Dacres . . . August 20, 1812', coloured aquatint engraved by S Seymour after his own original, published by J Pierie and F Kearney, 1812.
NMM ref PAG9065

9. 'Explosion of the British frigate *Guerriere* . . .', line engraving by B Tanner after an original by J J Barralet, published by B Tanner, Philadelphia, 10 November 1812.
Beverley R Robinson collection ref BRR51.7.475

1

2

Frolic **versus** *Wasp*

1. 'Jacob Jones, Esq of the United
States Navy', engraved by D Edwin
after an original by R Peale, engraved
for the *Analectic Magazine*, no date.
Beverley R Robinson collection ref
BRR51.7.732.43

2. 'Capture of H.B.M. Sloop of War
Frolic 22 guns Captain Whinyates By
the US Sloop of War Wasp 18 guns
Capt Jones . . .', coloured aquatint
engraved by S Seymour after an
original by J J Barralett, published by
W J Morgan, Philadelphia, no date.
NMM neg 9212

3. 'The Capture of H.B.M. Sloop of
War Frolic Captain Whinyates, by the
US Sloop of War Wasp, Capt Jacob
Jones, after a close Action of 43
Minutes, October 18, 1812', coloured
aquatint by F Kearny, from a sketch by
Lt Claxton of the *Wasp*, published by
Prentiss Whitney, Boston, no date.
Beverley R Robinson collection ref
BRR51.7.479

4. '*Poictiers* takes *Wasp*, 19 October 1812',
watercolour by Irwin Bevan (1852-
1940), no date.
Mariners' Museum, Newport News ref
QW290

SAILING FROM the Delaware on 13 October 1812, the ship sloop *Wasp*, 18 ran into a fierce gale three days later, when she lost her jibboom and two men overboard. However, late the following evening she spotted several sail, two of them large ships. The *Wasp* was commanded by Master Commandant Jacob Jones (1), a man of mature years who was already thirty-three when he joined the navy as a midshipman in 1799. Since then he had seen some active service, although not all of it successful: he was a lieutenant aboard Bainbridge's *Philadelphia* when she stranded off Tripoli in 1803 and was incarcerated for twenty months in a Barbary prison. Not surprisingly, he treated the unknown vessels with caution, hauling off until daylight revealed six merchant ships and an escort brig.

They were the remnant of a British convoy that had sailed from Honduras in September and been scattered by the same storm that had struck the *Wasp*. The escort was HMS *Frolic*, a standard 18-gun brig sloop of the *Cruizer* class, Commander Thomas Whinyates. She had also been damaged in the storm, losing her crossjack yard and springing the main topmast, and was repairing damages when the suspicious sail was sighted. When the American sloop did not respond to signals, the *Frolic* hauled her wind under what small amount of canvas she could set, running up Spanish colours to make her opponent hesitate and gain a few minutes, allowing her charges to escape a few extra miles to leeward. It is

unlikely that Jones was fooled for a moment, but he did hail as he came within range, and *Frolic* ran up her true colours before opening fire.

The vessels were fairly evenly matched, both having a main armament of sixteen 32-pounder carronades, although as in most of the engagements of this war, the American was somewhat larger and better manned. The sea still ran high after the storm, and having the advantage of the weather gage in the ensuing close action, *Wasp*'s shot tended to strike the hull, whereas *Frolic*'s went high. As a result, the *Wasp* lost her main topmast, mizzen topgallant and gaff, but the superiority of the ship rig was manifest when *Frolic* had her gaff shot away, losing any after sail and with it all means of manoeuvring. The battle was conducted at very close quarters – according to Jones 'so near while loading the east [?lee] broad side that our rammers were shoved against the side of the enemy' – but although the *Frolic* fired faster, the *Wasp*'s fire was a lot more effective. For the last half-hour of the 45-minute engagement, *Wasp* enjoyed a raking position, and when the battle was concluded by the Americans boarding the stricken brig, less than twenty of the British crew remained uninjured (2, 3). Shortly after the firing ceased, both the *Frolic*'s lower masts went over the side.

As Jones himself explained in his report, 'I could not ascertain the exact loss of the enemy as many of the dead lay buried under the masts and spars that had fallen upon deck, which two hours exertion had not sufficiently removed.' In fact, of 110 on board, the brig lost 17 dead and 45 seriously wounded; the American casualties were 5 killed and 5 wounded, and the disparity speaks for itself. However, the *Frolic* had done her job, all the merchantmen escaping, and the the *Wasp* was so badly damaged that when the 74-gun *Poictiers* appeared two hours later flight was impossible; both vessels were promptly taken (4).

Midshipman Charles Loftus of *Poictiers*, with the envy of an officer who had spent years trying to round up scratch crews for the undermanned Royal Navy, said the Wasps were 'the finest-looking fellows I think I ever saw.' Nor were their spirits dampened by capture, for he also recounts with admiration a failed plot to take over his ship: 'I cannot blame them, for it would have been a glorious thing for them to have taken one of His Britannic Majesty's ships of eighty guns into New York or Boston.'

Although brought into port safely, *Frolic* was not worth repair, but *Wasp* was taken into Royal Navy service and renamed *Loup Cervier*, after a Canadian wildcat. In 1813 she was again renamed *Peacock* to revenge the loss of the brig of that name, and foundered in August 1814 off the southern coast of the USA.

U   United States
M   Macedonian (shaded)
a, b, c, etc., synchronous positions
For 1 and 2, see text

United States **versus** Macedonian

AMONG THE US Navy's fine crop of officers, Stephen Decatur was probably the most dashing, having literally leapt to fame when he boarded and burned the captured *Philadelphia* in Tripoli harbour – in Nelson's view 'the most bold and daring act of the age'. Now raised to Commodore's rank, he always expressed a strong preference for operating alone, so although his division of the frigate *United States* and brig *Argus* originally sailed as part of Rodgers' formidable squadron, it soon parted company, on 11 October, and shortly thereafter his own two vessels also separated. *United States* headed southeast in the general direction of Madeira and was therefore sailing alone when on the morning of 25 October she sighted a large sail fine on her weather bow.

The stranger was HMS *Macedonian*, one of the best of the British-built frigates of the 38-gun class, but of course armed with a main battery of 18-pounders to her opponent's 24s. Fresh from refit, she was well found, and possessed a distinct advantage in speed and handling; she also held the weather gage, so in a battle of manoeuvre she should have had the initiative. She was not, however, a happy ship. A succession of heavy-handed captains, including Lord William Fitzroy (who was dismissed from HM Navy for oppressive conduct), had demoralised the crew, although they fought well enough when the time came. The current captain was John Surman Carden, no highflyer in the promotion stakes and rather an old man to be in command of a frigate. Like most British commanders of the period he had great difficulty manning his ship, but according to one of his seamen, he compounded his problem by quietly encouraging troublemakers, weaklings and the incompetent to desert at any opportunity.

But he was eager for glory, and on sighting the *United States*, his frigate was promptly turned towards her. There was some discussion on the quarterdeck about the tactics to adopt, and the 1st Lieutenant favoured crossing her bow and raking her from ahead, but Carden decided to fight a long-range battle of manoeuvre – it was claimed later that he thought his opponent was the *Essex*, which was armed predominantly with short-range carronades, but this was not mentioned at the court martial. At about 8.30am Decatur wore ship, which Carden saw as an attempt to seize the weather gage, and countered by hauling up; being thus thwarted, Decatur wore again and the ships passed one another at about a mile range. *Macedonian* fired three ranging shots from the port battery, which fell short, but a broadside from the American 24-pounders was more effective.

When safely past the bearing of *United States*'s main battery, Carden wore his ship, but Decatur bore away in a short jink before resuming his course, in order to increase the distance again and retain the advantage of his heavier guns. After suffering a battering for a quarter of an hour, Carden had to set the fore course in an attempt to close, but despite some depictions of the action (2), he was never able to get abreast the American frigate. By backing her mizzen topsail and letting go the jib sheets, *United States* kept enough way on to hold a position off her opponent's starboard bow at relatively long range (half musket shot). In this position, *Macedonian* was gradually shot to pieces, most of the damage being the work of the long guns. The British frigate lost her mizzen topmast, main yard and topsail, but fought on for a further bloody half hour, gradually losing the use of her carronades – they were mounted on what was known as the 'outside principle', designed to allow them to be run out far enough so their muzzle flash did not set fire to the shrouds, but also exposing the chock to which the fighting bolt was fixed; once the chocks were destroyed the mounting was useless. Eventually, both remaining topmasts and the whole of the mizzen went by the board.

This is the phase of the battle most popular with those more painstaking artists (3) who not only have the

3

correct relative positions of the ships, but also a fair representation of the damage, down to the only visible injury to the *United States*, her mizzen topgallant. Even those whose composition is less careful, like George Thresher, who has the *Macedonian* facing in the wrong direction chose this stage on which to base their work (5). At this point the battle was over and Decatur filled his mizzen topsail, crossed his opponent's bow, but without the raking broadside expected. There were some optimists in the British ship who interpreted an act of mercy as a sign that their antagonist had abandoned the fight, but after an hour repairing damages the American frigate ranged up again (4). The 1st Lieutenant was all for resisting until the ship sank, but wiser counsels prevailed and her colours were struck.

Macedonian had suffered grievously in human terms, casualties being 36 dead and 68 wounded. On the other hand Decatur's cautious tactics had paid dividends, his

ship suffering only 7 killed and 5 wounded. Being more strongly built than either *Guerriere* or *Java*, *Macedonian*'s structural damage was repairable, and Decatur decided that bringing the prize in would be a psychological boost for his country's war effort (and a personal fillip for his career) that would justify cutting short his cruise.

Samuel Leech, a young powder monkey in the *Macedonian*, has left a memorable description of the battle, but he also reveals how the seamen of this period often had more loyalty to their profession than to their nationality or even to their ship. After initial antagonism, the two crews got on famously:

All idea that we had been trying to shoot out each other's brains so shortly before, seemed forgotten. We ate together, drank together, joked, sung, laughed and told yarns; in sort, a perfect union of ideas, feelings and purposes, seemed to exist among all hands.

4

Like many before him, Leech was so at home that he transferred to the American service, clearly without any thought that it constituted desertion.

At this stage of the war, the American coast was not closely or consistently blockaded, and Decatur had little difficulty getting his prize into New York (6). He was correct in anticipating the reaction of the victory-starved public, and Leech recounts how

> we found the sound plentifully dotted with sloops . . . After we reached Hurl-gate, vessels here gave us plenty of employment. Most of them honoured us with three cheers, as they passed. Of course, the prize crew could do no less than cheer again, so that we passed our time amidst continued cheering.

The prize received many curious visitors, and the canny young Leech made himself a healthy sum showing civilians around and thrilling them with tales of the battle.

Even jury rigged the prize had sailed rings round 'The Wagon', as the *United States* was known in her service, suggesting that this benefit had not been exploited to maximum advantage during the battle. Carden's court martial took a similar line, for although he was acquitted, he was criticised for not using his ship's superior speed and manoeuvrability to close early in the engagement. It is highly unlikely that it would have changed the result, but Carden might have had the satisfaction of inflicting more damage. Of the three British frigate losses of the war, this is the only one in which the defeated ship possessed a single real advantage, and it is ironic that she was beaten on those very grounds. With a slow and relatively clumsy ship, Decatur completely outmanoeuvred his potentially agile opponent; in terms of pure tactical skill, it is probably the most impressive of the American single-ship actions, and all the more surprising from a man known for dash rather than circumspection.

5

1. Track chart of the engagement, from A T Mahan, *Sea Power in its Relation to the War of 1812*, Vol I. *Chatham collection*

2. '*United States* versus *Macedonian*', anonymous oil painting, nineteenth-century British school. *NMM ref BHC0599*

3. 'Engagement between the American Frigate the *United States* and the English frigate the *Macedonian* surrendered after 17 minutes of fighting', etching by Jazet after an original by Baugean, no date. *NMM neg X2072*

4. 'The English frigate Macedonian Captur'd by the American United States', etching by Baugean after an original by Montardier du Havre, published by Jean, no date. *NMM neg 9214*

5. A watercolour by George Thresher of the *United States* versus *Macedonian* action, no date. *US Naval Academy Museum ref 76.27.2*

6. '*United States* and *Macedonian* Frigates passing Hurl Gate for New York', engraved and published by P H Hansell, Philadelphia 1817. *Beverley R Robinson collection ref BRR80.26.16*

6

Constitution **versus** *Java*

EAVING THE *Hornet* blockading the British sloop *Bonne Citoyenne* in Bahia, Commodore Bainbridge (1) took the *Constitution* out to sea on 26 December, and was cruising offshore three days later when he sighted two sail at about 9am. They proved to be the British frigate *Java*, 38, and an American merchantman she had captured recently. Commanded by Captain Henry Lambert, *Java* was well into a long voyage to the East Indies, overcrowded with 68 supernumeraries of the new governor's staff and cluttered with stores and fittings for new ships building at Bombay, including a hold full of copper sheathing. She was heading for Bahia to water, but on seeing the American frigate immediately altered course towards her.

Bainbridge decided it would be diplomatic to fight well outside neutral Portuguese waters, so tacked and ran seaward for two hours, with *Java* in hot pursuit – she was an ex-French prize with a good reputation for her sailing qualities, and even deeply laden rapidly overhauled the American frigate at 10 knots. The engagement that followed was the most tactically elaborate of the three great American frigate victories (2), and the one in which the defeated British ship was most skilfully fought. Not surprisingly, therefore, it is the only one to inspire a sequence of paintings by Nicholas Pocock, the best known English marine painter of the day (3-6).

After the usual jockeying for position, *Constitution* fired the first gun about 2pm followed by two broadsides at a range of about half a mile. Running up her colours, *Java* replied when she reached a position just forward of her opponent's port broadside. Both ships then wore, but about 2.30pm the *Constitution*'s wheel was shot away, and for a while the British frigate enjoyed a manoeuvring advantage; this allowed her to rake the American ship from astern – although without any great effect – but as Bainbridge recovered control of his ship, relaying orders to the tiller relieving tackles, this benefit was soon lost.

Just before 3pm disaster struck the Java when her jibboom and the head of the bowsprit were shot away, depriving the ship of the use of her headsails and with it much of her handiness in tacking and wearing. From this point until the end of the action, *Constitution* was able to sail around her opponent at will and the battle was effectively lost. As the *Constitution* wore away in the smoke, *Java* attempted to tack, but paid off so slowly that she was raked from astern. In the following phase of broadside-to-broadside battering, the superior weight of the American long 24-pounders began to tell. However, despite damage to his fore and main masts, Captain Lambert believed that he might retrieve the day by boarding, but as the helm was put up, the wounded fore mast went over the side. The crippled British frigate drifted down on the *Constitution*'s port quarter and the stump of the bowsprit fouled the mizzen rigging, before the American frigate tore herself free and sailed ahead (3). A raking broadside brought down the *Java*'s main topmast, and shortly afterwards Captain Lambert was mortally wounded, but the British frigate fought on, until about 4.35pm when the mizzen also went by the board (4).

1. 'William Bainbridge', lithograph printed by Michelin, no date. *NMM ref PAD3484*

2. Track chart of the action, from the *Naval Chronicle* 29 (1813). *NMM neg D4539*

3. 'Plate 1. Situation of His Majesty's Frigate Java . . . Action with the American Frigate Constitution . . . rendered totally unmanageable', coloured aquatint engraved by Nicholas Pocock, Robert Havell and Daniel Havell after an original by Pocock and Lt Buchanan, published by Boydell & Co, 1 January 1814. *NMM neg C696*

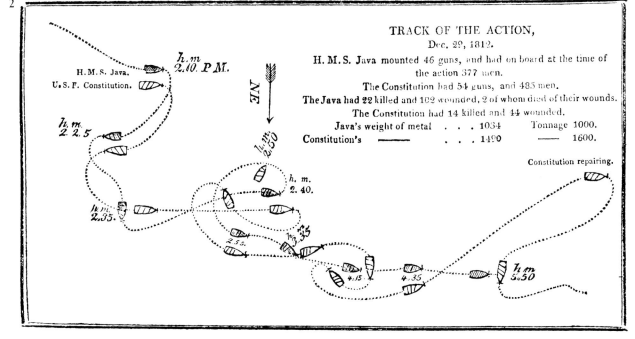

TRACK OF THE ACTION,
Dec. 29, 1812.

H. M. S. Java mounted 46 guns, and had on board at the time of the action 377 men.

The Constitution had 54 guns, and 485 men.

The Java had 22 killed and 102 wounded, 2 of whom died of their wounds.

The Constitution had 14 killed and 44 wounded.

Java's weight of metal . . . 1034   Tonnage 1000.

Constitution's ———— . . . 1490   ———— 1600.

Constitution repairing.

H.M.S. Java.
U.S.F. Constitution.

2.40. P M.
NE
h. m. 2. 2. 5
h. m. 2.50
h. m. 2. 40.
h. m. 2.35.
2. 55.
3. 35
4. 15
4. 35
h m. 5. 50

3

At this point, with his enemy irretrievably beaten, Bainbridge sailed ahead to repair damages, which took about an hour. This cautious tactic is noticeable in all three of the main American victories and contrasts sharply with the British approach in similar situations, which was to secure the prize before effecting repairs. It suggests a desire not to be caught unprepared by a fresh enemy ship – as happened to the *Wasp* after her battle with the *Frolic* – and reflects a realistic appreciation of the ubiquitous nature of British seapower. British captains were far less concerned about this, since there was every possibility that any new sail heaving into view would prove to be friendly.

With the *Constitution*'s rigging repaired, Bainbridge took station across the *Java*'s hawse about 5.30pm (5), and since there could be no question of renewing the defiance, her colours were struck immediately. American losses were higher than in previous single-ship combats at 14 dead and 20 wounded, but were still modest compared with

the 22 dead and 102 wounded in the British ship. It was said in extenuation of the loss that the British crew, although large, was poor in terms of skill and experience, and it is true that Lambert did lodge at least one formal protest about their quality with the Admiralty. However, the *Java* was handled very well, and being so completely outgunned by the American ship, it is difficult to decide if the precision of her gunnery was a major issue. There are many examples of frigate actions during the French wars in which the casualties were similarly disparate but the standard of the gunnery was not: after receiving only one well-aimed broadside, the rate and direction of return fire must deteriorate, and the differential in effectiveness widens very quickly thereafter. In none of the three major actions of 1812 were the 18-pounders of the British ships able to do enough damage to the main batteries of the American frigates even to begin to redress the balance. American tactics were specifically directed at first destroying their opponents' means of

4

manoeuvre by shooting away masts and rigging, before closing to take maximum advantage of the powerful 24-pounders firing into the hull to disable their enemies' guns.

Like *Guerriere*, another French prize, the lightly built *Java* was too badly damaged to warrant the risk of bringing her home. Despite the value of the military stores on board, she was set on fire on 31 December, and blew up (6). Her surviving crew was landed at Bahia on parole, and although there was some criticism of their treatment by the Americans, none of it came from the pris-

oners themselves; indeed, some of the officers of both ships remained friends for years afterwards. *Java* had, however, done enough harm to the *Constitution* to force Bainbridge to head for home: although he was careful to give more weight to the generally 'decayed state' of the ship in his decision, the ship's log reveals rather more injuries, including potentially disastrous damage to the lower masts. If any of these had fallen, it might have proved impossible to get the ship past British cruisers and safely into Boston, where she arrived to another rapturous welcome on 18 February 1813.

5

6

4. 'Plate 2. The Java . . . after having sustained several raking Broadsides from the Constitution whilst closely engaging her, until she became a perfect wreck . . .The Constitution making sail and getting out of Gun Shot', coloured aquatint engraved by Nicholas Pocock, Robert Havell and Daniel Havell after an original by Pocock and Lt Buchanan, published by Boydell & Co, 1 January 1814. *NMM neg C699*

5. 'Plate 3. The Java totally dismasted . . . the Constitution Crossing her Bow in a Raking Position Compels her to Surrender at 50 Min. past 5', coloured aquatint engraved by Nicholas Pocock, Robert Havell and Daniel Havell after an original by Pocock and Lt Buchanan, published by Boydell & Co, 1 January 1814. *NMM neg 552*

6. 'Plate 4. The Java in a Sinking state, set fire to, and blowing up – The Constitution at a distance ahead . . . on the Evening of 29th Decr 1812', coloured aquatint engraved by Nicholas Pocock, Robert Havell and Daniel Havell after an original by Pocock and Lt Buchanan, published by Boydell & Co, 1 January 1814. *NMM neg 1042*

1

Hornet

1. 'Hornet and Peacock', watercolour by Irwin Bevan (1852-1940), no date.
Beverley R Robinson collection ref BRR51.7.494.11

2. 'The Hornet sinking the Peacock', wood engraving by Abel Bowen after an original by Michéle-Félice Corné, no date.
NMM ref PAD5830

2

IN HER first war cruise the ship sloop *Hornet*, Master Commandant James Lawrence, had shared the frustrations of Rodger's abortive pursuit of the Jamaica convoy, and the failure to capture HMS *Belvidera*. Her second cruise, in company with Commodore Bainbridge in the *Constitution*, was to prove just as eventful, but far more successful. With orders that allowed him to chose his own cruising grounds, Bainbridge sailed from Boston on 9 September 1812, taking his ships across the Atlantic to the Cape Verde Islands and then back to the coast of Brazil.

At São Salvador (Bahia) in December they encountered the British sloop *Bonne Citoyenne*, 20, and blockaded her in the port for several days. The British ship was carrying specie reportedly worth £500,000, and when she showed no signs of coming out, Lawrence sent her captain a challenge to single-ship combat; Bainbridge promised to take the *Constitution* off, and not to interfere in the result. During the war there were to be a number of these chivalric flourishes—Lawrence himself being sent one of the most famous by Broke of the *Shannon*—but however sensitive in matters of honour, the officers of the two navies were bound by orders to put the interests of the service first. *Bonne Citoyenne* remained where she was, even after *Constitution* sailed for her encounter with the *Java*.

Hornet remained on station until on 24 January a British 74, *Montagu*, hove in sight, and Lawrence took shelter in the neutral port himself. During the night, however, he slipped out without being spotted, and following Bainbridge's orders sailed north, eventually reaching Demerara on 24 February. While going to investigate a brig at anchor in the river mouth, *Hornet* noticed another brig, apparently a sloop of war, on his weather quarter. The stranger was HMS *Peacock*, a sister of the *Frolic* taken by *Hornet*'s sister *Wasp* the previous October, and despite a reduced battery of 24-pounder carronades, the British brig attacked without hesitation.

Hornet having tacked to gain the weather gage, the two sloops fired a broadside in passing, and *Peacock* in turn then wore, but *Hornet* ran down on her starboard quarter and took up a raking position. The brig's main topsail and gaff halyards were shot away, rendering her unmanageable, and a storm of grape and musketry cleared the quarterdeck, Captain Peake being mortally wounded. Having lost so much canvas, the brig was wallowing before the wind in a big sea, and in this position at such close range the *Hornet*'s 32-pounder carronades did considerable damage between wind and water. The brig's main mast went by the board after about half an hour's fighting (1), and with six feet of water in the hold the senior surviving lieutenant had no alternative but to surrender.

The brig was in a parlous state and hoisted an ensign upside down in the fore rigging as a sign of distress (2). One of *Peacock*'s survivors claims Lawrence took over half an hour to send help, but despite the best efforts of the boarding party the brig sank in shallow water, drowning four of her crew and three of the *Hornet*'s. British casualties were severe (9 dead, 28 wounded), but *Hornet* escaped with only 2 dead and 3 wounded. Although broadside firepower and crew strength were significantly weighted in favour of the Americans, the action led to serious questions being raised about the state of British gunnery. In March 1813 the Admiralty instructed Admiral Warren to ensure that gunnery exercises as laid down in standing regulations were strictly adhered to, later ordering the abolition of such practices as scouring and polishing iron stanchions and ringbolts – *Peacock* was a well-known 'spit and polish' ship, nicknamed 'the Yacht' – and that 'the time thrown away on this unnecessary practice be applied to the really useful and important points of discipline and exercise at Arms.'

Hornet's damage was largely confined to masts and rigging, but Lawrence was concerned that the brig at anchor might sail out to her consort's rescue and hastened repairs. Actually, the brig *Espiegle* was too damaged in her tophamper to sail at all, and Lawrence brought his victorious sloop home safely. Lawrence was promoted Captain from 4 March 1813, and posted to the frigate *Chesapeake*.

Command of the *Hornet* was given to James Biddle (3), newly promoted Master Commandant as a reward for his success as 1st Lieutenant of *Wasp* in the action with the *Frolic*. However, the sloop's next cruise ended in frustration when she was chased into New London with the rest of Decatur's squadron on 1 June by the British blockading force. So tight was the British grip on the coast that most of the squadron never escaped again for the duration of the war, although the swift-sailing *Hornet* eventually managed to reach New York in November 1814. Here she was to remain until the beginning of 1815, when she took part in the US Navy's last, and most ambitious, mission – a squadron attack on British shipping in the Indian Ocean along with the frigate *President*, sloop *Peacock*, and two merchant brigs, *Tom Bowline* and *Macedonian*, hired as store vessels.

Taking advantage of winter gales, the ships tried to elude the watching British. *President* failed and was captured, but the sloops and one of the store brigs succeeded a few days later on 20 January, although they were soon separated. Rendezvous was to be the remote south Atlantic island of Tristan da Cunha, and *Hornet* was first to arrive. But the next sail that hove into view, on 23 March, proved to be HMS *Penguin*, another of the ubiquitous *Cruizer* class brig sloops. A close engagement followed, with much the same result as all of the actions between American ship sloops and British brigs (4). *Hornet*'s well-directed fire dismantled *Penguin*, Commander Dickinson was killed, and when the disabled brig attempted to board, the resulting collision carried away her bowsprit and fore mast. Surrender followed quickly,

3

3. 'James Biddle esqr of the United States Navy. Engraved for the Analectic Magazine', stipple engraving by Gimbrede after an original by Wood, published by M Thomas, no date.
NMM ref PAD3571

4. 'HM sloop of War *Penguin*, Captain Dickenson, captured off the Island of Tristan d'Acun-ha by the US Sloop of War *Hornet*, J Biddle, Esq, Commander, March 23, 1815', one of a pair of lithographs made by Samuel Walters from a sketch by Captain William Skiddy, published by Day & Haghe, London, about 1816.
Beverley R Robinson collection ref BRR51.7.536.1

4

by American reckoning a mere 22 minutes after opening fire.

The 'butcher's bill' was tolerably severe: 14 dead and 28
wounded out of a crew of 105 men and 17 boys; 1 died and
10 were wounded aboard the *Hornet*. One of the American
ship's crew claimed she was hit by nothing larger than
grape throughout the action (although all her boats
except the launch were destroyed), and that two of
Penguin's guns still had the tompions in them at the close
of the action. For their part, the British blamed poorly
mounted carronades that upset during the battle. The
truth is that by this stage of a war that had been in
progress for twenty years, British ships were not just
undermanned, but were poorly manned to boot. *Penguin*
had been in commission for over a year, and had had
plenty of time to identify, and eliminate, such problems.

Despite the arrival of the *Peacock* and *Tom Bowline*, there
was little chance of repairing the badly damaged prize,
and virtually none of getting her safely through the
British blockade to an American port, so *Penguin* was
scuttled. Employing the store ship as a cartel, the two
sloops sailed to continue their cruise into the eastern
seas, and on 27 April they spotted a large ship which they
took for an East Indiamen. Closer inspection disabused

them of this enticing prospect, the stranger turning out
to be the *Cornwallis* of 74 guns, and hunters became hunted.

Peacock soon separated, but surpringly the heavy teak-
built two-decker proved faster on a wind than the lithe
American sloop. Biddle jettisoned spare gear, stores, and
eventually some of his guns. By the morning of the 29th
Cornwallis was in a position to open fire, and *Hornet* then
threw most of her armament over the side (5). This gave
the chase a temporary advantage, but squally weather
later in the morning brought *Cornwallis* well within range
again; some shot struck home, but did no irreparable
damage. By this stage *Hornet's* crew had packed their
belongings in anticipation of surrender – as the ship's
2nd Lieutenant confided to his journal, 'I don't believe
there was an officer or man onboard, but what thought
of sleeping that night on board the 74' – except possibly
Biddle, who had the forecastle cut up and the rest of the
guns jettisoned in order to keep ahead. As the big two-
decker yawed to fire her guns, the sloop edged way, gradually leading her in one large circle until the sloop found
her own most advantageous point of sailing. On the 30th
after a 42-hour pursuit, the 74 gave over the chase.

Of course, with no armament *Hornet's* war was also
over, and she cautiously made sail for a US port.

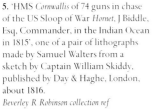

5. 'HMS *Cornwallis* of 74 guns in chase
of the US Sloop of War *Hornet*, J Biddle,
Esq, Commander, in the Indian Ocean
in 1815', one of a pair of lithographs
made by Samuel Walters from a
sketch by Captain William Skiddy,
published by Day & Haghe, London,
about 1816.
*Beverley R Robinson collection ref
BRR51.7.536.2*

5

Shannon **versus** Chesapeake

AFTER A year of war the British had still not gained a victory in a single-ship action. American successes might be explained by superior force, but until an engagement was won on terms approaching equality, it sounded like an excuse. Any Royal Navy officer would have given his eye-teeth to even the score, and none yearned for such an event with more fervour than Captain Broke of the *Shannon*, 38.

Philip Bowes Vere Broke (1) was a well-to-do landed gentleman of a type common in the British service, but was highly unusual in his passion for gunnery. This reached far beyond frequent practice – which despite the conventional view was not universally ignored in the late-war Royal Navy – but he aspired to more accurate and effective fire than could be obtained by conventional means. He had tried and tested many innovations in his ship, all guns having dispart sights and wooden tangents to determine angles of elevation; the decks were marked with bearing angles, and the gun carriages were asymmetrically cut down to level the trunnions horizontally despite the sheer of the deck. He even had his chase guns fitted on a traversing and elevating carriage of his own design, and in battle given specific targets like the enemy's wheel or his headsails. To date his zeal had earned him nothing except the occasional rebuke from the Admiralty for the unauthorised alterations which upset the Board of Ordnance.

He had commanded *Shannon* since 1806, but despite the most meticulous preparations, he had yet to find a worthy opponent. His squadron had unsuccessfully chased the *Constitution* in July 1812, and in May 1813 he was off Boston, smarting from losing *President* and *Congress* which had escaped his vigilance in bad weather. For nearly a year he had burned every prize rather than weaken *Shannon*'s complement, but the absence of a glorious victory by way of compensation for the lost prize money was beginning to dispirit the crew. There was still one frigate in Boston, said to be the *Chesapeake*, but Broke was concerned that the poor material state of the *Shannon* might force her into refit before the American emerged; she had been built with an experimental light-weight fastening system, and in Broke's own words 'her topsides are slight and *work like a basket*'. In this frame of mind, Broke sat down to write his famous challenge to Captain James Lawrence (2), the man promoted into the *Chesapeake* after his convincing victory over the *Peacock* in February.

The letter was never received, but Lawrence was known to be aggressive, self-confident and sensitive on matters of honour – he had once issued his own challenge to the commander of the *Bonne Citoyenne* and was outraged when it was refused – so it was calculated to goad him into fighting. The goad was unnecessary because Lawrence had already decided to set sail. He had

1. 'Captain Sir Philip Bowes Vere Broke Bart. &c.&c.', mezzotint engraved and published by Charles Turner after an original by Samuel Lane, 25 March 1816. *NMM ref PAH5546*

2. 'James Lawrence, Esq, Late of the United States Navy', stipple engraving by Edwin after an original by Stuart, published by Moses Thomas, Philadelphia, December 1813. *Beverley R Robinson collection ref BRR51.7.732.57*

3. 'This View of His Majesty's Ship Shannon hove to, & cooly waiting the close approach of the American Frigate Chesapeake who is bearing down to the attack', coloured aquatint engraved by Robert Dodd (1748-1815) after his own original, published by the artist and G Andrews, August 1813. *NMM neg X2060*

4

5

6

only commanded the ship for two weeks, with a number of fresh officers and a newly enlisted crew. They were trained and experienced seamen, but they had had no opportunity to shake down into a well drilled team. The ship herself was almost identical in most respects to *Shannon*, although slightly larger and considerably stronger built – her eventual captors described her as 'over-built' – having been originally intended as a sister to the *Constitution* class. It would be the most equal match of the war so far, but the confidence in an easy American victory was universal, from Lawrence himself down to the small armada of rubber-neckers who followed him out to watch the fun.

After months of frustration, just after midday on 1 June 1813 brought the first sight of the *Chesapeake*'s sails. The effect on the *Shannon* was electric, but Broke knew he dare not fight so close in, where a damaged ship could be boarded by boats from the shore, so he stood out to sea under easy canvas for nearly five hours. *Chesapeake*, flying three ensigns and a large flag embroidered with the slogan 'Free Trade and Sailor's Rights' followed in the light breeze and at about 5pm she took in her studding sails (3). *Shannon* now waited her attack, beating to quarters at 5.10.

As the *Chesapeake* came on steadily, Broke called his men aft and delivered the usual short exhortation. After stoking up their passion by reminding them of the

calumnies of the American press, he instructed them: 'Don't try to dismaster her. Fire into her quarters; maindeck into maindeck; quarterdeck into quarterdeck. Kill the men and the ship is yours.' Broke was a man of fixed views – some would say quirks – and one of his prohibitions was cheering; most services, the Royal Navy included, encouraged the martial yell, but the Shannons dispersed in silence. Another mark of his austere professionalism can be gauged from his response to one seamen's request to fly three ensigns as the *Chesapeake* had: 'No, we have always been an unassuming ship.'

Under fighting sail, the *Chesapeake* gradually overhauled her opponent, and as soon as it was clear that she would not try some raking manoeuvre under *Shannon*'s stern but was going to attack on his starboard quarter, Broke ordered his maindeck gun captains to 'fire as soon as the guns bore on his second bow-port'. In response to a great cheer from the Chesapeakes, the *Shannon* remained ominously silent, but when the *Chesapeake*'s bow came into view from the aftermost gunport, No 14, its double-shotted 18-pounder gun opened the battle (4). It was over in less time than it takes to describe. As the American frigate slowly fore-reached down *Shannon*'s starboard side, she was systematically destroyed from bow to quarter by accurate and deadly fire; the chase guns did their appointed work, one killing the American quartermasters and eventually destroying the wheel,

4. 'A Series of Four Views . . . No. 1 . . . HMS Shannon commencing the Battle with the American Frigate Chesapeake on the 1st June 1813', lithograph engraved by Louis Haghe after an original by Capt. R H King and John Christian Schetky, printed by W Day and published by Smith, Elder & Co, 1830. *NMM ref PAH8115*

5. 'A Series of Four Views . . . No 2 . . . the American Frigate Chesapeake crippled and thrown into utter disorder by the first two broadsides fired from HMS Shannon', lithograph engraved by Louis Haghe after an original by Capt. R H King and John Christian Schetky, printed by W Day and published by Smith, Elder & Co, 1830. *NMM ref PAH8116*

6. 'A Series of Four Views . . . No 3 . . . HMS Shannon carrying by Boarding the American Frigate Chesapeake after a Cannonade of Five Minutes, on the 1st June 1813', lithograph engraved by Louis Haghe after an original by Capt. R H King and John Christian Schetky, printed by W Day and published by Smith, Elder & Co, 1830. *NMM ref PAH8117*

7

the call. The first officer coming up on deck, Lt Cox, instinctively turned to help his captain down to the surgeon, and in the cockpit Lawrence issued his famous order: 'Tell the men to fire faster! Don't give up the ship!'

After about 6 minutes from the first shot the shattered port quarter gallery crashed into the *Shannon*'s bow, and a grenade which ignited a small explosion of ammunition having cleared his opponent's quarterdeck, Broke seized his chance and led a boarding party himself (6). The hand-to-hand combat was as brief, bloody and hard-fought as the gunnery duel, and as the wind tore the ships apart and twisted the *Chesapeake* across the *Shannon*'s bow, the original British boarding parties of about 50 men were left stranded. But by this stage the victory was certain, and Broke was trying to restrain the blood-lust of his men when he was himself attacked by three American seamen chased out of the fore top by a British assault along the fore yards. Broke always favoured a top hat in action (another of his eccentricities), but it could not save him; he was clubbed by a musket butt and then struck a deep cut by a cutlass, before his enraged crew dispatched the Americans (7). Aft there was another unnecessary loss when 1st Lieutenant Watt and his group, in a mix-up over ensigns, were mistaken for Americans and cut down by well-directed grapeshot

while the other blew away her headsail sheets, so she luffed up out of control, head to wind, and eventually began to make a stern-board towards the *Shannon*'s bow (5). At this point she had few guns that could bear, but was suffering an oblique raking from the British ship. Lawrence, already seriously wounded, was hit again, and the efforts to assemble boarders were hampered by the disappearance of the bugler who should have sounded

8

from one of *Shannon*'s guns. But the mistake was soon rectified, and 11 minutes from the opening round the *Chesapeake* was given up.

It was a most sanguinary battle. Of the 395 men on board when she started the action, *Chesapeake* lost 69 dead or mortally wounded and 77 others injured; *Shannon* had 26 killed outright and the captain and 57 wounded, 8 of whom did not recover, from her total of 330. As modern studies of the battle have pointed out, on a casualty-perminute basis it is one of the bloodiest combats of the whole age of sail. Despite being a new crew, the Chesapeakes did a lot of damage in the few minutes' firing they were allowed, landing 25 round-shot hits, and over 130 others; over a slightly longer period, she was hit by 56 round-shot and 306 of grape, and it is the disparity that explains her defeat.

Neither ship was seriously damaged aloft, however, and on Sunday 6 June they entered Halifax. One eyewitness describes how, as the rumour spread around the church he was attending, the service was gradually deserted, and by the time the ships were in full view, 'Every housetop and every wharf was crowded with groups of excited people, and as the ships passed, they were greeted with vociferous cheers. Halifax was never in such a state of excitement before or since . . .' Wearing the huge White Ensign that had cost Watt his life, *Chesapeake* was led past cheering ships with yards manned in tribute by the *Shannon* conned by Lieutenant Provo Wallis; himself a native of Halifax, it must have been the proudest moment of his life (8).

More sober events were to follow. Lawrence had died from his wounds and was buried with full military honours, six senior Royal Navy captains acting as pallbearers; the ship's 1st Lieutenant, Ludlow, only survived him by a few days and was buried near Lawrence. Broke's life was also despaired of for a while, but he eventually made a slow recovery, although he never saw active service again. He had done his duty, and a grateful (and relieved) country showered him with honours. He was made a Baronet and later a Knight Commander of the Military Order of the Bath; he was granted the Freedom of the City of London; he received addresses, ceremonial swords and valuable pieces of plate from organisations as far apart as the underwriters of Halifax to the gentry of Suffolk (9). And a popular naval toast became 'An Irish river, and an English Brook [the usual pronunciation of Broke]'.

Broke's influence on the post-war Royal Navy was enormous, but it was achieved mostly through correspondence and encouraging the efforts of others – particularly reforming officers like Captain John Pechell, RN and gunnery zealots like General Sir Howard Douglas. Broke was the inspiration for a movement that climaxed

9

in the establishment of the world's first school of naval gunnery, HMS *Excellent* in 1830, but his practical impact in the service was more direct and immediate. His methods were soon imitated by many captains, and as early as October 1815 Admiral Codrington was reporting:

> The *Tenedos* is quite in the *Shannon* style, and it is thought Captain Hyde Parker, who commands her, would on a similar occasion acquit himself à la Brook. The *Acasta* is also a pattern ship now, having left off that over-polishing which has done so much mischief.

The widely held belief that the British had ignored gunnery in the later years of the war was an over-simplification. Some ships were clearly better than others, and many British officers were of the opinion that merely reviving the early-war level of drilling would be enough to restore the Royal Navy to its previous eminence. However, the achievement of Broke and his followers was to convince that service that a whole new order of accuracy was possible at sea: using techniques derived from his methods, the last generation of smoothbore muzzle-loaders, with aimed and concentrated fire, was far more deadly than to anything previously achieved by any navy.

7. 'The Boarding of the Chesapeake by the crew of the Shannon', anonymous steel engraving, no date. It shows Broke, cut down by the blow to the head, and his crew taking revenge on his attackers. *NMM ref PAD5835*

8. 'A Series of Four Views . . . No 4 . . . HMS Shannon leading her Prize the American Frigate Chesapeake into Halifax Harbour, on the 6th June 1813', lithograph engraved by Louis Haghe after an original by Capt. R H King and John Christian Schetky, printed by W Day and published by Smith, Elder & Co, 1830. *NMM ref PAH8118*

9. 'Commemorative silver plate given to Commander Broke by the County of Suffolk for his part in capturing the Chesapeake', aquatint engraved by Henry Meyer, published by S Hougham & Co, 2 December 1816. *NMM ref PAG9073*

1

2

Brigs at war, 1813

IT HAD always been Commodore John Rodger's contention that the best place to attack British commerce was in the coastal waters around the British Isles, where the convoy system tended to break down, leaving many ships making their independent way to their final destinations. This theory was proved beyond doubt by the cruise of the brig USS *Argus*, Master Commandant William Allen, in 1813. She sailed from New York on 18 June to convey the new US minister to France, a task accomplished by 20 July, and she then set out on the single most destructive cruise of any US warship during this war. Operating in what a later age called the Western Approaches—between the mouth of the English Channel and southern Ireland, the brig took nineteen merchant ships in about three weeks (compared with only one on the transatlantic crossing).

While Rodgers was correct in asserting that the preponderance of the naval power of Britain was disposed on the coast of her enemies, it did not mean that there were no warships in home waters. *Argus* did encounter an escorted convoy on the 25th, which she had to leave well alone, while on the 28th she was chased by a naval schooner, cutter and brig. Nevertheless, she carried out a daring raid in the Shannon estuary, and by 9 August her surgeon noted the brig 'Much incommoded with prisoners'. Her greatest single success was taking six vessels on 11 August, mostly stragglers from a convoy she was stalking. This was a dangerous tactic, and *Argus* had a number of close shaves with escorting warships, on one occasion gliding past a frigate in a fog bank: 'we could perceive her hull and ports but not her masts or rigging.'

Successful commerce raiders survive by frequent and rapid changes of cruising ground, and in this respect Allen was not quick enough. The British could not be expected to ignore so much destruction on their doorstep, and a number of vessels were on the lookout for the American brig. One of these, HMS *Pelican*, Commander John Maples, was attracted by the burning of one of *Argus*'s victims early on the morning of 14 August, and gave chase. With 32-pounder carronades to *Argus*'s 24s, for once the British brig was more powerful, and the action was settled by the *Pelican* shooting away her opponent's main braces and after running rigging (1). Like a number of British brigs in earlier actions, *Argus* then became unmanageable, and *Pelican* raked her from astern and forward until the American surrendered after a total of 43 minutes firing (2). She suffered 29 casualties, 11 of whom were killed or mortally wounded, including Allen, who was buried at Plymouth with full military honours. Damage to the British brig was surpringly light by the standards of this war, which the surviving US officers put down to the absence of 20 of the *Argus*'s 151-man crew, and the fatigue of the remainder after their efforts boarding and burning merchantmen.

Argus had proved the vulnerability of English waters, and combined with the tight British blockade, from the spring of 1813 American naval operations tended to gravitate away from her own coasts. One exception was in northern New England, where instead of a formal blockade an obscure but fierce little *guerre de course* was in progress: American and Canadian privateers preyed on the coasting trade that was the essential mode of transport for both peoples in those trackless countries. One of the US Navy's smaller warships, the *Enterprise* (a schooner rerigged as a brig) was ordered into the fray, but doubts about the ship's sailing qualities as well the overwhelming force of the enemy can be inferred from her orders of 28 August.

As the object of your cruise is to protect the coasting trade to the eastward which has been so much interrupted by small cruisers of the enemy of late, you will keep as close along the land as the safety of your vessel will admit, and by all means keep so close as not to let the large Cruisers of the Enemy get in shore of you to cut you off, and great care must be taken to keep so near a port that your vessel will enter as to be sure of reaching it in a few hours chace as the enemy's cruisers are so numerous that you hardly hope to be long out without being chaced by a superior force, in which case it would be desirable to have a port under your lee or near you, that you may run for.

However, a week later on 5 September when she encountered a British brig some thirty miles east of Portland, *Enterprise* showed no inclination to run.

Her opponent announced her nationality by hoisting four ensigns, one of which was nailed to the mast. She was HMS *Boxer*, 14 guns, originally built as a gunbrig (3) but later reclassified as a brig sloop so now under the

1. 'Capture of the Argus, Augt 14th 1813', coloured aquatint engraved by Thomas Sutherland after an original by Thomas Whitcombe (born *c* 1752), no date.
NMM ref PAD5840

2. 'Capture of the Argus August 14th 1813. From a painting in the possession of Capt Maples', coloured aquatint engraved by Thomas Sutherland after an original by Thomas Whitcombe (born *c* 1752), no date.
NMM ref PAD5839

3. Sheer draught for the brigs of the *Confounder* class of which *Boxer* was one.
NMM ref DR3592

4. 'Boxer and Enterprise', watercolour by Irwin Bevan (1852-1940), no date.
Beverley R Robinson collection ref BRR51.7.494.14

5. 'The Enterprize and Boxer', wood engraving by Abel Bowen after an original by Michèle-Félice Corné, no date.
NMM ref PAD5841

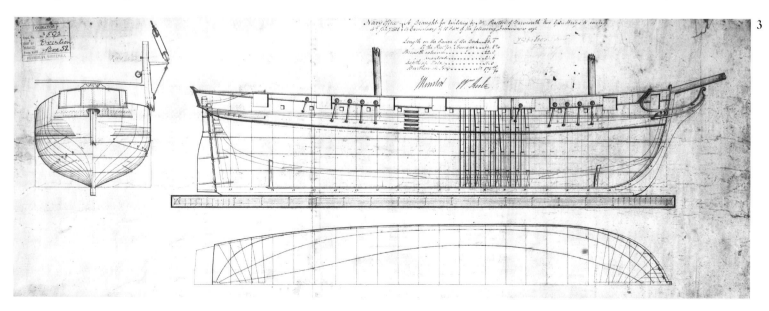

3

4

5

orders of a Commander, Samuel Blyth. She was slightly smaller, carried a couple less guns and, as was usual at this time, was far less numerously manned than the American vessel, but in overall terms the brigs were a fair match. And they were equally eager for battle, although light and fluky winds baffled their attempts to close until

the afternoon. Burrows of the *Enterprise*, not to be out-done in bravado, ran up three sets of stars and stripes, fired a gun in defiance, and at about 3.15 the two vessels exchanged broadsides at half pistol shot (4).

In most actions the first broadside — often the only properly directed fire — was usually the most telling, and was often decisive. Disabled guns and disrupted gun crews meant that return fire could fall off rapidly in a damaged ship, enhancing the difference in firepower to the point where recovery was impossible. The pattern is clear in this engagement, where although the fighting lasted 45 minutes, the battle was won early on. Both commanders were mortally wounded in the opening moments, but *Enterprise*'s 18-pounder carronades were more effective than *Boxer*'s. With her main topmast gone, and much of her rigging disabled (5), after about an hour's fighting, the latter hailed that she had surren-dered (the colours nailed to the mast being impossible to strike). Both protagonists lost 4 dead, but the British suffered more wounded (18 to 10). The existence of a friendly port under her lee allowed *Enterprise* to bring the badly damaged *Boxer* in to Portland.

American privateers

THE PRIVATEERS of 1812, along with the US Navy's big frigates and ships sloops, were instrumental in focusing the world's attention on the skill and innovation of American ship design. For anyone with more than a passing interest in maritime history, the image of the American privateer is clear — a low racy schooner, with heavily raked masts, a tower of canvas, and a witch-like performance on a wind (1). This is not entirely untrue, but it is not the complete truth either.

The majority of what are described in general histories as 'privateers' were actually traders with letters-of-marque (that is, a commission to commit hostile acts against enemy shipping if the opportunity arose), but deriving their profit from the cargo in the hold. The true privateer cruised like a warship with the sole intention of capturing enemy merchant vessels. Since it took time to build craft specifically for the task, the first privateers fitted out were necessarily converted cargo carriers, but in this regard the Americans had a distinct advantage. Two decades of European war, blockade and embargo had placed a great premium on speed and allowed substantial profits to be made from low-bulk, high-value goods. The United States not only became the world's neutral carrier, but developed sharp-hulled vessels of small capacity that made ideal blockade-runners (2), and were suitable for rapid fitting-out as commerce-raiders.

Because of these early conversions, the list of commissioned private warships contains most rigs: 26 ships, 67 brigs, 364 schooners, 35 sloops, and 34 others (including small craft, and — oddest of all — one three-masted xebec). This is a total for the whole war, and schooners certainly predominate, but even here there were regional variations. Only half of the commissioned vessels from

Massachusetts were schooners and two-thirds of those registered in New York, but considering the reputation of the 'Baltimore clipper', it is not surprising that Baltimore only commissioned three ship rigged letters-of-marque; brigs were often a matter of definition, since vessels like *Chasseur* carried the square yards that could convert them from schooners to brigs or brigantines without too much effort.

Armament was usually mixed, with one or two long guns, often on centreline pivot mountings and occasionally of large calibre, designed to intimidate merchant ships from beyond a distance where their weak guns could reply (and also potentially useful for dissuading pursuing warships from pressing too hard); the rest were short guns or carronades that were only used if the target put up more resistance than usual. The other arm was a large crew, necessary to man prizes, but often

1. 'An American privateer schooner', oil painting by C Burton, signed and dated 1815. The epitome of the late-war purpose-built privateer. *NMM ref BHC1089*

2. 'A Draught of His Majesty's Schooner *Grecian*', as taken off, Portsmouth Yard, 10 May 1816. She was a Baltimore letter-of-marque captured in Chesapeake Bay by *Jaseur* in May 1814. *NMM neg DR4555*

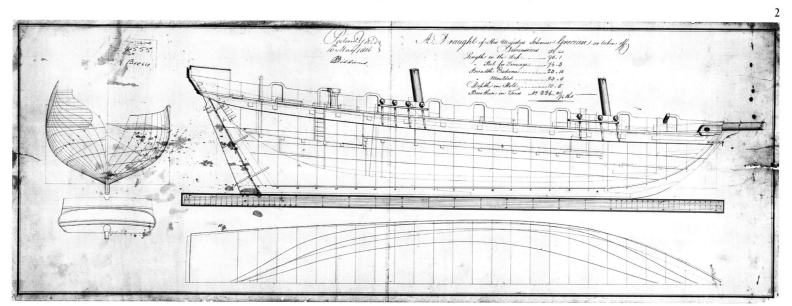

3

containing an element of waterfront ruffians who were a very effective terror-weapon in boarding.

The first ad hoc privateers (3) to sea had a relatively easy time, but as the British response geared up, and the combination of convoys and coastal blockade made operations more difficult, it became necessary to design and build more powerful vessels specifically for their calling. The speed requirement was, if anything, more crucial, and without any thought for cargo capacity they became even sharper in hull form. There was a tendency

to operate further and longer, which meant larger crews and bigger hulls, while a more powerful armament was useful if they were to fight their way past the increasing number of small British cruisers. As a result, the average size of Baltimore privateers at the end of the war rose to 286 tons and 116 men, whereas the first twelve to sea had averaged 155 tons and 97 men. If Baltimore is a guide, the vast majority of privateers during the war as a whole were in the 100-300-ton range, although there were small boats registered in some ports and large ships in

4

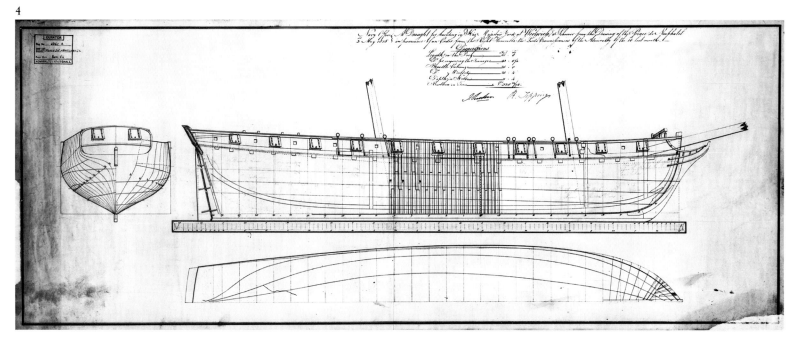

others. The biggest schooners passed the 300-ton mark with vessels like the famous *Prince de Neufchatel* of New York at 310 tons (4), and, Baltimore's largest, the 376-ton *Mammoth*.

Being involved in a high-risk enterprise, the investors in privateering did their best to design, build and equip their vessels to the highest standards. Historically, the Baltimore clipper schooner or pilot-boat model has always been awarded the palm. Much of the design was intuitive, but based on nearly two decades of demand for fast-sailing vessels, so the work of a builder like Thomas Kemp (who produced, among others, the *Rossie, Comet* and *Chasseur*) was a guarantee of quality. Although using the best materials, these schooners were necessarily lightly built and enjoyed short lives, but the result was a very young fleet: of 111 known vessels commissioned at Baltimore, only two were older than five years. In fact, Baltimore's construction programmes reflect the declining prospects of privateering during the war: 45 built in 1812, 28 in 1813, 8 in 1814, and only 1 in 1815. Attention to detail extended to features like their sails, for which the best cotton duck, rather than flax, was employed wherever possible – indeed, it was said that an American privateer was instantly recognisable by her snowy white canvas.

The seafarers of Chesapeake Bay were inordinately proud of their clipper schooners, but were inclined to exaggerate their sailing for good commercial reasons. In January 1814, the local newspaper, *Niles Weekly Register*, claimed 'These wonderfully constructed schooners cannot easily be taken, if not overloaded, if they have sea room and are uncrippled, and properly managed.' The statement contains a lot of *ifs*, and its conclusion is even more tendentious: 'They go where they please; they chase and come up with everything they see, and run away at pleasure.' Less technically minded historians have tended not to question such claims, whereas common sense suggests that it was in the business interest of every merchant, shipowner and shipbuilder in the Chesapeake Bay area to persuade firstly the rest of America and then the rest of the world that they had a superior product. To take such statements at face value is akin to evaluating an industry purely on its advertising.

There is no doubt that Baltimore schooners were among the best suited for their task, and at the end of the war the US Navy considered acquiring twenty of them for commerce-raiding; but the number of them captured simply disproves the crude notion that they could always escape from any warship. Being fore-and-aft rigged, schooners were inherently better to windward than any square-rigger, and many of the apparently cheeky incidents involve less risk than first appears, and

5

less requirement for pure speed (5). Nevertheless, they were extreme machines, with little reserve of stability and not much concern for seakeeping, so needed to be handled with the greatest of skill and seamanship (6). Even in experienced hands they could be dangerous, a point reinforced by the loss in 1986 of the modern replica *Pride of Baltimore*. This vessel was generally regarded as a very accurate imitation of the original form, yet she was never logged at more than 9 knots.

Among the most beautiful of all sailing ship designs, the clipper schooner was certainly capable of outstanding performance under sail, but it was not supernatural.

6

War as business: privateers in action

ALTHOUGH PRIVATEERING was first and foremost a business venture, none of the everyday aspects of the trade – fitting out the vessels, signing on hands, or even condemning the prizes - attracted the attention of the artists and printmakers. In the public mind it was regarded as an aspect of the war effort, and it was the spectacular captures and hard-fought actions that proved the most popular subjects. A selection of these reproduced in this section serves to demonstrate at least some of the combat aspects of privateering and the attitudes of those involved on both sides.

Conditions for the privateersmen were most favourable in the early months of the war, and those that got to sea quickly ran the least risk and were offered the greatest potential reward, before British convoys and cruisers became better organised and more alert. One such was David Maffitt of the Philadelphia schooner *Atlas* which surprised two rich merchantmen homeward-bound from Surinam on 5 August 1812 (1). They put up some resistance, but both the *Pursuit* of 450 tons and the *Planter* of 280 were taken. Their armament is represented as 16 and 12 guns respectively, but with crews of only 35 and 15, they would not have had enough men to work even one broadside. In later stages of the war such valuable but ill-defended ships would have been forced to join a convoy.

As the war developed, privateers were forced to look for new cruising grounds, where their presence would be unexpected and the enemy would consequently be unprepared. The classic example was to be the waters around the British Isles, and privateers preceded US Navy warships into these dangerous hunting grounds. However, there were other strategic areas where British trade was bound to pass, one being Cape St Vincent in southern Spain, which was not only rounded by all traffic to and from the Mediterranean, but also formed a landfall for much more distant trades. The schooner *Dolphin*, Captain W S Stafford, which carried Baltimore's privateering commission No 2, was quick to choose this area, but as if to demonstrate the vastness of the seas found no targets for two months. However, Stafford's patience was finally rewarded in February 1813 by the capture of the ship *Hebe* and the brig *Three Brothers* (2). Captain Brigham of the former openly expressed his surprise at encountering 'a damned Yankee privateer' in that location. Having experienced the rewards of privateering, Stafford was soon to feel its risks: not only was the *Hebe* recaptured before she could reach America, but *Dolphin* herself was taken after a desperate resistance in the Rappahannock by the boats of the British blockading squadron in April 1813. Three other first-class letter-of-marque schooners were taken at the same time.

The British found it difficult to capture these fast and weatherly vessels at sea, but there were situations in which superior sailing would not avail the swiftest privateer. Boat attacks on becalmed or moored privateers were common, but were not always successful: privateers had no incentive to pick a fight with a warship, but the horrors of prison or the hulks gave them every motivation to defend themselves when attacked. Probably the bloodiest repulse of the war was dished out by the *General Armstrong* against the boats of the *Plantagenet*, 74, frigate *Rota*, and brig sloop *Carnation* on the night of 26/27 September 1814. Although the privateer was moored in the neutral harbour of Fayal in the Azores, she was

1

2

3

provoked into firing on a reconnoitring boat from the squadron, which gave the British the necessary excuse to mount a cutting-out attempt. Seven boats containing 180 men attacked the well-prepared privateer, but were beaten off with the destruction of two boats and the loss of 34 dead and 86 wounded (3). Despite the success, there could be no escape for the privateer, and she was burned by her captain, Samuel Reid.

Prizes taken without loss of life or damage (particularly to the privateer) made the best business sense, and intimidation was a much-tried tactic; but all privateers had to be prepared to fight if bluster failed. A good exam-

4

5

1. 'Battle between the Schooner Atlas and two British Ships, on the 5th of August 1812', tinted lithograph engraved by A Weingartner, no date. These prints were originally produced as illustrations to George Coggeshall's *History of American Privateers . . .* (New York 1856), so although they are not strictly contemporary it is reasonable to assume that the author, an old privateersman himself, would have insisted on accuracy.
NMM ref PAD5818

2. 'Battle between the Schooner Dolphin, the British ship Hebe and a Brig off Cape St Vincent on the 25th of Jan 1813', tinted lithograph engraved by A Weingartner, no date.
NMM ref PAD5831

3. 'The American Privateer *General Armstrong . . .* Oct 26th 1814 repulsing the attack of 15 boats containing 400 men . . . The British loss was 120 killed and 130 wounded -Americans lost 2 killed and 7 wounded,' lithograph by N Currier, New York. Mistakes with the date and details of the privateer (she should have been schooner rigged), and the wildly exaggerated numbers are not uncommon in the prints of this period.
Beverley R Robinson collection ref BRR51.7.529

4. 'Battle between the Schooner Saratoga and the Brig Rachel on the 15th of Dec 1812', tinted lithograph engraved by A Weingartner, no date.
NMM ref PAD5826

5. 'Battle between the Schooner Rossie and the Ship Princess Amelia on the 16th Sept 1812', tinted lithograph engraved by A Weingartner, no date.
NMM ref PAD5823

6. 'To Francis Freeling . . . the situation of H.M. Packet Hinchinbrook at the close of the Engagement with the American privateer Grand Turk of Salem on the 1 of May 1814 . . .', coloured aquatint engraved by Baily after an original by Lt William Innes Pocock, published by Colnaghi & Co, 1 February 1819.
NMM neg 798

7. '*Hibernia* beating off the privateer *Comet*, 10 January 1814: firing her starboard broadside', oil painting in the style of Thomas Whitcombe.
NMM neg B5539

8. '*Hibernia* beating off the privateer *Comet*, 10 January 1814: on quarter, firing her port broadside', oil painting in the style of Thomas Whitcombe.
NMM neg B5541

9. '*Hibernia* beating off the privateer *Comet*, 10 January 1814: sailing off', oil painting in the style of Thomas Whitcombe.
NMM neg B5540

ple was encounter between the New York schooner *Saratoga* and the brig *Rachel* in the Caribbean in December 1812 (4). Under Captain Charles Wooster, the *Saratoga* was to take twenty-two prizes, but *Rachel* was one of the most stubborn. When the vessels first met, Wooster sent a boat with an officer to inform the the brig of the force of his own vessel and threatened to put to death every man if there were any resistance. Captain Dalmaroy of the

Rachel had a letter-of-marque, 14 guns, a larger than average crew of 36, and no desire to surrender. Literally nailing his colours to the mast, he set sail and prepared to make his defence. As *Saratoga* came up, she twice hailed the brig to strike or take the consequences, but it needed a raking broadside, several vollies of musketry, and a large boarding party on her deck before *Rachel* gave up — and even then only after the death of her captain.

6

One much sought after class of prey was the government mail packet. These relatively small craft often carried specie or other particularly valuable cargoes so were desirable prizes. However, they were also fast-sailing and relatively well-armed – usually with powerful but light brass 9-pounders – and were inclined to put up a fight. Even the most skilful and experienced privateer captain found them troublesome. The veteran Joshua Barney, sometime naval officer, who ran his highly successful *Rossie* on naval lines, encountered the *Princess Amelia* in the West Indies in September 1812. The packet carried 8 guns and 28 men, but *Rossie*, with 12 and 95 respectively, still took two hours (50 minutes in close action) to subdue her opponent (5). The latter's captain, master and a boy were killed and eleven more of the crew wounded, before the mails and dispatches were jettisoned and the ship surrendered.

Although badly damaged, the prize was taken into Savannah by Barney, and as a tribute to her sailing qualities purchased for the US Navy as the *Georgia* and later *Troup*. The British government, keen to encourage similarly stout defences of their mails, awarded survivors 'gratuities' and the families of the dead were granted pensions in recognition of the gallant behaviour of the packet's crew. Throughout the war, serious resistance was common, and sometimes successful, even against the most powerful attack. The famous brig *Grand Turk* of Salem, a big purpose-designed privateer of 309 tons and 14 guns, made around thirty prizes in the course of five cruises – but she failed against the packet *Hinchinbrook* in May 1814. Although heavily outgunned, the British vessel prevented the privateer boarding, and after a long gunnery duel, beat her off (6).

From the perspective of a British merchantman, merely surviving an attack was a victory, but occasionally a creditable defence could be raised to the status of an epic if it caught the imagination of a prominent artist. One of the foremost marine painters of the age, Thomas Whitcombe (or possibly one of his followers), produced a sequence of four canvases depicting the nine-hour battle between the Baltimore schooner *Comet* and the big transport *Hibernia* on 10 January 1814. Commanded by Thomas Boyle, one of the very best privateer captains, *Comet* was highly successful, having twenty-seven prizes to her credit, but there were to be no more. Having survived attacks first on her bow (7) and then her stern (8), the transport eventually forced the privateer to sheer off with casualties of 3 dead and 16 wounded (9). The *Hibernia*'s high sides and anti-boarding netting (carefully depicted in the painting), prevented the usual hand-to-hand tactics favoured by privateers. A shattered *Comet* was brought into Wilmington, but she never again cruised as a privateer.

1

Irwin Bevan's War of 1812

2

MANY OF the best – and sometimes the only – representations of the minor actions of the war come from the Bailey Collection of the Mariners' Museum, Newport News, Virginia. Comprising a total of 254 watercolour drawings, when acquired in 1940 they were thought to be the work of the engraver Charles T Warren (1763-1823). However, the coverage ranges between events of 1745 and 1850, so they could not be both contemporary and the work of one person. The Museum's research eventually showed them to have been produced by Irwin John Bevan (1852-1940), a Welsh-born artist and book illustrator. His work is reproduced, for example, in *Sea Fights of the Great War* by W L Wyllie and

M F Wrenn, published in 1918. Further examples of his work can be found in the holdings of the National Maritime Museum at Greenwich and the Beverley R Robinson Collection at the US Naval Academy Museum, and may indeed be from the same series. They all relate to the navy in the age of sail, and are strongly American in focus, so it is assumed that they were produced for an abortive book project.

Bevan was a keen naval historian and his work reveals a thorough knowledge of contemporary sources, although mostly written rather than visual. Some of his watercolours include long manuscript captions, quoting almost verbatim from sources like *Gazette* letters, but also the standard nineteenth-century historians like William James. He undoubtedly understood sailing ships, so his representations are convincing on a generalised level, but there are anachronistic mistakes in some ship portraits, and the topography could not have been based on firsthand knowledge. Occasionally, the composition of a painting suggests familiarity with a contemporary print, but in general his conceptions seem to have been based on his reading. If they were meant as book illustration, they certainly work well in their intended role, and a number have been used in this book to fill gaps in the contemporary coverage. These are mostly of minor events, unlikely to attract the market-oriented painters and printsellers of the day, keen to sell glorious images flattering to the national self-image; but for this reason Bevan's work better illustrates the run-of-the-mill actions that made up the experience of so many involved in the naval war.

We have chosen four relating to the eternal battle between hunters and hunted in the war on trade.

Highflyer was one of the most fortunate Baltimore privateers, having taken nine prizes that managed to find their way back to American ports, producing an estimated $187,000 for her backers. However, despite the vaunted sailing qualities of Baltimore clipper schooners, she was captured twice, the first time by the frigate *Acasta* and the *Poictiers*, 74 on 9 January 1813. Taken into the Royal Navy under the same name, she was found very useful by the British during their Chesapeake operations, but was retaken on the Nantucket shoals by the returning USS *President* on 23 September 1813 – although in this case it was due to the inattention of the lieutenant in command, who assumed that the frigate he could see through the mists was one of the British blockading squadron he was ordered to join (1). All the schooner's papers were capture intact, as was the secret private signal book.

Inca, another Baltimore letter-of-marque schooner, was a successful blockade runner, having made a number of transatlantic voyages to France. Her luck ran out off Charleston in November 1813 when she was chased ashore by the brig sloop *Recruit* (2). The cargo, however, was saved, and the owners eventually negotiated its ransom from the British blockaders.

The tight cordon around the American coast drove the privateers into distant waters, although there was nowhere completely safe from a navy with over 500 cruising warships. In the Bay of Biscay the *Bunker Hill* of 14 guns and 86 men endured a long chase in light condi-

3

tions by the frigate HMS *Cydnus*, 38 guns, but was finally overtaken and compelled to surrender on 4 March 1814 (3). Even if they could not be caught, there were other methods of neutralising privateers – in the case of the *True Blooded Yankee* literally, since she was driven into the Brazilian port of São Salvador by the British brig sloop *Albacore* in December 1814 (4). Although an ally of Britain, Portugal was not a belligerent in the American war, so the *Albacore* kept the privateer blockaded rather than cutting her out. Unable to slip past the watchful sloop, eventually the privateer had to be sold to defray the costs of her stay. The *Albacore*'s action was credited with saving at least two packet ships and numerous merchantman.

4

1. '*President* and *Highflyer*, 23 September 1813', watercolour by Irwin Bevan (1852-1940), no date.
Mariners' Museum, Newport News ref QW341

2. '*Recruit* and *Inca* off Charleston, 2 November 1813', watercolour by Irwin Bevan (1852-1940), no date.
Mariners' Museum, Newport News ref QW324

3. 'Capture of *Bunker Hill* in Bay of Biscay, 4 March 1814', watercolour by Irwin Bevan (1852-1940), no date.
Mariners' Museum, Newport News ref QW357

4. '*Albacore* and *True Blooded Yankee*, December 1814', watercolour by Irwin Bevan (1852-1940), no date.
Mariners' Museum, Newport News ref QW400

Privateers *v* small cruisers

IN THE balance sheet of a privateer's business combat with naval vessels was usually regarded as an avoidable liability. Even though many privateers were larger than minor warships, battle offered only great risk of damage and little potential reward. However, a privateer might be forced by mistake or tactical necessity into combat with one of the King's smaller cruisers, and occasionally overturned the odds of better discipline and superior training by sheer force of numbers or unbridled aggression.

An example of the advantage of a larger (and more ferocious) crew was demonstrated by the *Decatur*, nominally registered in Charleston but with a French captain, Diron, and a largely Gallic crew. The British schooner *Dominica* was escorting a packet from St Thomas in the West Indies when on 5 August 1813 she was attacked by the *Decatur* with obvious intention to board. The British vessel had more firepower but the privateer carried a bigger crew; after skillfully fending off two attempts to board, the *Dominica* finally succumbed to a fierce assault over her quarter, but did not strike her colours until 60 of her crew of 88, including the young lieutenant in command, were either killed or seriously wounded; only two escaped injury altogether (1). The loss of 19 of his own crew, not to mention the valuable packet which escaped, must have led Diron to question the wisdom of this engagement.

Dominica was a large ex-privateer, but some Royal Navy vessels barely warranted the description 'warship', a notorious example being the dispatch vessels built on the lines of Bermudan sloops. With a total broadside of two 12-pounder carronades, if they could be overtaken they were easy prey for even modest-sized privateers. *Rook, Whiting* and *Pike* were taken by French corsairs and *Ballahou*

2

and *Landrail* by Americans. On 12 July 1814 this last was chased in the Channel while carrying important dispatches by the swift-sailing Baltimore privateer *Syren*, which gradually overhauled the cutter rigged *Landrail*. Having no long-range weapon to answer the American 'Long Tom', the cutter shortened sail and then sustained a remarkable fight against overwhelming odds for well over an hour (2) before damage to her carronades and the expenditure of all her small-arms ammunition compelled her to strike. Five of her crew of 20 were wounded, but they believed they had killed 3 and wounded 15 of their 50 opponents. It is difficult to be certain because *Landrail* was recaptured, and *Syren* herself never reached safety, being driven ashore and destroyed by the Delaware blockading squadron on 16 November the same year.

Even the most experienced privateer captain could be guilty of an occasional lapse of judgement, and there was none more able than Thomas Boyle of the famous 'Pride of Baltimore', the brig *Chasseur*. On sighting a schooner off Havana on 26 February 1815, Boyle gave chase, the stranger apparently making off under such a press of sail that she soon carried away her fore topmast. As *Chasseur* came up Boyle could see only three gunports on his target's port side, and convinced himself that she was a weakly armed trader, especially since she had few men on deck. Somewhat careless in his preparations therefore, Boyle was surprised when the schooner hauled up a broadside of ten gunports and promptly opened fire (3).

The stranger was HMS *St Lawrence*, once the Philadelphia privateer *Atlas*, but now in Royal Navy service and armed with a battery of fourteen 12-pounder carronades and one long 9-pounder. Carrying too much sail, *Chasseur* surged past, whereupon the British schooner attempted to cross her stern, but was thwarted by Boyle's quick response in also turning to meet broadside with broadside. However, the gunfire soon told against the *Chasseur*, and since she was unlikely to be allowed to break off the action, Boyle was forced to trust in the traditionally larger crew of a privateer. Running alongside the British vessel, his boarding party soon compelled her to surrender, with 6 killed and 17 wounded (4).

Boyle's skill had offset his earlier complacency, but he himself lost 5 dead and 8 wounded, which he felt necessary to explain to his owners.

> I should not willingly, perhaps, have sought a contest with a King's vessel, knowing that is not our object; but my expectations at first were a valuable vessel and a valuable cargo also. When I found myself deceived, the honor of the flag intrusted to my care was not to be disgraced by flight.

3

Nobody would argue with the first point, but since privateers were encouraged to run from regular warships there could be no disgrace: the only disgrace was being caught napping in the first place, and Boyle's embarrassment is clearly visible through the smokescreen of patriotism.

4

1

The destruction of American trade

IN COLONIAL days American-built ships had provided one-third of the tonnage flying the British flag, and from the 1790s, with most of Europe at war, US shipowners had seized a high proportion of the neutral carrying trade. They already enjoyed a significant advantage in more cheaply constructed ships (thanks to plentiful supplies of accessible timber), but the relative safety of neutrality and wartime shortages that drove up prices made shipowning an attractive investment (1). Despite self-inflicted wounds like Jefferson's Embargo Act of 1807 – it was estimated to have cost 55,000 seamen's jobs and perhaps 100,000 more in related industries – the freeing

2

3

of restrictions in 1810 led to a rapid resurgence. After Macon's Bill No 2 American-flag shipping reached 981,019 tons; on a per capita basis this was not to be exceeded for thirty-seven years, and equated with about 40 per cent of the massive British merchant marine. Even the coastal trade shared in the reflected glory, doubling in tonnage each decade from 1790 to 1810 when it stood at 405,000 tons.

All this quickly changed on the outbreak of war and the disappearance of neutral status. Despite Madison's 90-day embargo, designed to see as many merchant ships as posible safely home before the formal declaration, many never made it. Salem had 73 ships at sea in June 1812, 17 of which were definitely captured and another 18 of which are not known to have arrived (2). When the British introduced the commercial blockade, at first the New England states were exempted, partly to encourage their political isolation from the pro-war southern states, but mainly because the British needed American grain to feed Wellington's army in Spain and licensed Yankee ships to carry it.

Many American ships had a reputation for being fast-sailing, but nevertheless hostilities reduced their appeal as carriers. To quantify this, in 1805 New England had re-exported foreign goods to the value of $15.6 million, which was reduced to $5.9 million in 1811, but no more than $0.3 million in 1813; using another indicator, of the 44 vessels cleared from Boston for overseas in December 1813, only 5 were American. If unlicensed, those that put to sea had to run the gauntlet of British seapower, and few survived a round trip (3). Insurance premiums on American ships reached 50 per cent, reflecting an actuarial assessment of the risk.

As a result, by September 1813 there were 245 vessels laid up in Boston, not including coasters. Not surprisingly, over 200 were square rigged, the few active

shipowners turning to sharp-lined schooners to max-imise the chance of escape. The fore-and-aft rig was far superior to windward than any square rig, but the schooner still needed the right tactical situation and weather conditions to be able to escape up-wind (4).

By 1814 the blockade was so tight that even the coastal trade almost entirely halted. Shipowning ceased to be an attractive investment, and capital migrated into manu-facture, many economic historians viewing the war as the catalyst for the American industrial revolution. Whereas 250 ships had been registered in Salem in 1805, there were only 57 by 1815; although the US retained the advantage of cheaper ships for at least two decades, the war cost America its status as neutral carrier to the world.

4

1

Ships of the Royal Navy: schooners

THE SCHOONER rig is strongly associated with North America, and as far as the Royal Navy is concerned rightly so. The first Navy schooners were purchased in New England in the 1760s in an attempt to enforce the unpopular excise and trade regulations. They were useful against smuggling vessels and privateers of their own type, but in Britain the rig was never regarded as suitable for serious fighting vessels.

Square canvas could be backed, which made square riggers more handy in battle, and the few sails of the schooner made them very vulnerable to damage aloft – the loss of either of the big gaff courses would render a schooner completely unmanageable.

After 1783, the Royal Navy continued to employ a few schooners, acquired through hire, purchase or capture. With cutters, they ranked as the smallest cruising war-

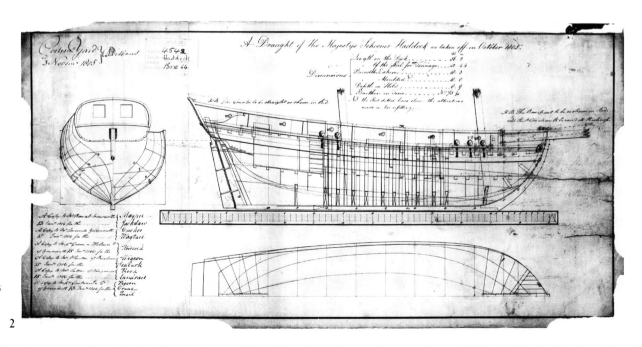

2

ships, but whereas cutters were used quite agressively, operating against minor commerce raiders and defending friendly trade, schooners tended to be used for carrying dispatches, and also undertaking reconnaissance in places where the superior windward performance of their fore-and-aft rigs made them a better bet than the less weatherly square-riggers. The Navy's first purpose-built schooners were experimental: Samuel Bentham, the Inspector General of Naval Works, pursuaded the Admiralty to acquire four schooner rigged vessels of his design – in many ways reduced versions of his eccentric sloops *Dart* and *Arrow* – but although they were to enjoy active careers, these were rated first as advice boats and then as gun vessels.

As the Navy's areas of operations expanded so did the need for fast-sailing craft to carry orders to far-flung stations and bring home reports. Cutters and schooners were obvious candidates, but ex-merchant types were often lightly armed and not particularly fast, making them easy prey to more powerful privateers of traditionally speedy forms like xebecs and luggers. In April 1804, for example, Nelson's dispatches were lost when the 77-ton hired cutter *Swift* was taken by a big privateer xebec; but earlier the schooner *Flying Fish* had been captured in the West Indies in 1795, and the cutter *Sprightly* in 1801, both carrying important dispatches.

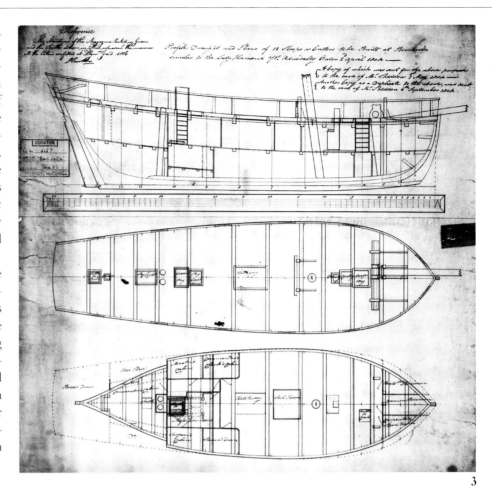

3

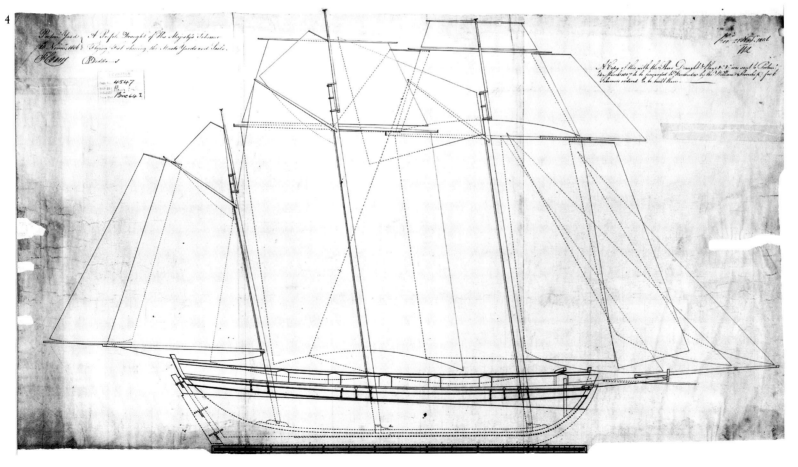

4

The Admiralty revived the old concept of an advice boat, a craft intended to carry information (a seventeenth-century meaning of 'advice'), either in the form of dispatches or in the form of intelligence from reconnaissance. Speed was a prime requirement, and the *Express* class of 1800 were extremely long and sharp-lined. These were not entirely successful, and since the Surveyors were not very highly regarded by the encumbent Admiralty Board of the time, a new schooner design was produced by a commercial builder in Bermuda, 'similar to a Bermudian dispatch boat' (1). These 70-ton schooners (2), with their almost nominal armament of four 12pdr carronades, were much criticised at the time: William James poured scorn on these 'tom-tit cruisers' which he flatly declared were 'a disgrace to the British Navy', pointing to their remarkably high fatality rate — some were even captured by privateers, *Ballahou* and *Landrail* by the Americans and at least three others by the French. They certainly suffered greatly from the elements and the enemy, but James misunderstood their purpose — they were principally designed to carry dispatches (to save more important warships being diverted), and it was inevitable that some would be captured by more powerful ships in situations where the schooners' superior sailing could not be employed to advantage.

However, criticism also came from more influential quarters. St Vincent, then C-in-C of the Channel Fleet, wrote to Admiral Markham of the Admiralty Board in July 1806:

I have omitted to write to you an account of the schooners, which are no more like Bermudian vessels than they are like Indian Praams; if any more are built, Surveyor Rule must have nothing to do with them, but the [Ber]Mudian builders left to their own discretion; in fact, they are a plague and bother to all who have them under their orders.

At this date he can only have been referring to the *Ballahou* class, and although St Vincent is never very objective on the subject of the Surveyors, it may be that Sir William Rule had some say in the design of these craft. That being said, surviving evidence suggests that they certainly did resemble Bermudian sloops, and it was not the model but the restricted dimensions which were at fault.

Another Bermudian prototype, the sloop *Lady Hammond*, had just been chosen for a new design of twice the tonnage (2), and some of these were rigged as cutters — court martial records show *Alban, Cassandra, Claudia* and *Laura* were cutters when lost, and *Alphea, Barbara* and *Zenobia* were schooners. The hull form of these Bermudian vessels, with their sharp V-section and deep drag aft were closer to traditional English cutters — hence the alternative rigs — than to the shallow American Virginia pilot boat model. However, it was one of the latter that was chosen as the prototype for the Navy's last purpose-built schooner design of the war, the three-masted *Shamrock* class of 1808, modelled on the Baltimore-built *Flying Fish* (4), ex-*Revenge*. This was actually a reversal of policy since the original design proposed for the advice schooners that became the *Ballahous* was the Virginia pilot boat *Swift* of 1794, which had a very flat 'skimming dish' hull form quite unlike the Bermudian model eventually chosen. Curiously, though, the apparent success of large American privateer schooners in the War of 1812 had no immediate effects on the Navy's building policy, although there was a short-lived desire to copy the *Prince de Neufchatel*.

Like cutters, schooners served on virtually every station, but there was a tendency to prefer the latter on the North American and West Indies stations and the cutter nearer home. Even the advice schooners sometimes served in offensive roles — the *Snapper*, for example, was captured while interrupting local shipping on the French coast in July 1811 — and both were often attached to blockading squadrons for inshore scouting. One particular task — coping with the swarm of small privateers — required large numbers of small craft, mostly schooners, on the West Indies stations throughout the war, and on the American coast after 1812.

The post-war years saw the schooner gain some renewed popularity for packet and anti-smuggling duties (5).

5

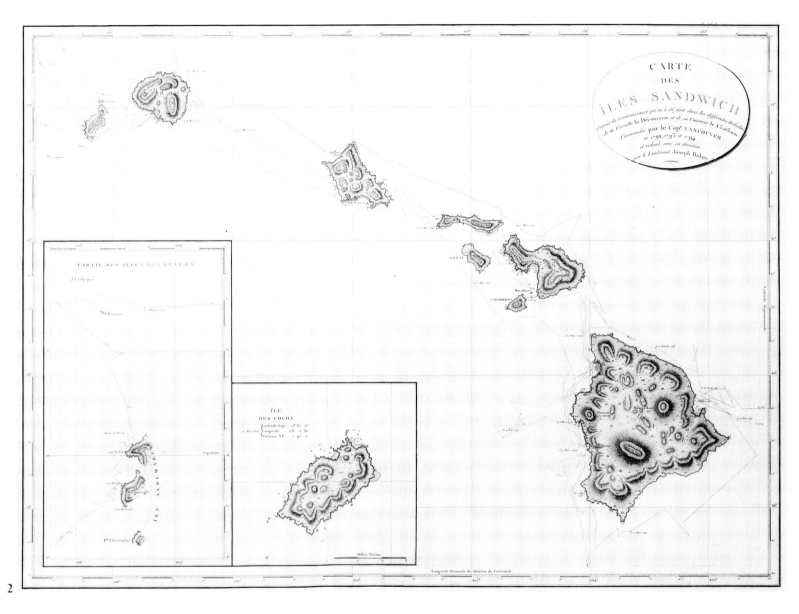

2

Cruise of the *Essex*

1

PROBABLY THE single most outstanding achievement of the naval war was the frigate *Essex*'s invasion of the British sphere of influence in the Pacific and the devastation of the South Sea whaling industry. Undertaken on the individual initiative of her captain, David Porter (1), it is also the best known, since Porter possessed a flair for publicity unusual for his day and profession, culminating in an autobiographical account of his exploits published in 1822. Porter had earlier tried to interest the Secretary of the Navy in a voyage of exploration and colonising in the Pacific, so when he missed Bainbridge's squadron at all three of the arranged rendezvouses, his discretionary orders to act 'for the good of the service' allowed him, quite legitimately, to fulfil his ambition.

Porter knew that he would possess three advantages,

in the short-term at least. It would take the British many months before they could send forces strong enough to oppose him, their nearest naval station being Brazil. The political situation on the west coast of south America had been confused since the French occupation of Spain, and he could probably find some local authorities sympathetic enough to assist with refitting and supplies. There was also a well developed but unprotected British whaling industry in these waters, and once captured these whalers – equipped and stored for long voyages – could also provide the resources he might need to prolong his cruise.

Having endured the inevitably stormy rounding of the Cape, when he arrived at Valparaiso on 15 March 1813 his ship was well received by the revolutionary junta, as he anticipated. Refitted and revictualled, the frigate

3

Massachusetts Bay (4), and by 12 December Porter could set sail for the Chilean coast with a well found ship victualled for six months. Having achieved his ambitions as an explorer and his goal as a commerce destroyer, he now looked forward to the ultimate glory of a victorious single-ship engagement with another frigate. On the eight-week passage his crew were exercised thoroughly in the use of great guns and small arms in preparation.

They did not have long to wait. *Essex* and *Essex Junior* had only been at anchor at Valparaiso a few days when on 3 February 1814 the British frigate *Phoebe*, 36, James Hillyar, and ship sloop *Cherub*, 18, arrived. Ironically, the frigate had not been sent in response to Porter's activities, but was on a secret mission to destroy American fur trading outposts in the Pacific Northwest. At Rio de Janiero the admiral of the South America station, aware of the situation, had added two sloops to Hillyar's command to give him local superiority over the *Essex*. Hillyar had then sent one of these, HMS *Racoon*, to fulfil the original mission while he sought out Porter.

Both Hillyar and his ship were veterans: in her earlier years *Phoebe* had been the victor in single combats over the French corvette *Atalante*, 16, and the 36-gun frigates *Néréide* and *Africaine* (each larger than *Essex*); and under Hillyar's command the ship participated in a series of hard-fought squadron actions off Mauritius in 1811 which culminated in the capture of a number of frigates (including the *Java*, the ship later taken by the *Constitution*). The tactical problem for Porter was that the main battery of *Phoebe* comprised twenty-six long 18-pounders, whereas his own ship was armed almost entirely with 32-pounder carronades. These were devastating at short range, but he had frequently cast doubt on the sailing abilities of the *Essex*, and he could not believed *Phoebe* would allow him to close. *Cherub* was another factor, since she was superior in every way to the converted whaler he had as a consort. Furthermore, Hillyar and Porter were acquainted, having met in the Mediterranean some years before, so Porter knew his opponent was a skilled but cautious man – in fact, Hillyar had once provoked some dissent in his squadron by refusing to pursue a superior French frigate force, preferring to wait for reinforcements he knew to be on their way.

In the circumstances, therefore, Porter could only wait and hope for luck or a British mistake to even the odds. In the event the weather forced his hand, when on 28 March a southerly gale drove *Essex* from her anchors, and Porter decided to try to weather the British ships that were then blockading the bay. Unfortunately, a squall carried away his main topmast and the frigate was forced to run back towards the shore, followed closely by the British ships. As Porter let go the spare anchor, the

sailed north to the Galapagos Islands (2) in pursuit of the main target of the cruise, the British whale ships (3). Over the next few months Porter was to capture twelve of these, and retake an American whaler prize to a British privateer. They were either overawed by *Essex* herself, her boats, or by the *Georgiana* or *Atlantic* (renamed *Essex Junior*), two of the prizes armed by Porter to act independently. Taking about sixty per cent of the whalers in the south Pacific was a serious blow to British trade, although Porter's own estimate of $5 million was a wild exaggeration of its value, and not one of the prizes ever reached the United States.

By the end of September *Essex* had been at sea eleven months and was in dire need of a major refit. This had to be somewhere remote, so there was no chance of the frigate being surprised when unable to defend herself – especially since Porter had heard rumours of a British squadron of a frigate and two sloops on its way to the Pacific. These were still some months away, but Porter took no chances, choosing the Marquesas Islands, far out in the Pacific and well away from any trade routes. Along with four remaining prizes, *Essex* arrived off Nuku Hiva on 25 October, and repairs began as soon as the frigate could be warped into the bay. True to his self-image of an explorer and coloniser, Porter annexed the island for the United States renaming it Madison's Island, but his government never acknowledged the acquisition. Meanwhile the refit proceeded apace in what was now

4

Phoebe opened fire, and a short but destructive cannonade followed, before the British ships wore round and stood further off. The attack was renewed about an hour later, and although Porter cut his cable hoping to drift closer to his enemy, Hillyar manoeuvred to retain his range advantage, *Essex*'s return fire being largely confined to three 12-pounders (5).

Porter's final gambit, an attempt to run the ship ashore, was foiled by the wind dying away, and after enduring 45 minutes of remorseless destruction, he struck his colours to save further bloodshed. As might be expected by the one-sided nature of the battle, the casualties were disproportionate: *Phoebe* lost 4 killed and 7 wounded, and *Cherub* 1 and 3 respectively, but Porter claimed 58 dead and 65 wounded in his ship, although having allowed some of the crew to swim for shore before surrendering there was no way of confirming the figures. Hillyar paid generous tribute to his enemy's resistance, but neither ship was seriously damaged, and the prize was brought back to England without difficulty. The *Essex Junior* was disarmed and sent as a cartel with the prisoners to America.

5

1

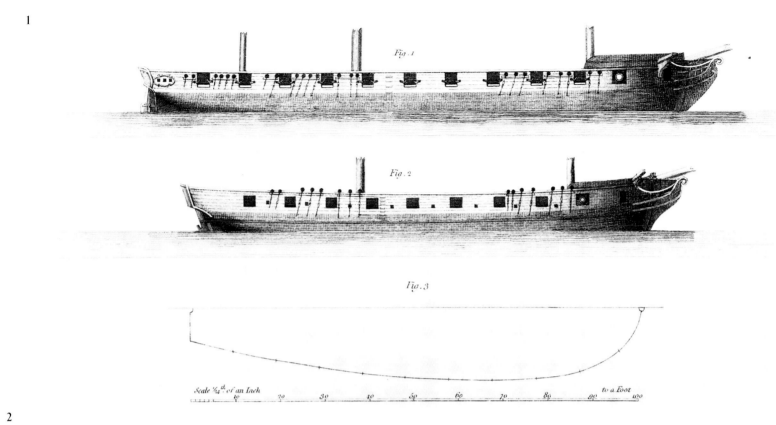

2

Sloops of war – the new generation

THE ONLY ships of the new construction programme to see any real service during the war were the three sloops of the *Frolic* class. Generally regarded as enlarged and improved versions of the original *Wasp* and *Hornet*, the new *Wasp, Peacock* and *Frolic* proved almost perfect commerce raiders. They were fast and powerful under sail, with a low flush-decked hull that made them weatherly; although fairly sharp in hull form, they could stow enough provisions to make long-distance cruises. With a length of 118 feet, there was plenty of room for eleven guns (plus a chase port) on the broadside, and an armament of twenty 32-pounder carronades and two long 18s gave them significant superiority over any British sloop they were likely to meet, especially the ubiquitous *Cruizer* class brigs (1).

In fact, the British had an ideal counter in the *Hermes*, based on the French *Bonne Citoyenne*, which had two guns less than the American design but was otherwise similar. On hearing of the new US sloops the British mass-manufactured a modified version of this design, but while adding two extra guns actually reduced the dimensions of the hull. None of these ever met an American sloop in combat, but one, the *Levant*, was unfortunate enough to meet the *Constitution*.

The service careers of the new American sloops did not get off to an auspicious start. First to sea was the *Frolic* (named after the brig defeated by Jacob Jones's *Wasp* in 1812), which sailed from Portsmouth, New Hampshire in February 1814 under the command of Joseph Bainbridge. By April she was off Florida, when on the 20th lookouts spotted a frigate and a schooner to the northwest. Not being able to weather the Florida shoals, *Frolic* tacked in the hope of weathering the strangers, by this time clearly enemies, and making for Havana. The schooner was the *Shelburne*, which had started life as a speedy Baltimore letter-of-marque, with the legendary windward performance of the type. She had soon cut off *Frolic*'s escape route, and Bainbridge considered beaching the ship, but the Cuban coast was very rocky, and as the pilot later reported, 'should the Cap. run her on shore we must all been lost.'

As a final gamble, the sloop was tacked across the

3

4

5

bows of the oncoming frigate, but a wind shift headed the ship off, and in a trice she was within range. Lightening the sloop by cutting away her anchors and throwing overboard her larboard guns had no effect and the enemy was soon on her quarter (2). The frigate was the 18-pounder 36-gun *Orpheus*, Captain Hugh Pigot, and – 'being under the frigate's guns one broadside would have sent us to eternity' – Bainbridge wisely struck his colours. Although criticised for an apparently pusillanimous surrender by some historians, Bainbridge was exonerated by his navy, and in truth it is difficult to see what more he could have done. *Frolic* was taken into the Royal Navy, and renamed *Florida* to celebrate the scene of her capture.

Far more fortunate was the cruise of the *Wasp*, which, benefiting from the experience of the *Argus* the previous year, was sent to operate in the English Channel approaches. Under the command of Johnston Blakely (3), the sloop sailed from Portsmouth on 1 May and

although many of the chases turned out to be neutrals, by the end of June *Wasp* had taken seven British merchantmen. By this stage of the war there was little chance of prizes reaching a friendly port, so Blakely burned most of his captures, employing one as a cartel to send his prisoners to England.

In these waters he was unlikely to remain unmolested for long, and on 28 June he sighted a naval brig, HMS *Reindeer*, another of the *Cruizer* class, but built of fir and armed only with 24-pounder carronades. This brig had a far better crew than was usual at this time, and under Commander William Manners had been worked up to a high level of efficiency, earning them the sobriquet 'Pride of Plymouth'. According to a colleague, they had frequently discussed the 'best way of dealing with our disproportioned American foes', and Manners' opinion was 'Yardarm and yardarm, three broadsides double-shotted, and board.' In the event, although his attack was unhesitating, it was rather more intelligent. Having retained the weather gage, *Reindeer* took station on the *Wasp*'s weather quarter, where none of her guns could reply, and opened the action by firing her 12-pounder boat carronade in an attempt to damage the American's rigging. (Mounted on the brig's topgallant forecastle, this small gun so impressed Blakely that he had it removed to the *Wasp* after the battle for use in the same way.) After enduring this galling fire for ten minutes, Blakely luffed up and let go his starboard broadside, and thereafter the close-range engagement became ferocious. *Wasp*'s crew were also well trained, and their superior weight of metal soon told. After about half an hour the bow of the totally disabled brig crashed into *Wasp*'s starboard quarter (4), and with a crew reduced to half its original very inferior numbers, Manners decided that boarding was his last chance. Already seriously wounded, as he climbed into the rigging to lead the assault, he was shot down by sharpshooters in the *Wasp*'s tops; thereafter British resistance crumbled.

It was a very bloody action. American casualties of 11 dead and 15 wounded were far outweighed by the 23 killed and 42 wounded in the British crew. The *Reindeer* was shot to matchwood and had to be burnt the following day. Although not badly damaged, Blakely took his sloop to L'Orient, where despite the neutrality of the new Bourbon government he was allowed seven weeks to refit and reprovision his vessel. Sailing again on 27 August, he took three more merchantmen, before falling in with yet another British brig, this time the *Avon*, with her full complement of 32-pounder carronades. In the evening of 1 September a confused night action took place, in which the brig's gaff was quickly shot away (5), followed by her main mast; in this unmanageable state she was battered for half an hour before surrendering.

Blakely's account of the preliminaries to the action mentions four sail, from which he deliberately selected the furthest to windward, in order to minimise the possibility of intervention by the others. However, as he was securing his prize, one of these, *Avon*'s sister *Castilian*, approached close enough to fire a broadside — although to no effect (6). Fearing that he might soon be facing three fresh opponents, Blakely made sail, leaving a badly damaged *Avon* to sink a few hours later. *Wasp*'s damage was confined to her top hamper in this one-sided fight, and compared to the British losses of 10 dead and 32 wounded, her 1 killed and 2 wounded speaks volumes for the poor quality of British gunnery and the excellence of her own.

Moving his cruising grounds further south, Blakely captured a few more prizes off Madeira, including the brig *Atalanta*, which was so valuable that he risked sending her home with his dispatches. On her safe arrival, Blakely was promoted to captain and voted the thanks of Congress for his victory over the *Reindeer*. He did not live to benefit, however. *Wasp* disappeared without trace, some time after 9 October 1814, when she was last seen by a Swedish ship 900 miles south of Madeira. Two of the surviving officers of the *Essex* travelling in the Swedish ship joined the *Wasp*, and as a result never reached home at all.

1. Comparative profiles of the American *Frolic* class sloops (top) and the British *Cruizer* class brigs, prepared by William James for his book *A Full and Correct Account of the Chief Naval Occurrences of the late war . . .* published in May 1817.
NMM neg D9543

2. '*Frolic* and *Orpheus*, 20 April 1814', watercolour by Irwin Bevan (1852-1940), no date.
Beverley R Robinson collection ref BRR51.7.494.17

3. 'Johnston Blakely Esqr of the United States Navy, engraved for the Analectic Magazine', stipple engraving by Gonbrede, published by M Thomas, no date.
Beverley R Robinson collection ref BRR51.7.732.53

4. 'Action between USS *Wasp* and HMS *Reindeer*, 28 June 1814', oil painting by Edwin Hayes (1819-1904), no date. Note that the artist has reversed the action in mirror-image.
NMM ref BHC0610

5. '*Wasp* and *Avon*, 1 September 1814', watercolour by Irwin Bevan (1852-1940), no date.
Beverley R Robinson collection ref BRR51.7.494.23

6. 'The Wasp and Avon', wood engraving by Abel Bowen after an original by Michèle-Félice Corné, no date.
NMM ref PAD5852

6

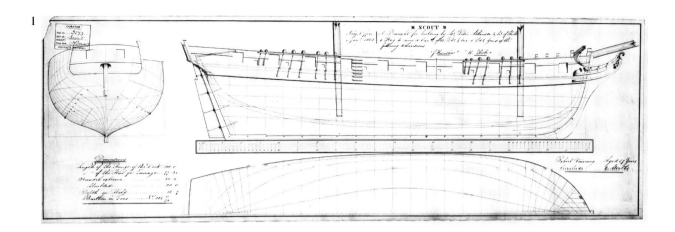

Ships of the Royal Navy: brig sloops

STRICTLY SPEAKING, in the Royal Navy the term 'sloop' applied to any vessel in the charge of an officer with the rank of Master and Commander (or Commander for short), such as a bomb or fireship when cruising, or even a ship of the line when armed *en flûte* as a troopship or store ship. However, the vast majority of such commands were small cruisers, generically called 'sloops of war', which varied in both rig and hull design. Some were miniature frigates with quarterdeck and forecastle; some that were also ship rigged were flush-decked; but the vast majority were rigged as brigs and with one or two exceptions carried their single tier of ordnance on an exposed weather deck.

Brig sloops were introduced into the Royal Navy in 1778, a generation after the new ship rigged sloops, which had proved to be seaworthy but slow. The hull form was very sharp, with a lot of deadrise in the midship section, and the layout was flush-decked. Small craft features, like the exaggerated sheer, tiller worked on deck, and a lack of quarter galleries, suggest a vessel scaled up from a cutter rather than reduced from a ship sloop, and the first class carried the same armament of ten 4-pounders as the biggest cutters. Brigs soon grew to be much the same size and gun power as ship sloops, but a clear dichotomy in their employment is apparent after 1793. Ship sloops were rather like post ships in that they were seaworthy and more habitable than brigs but simply not as fast or weatherly. As a result, almost all the sloops attached to the Channel Fleet in the early years of the war were brigs. This was true of the detached squadrons as well as the main force: *Kingfisher* was with Cornwallis in 1795, *Childers* with the Quiberon expedition of the same year, and *Kangaroo* was the only sloop present in Warren's clash with Bompard in October 1798. High-profile forces like Kingsmill's Irish squadron had almost all brigs amongst its sloops, in contrast to Duncan's cinderella fleet in the North Sea that had many ship sloops (perhaps reflecting its heavy workload of convoys, and many small ports requiring blockade).

Brig sloops, on the other hand, grew relentlessly in numbers during the French wars. They were found capable of discharging a very wide range of duties, associated with both a fleet role and trade protection. Once rearmed with carronades they enjoyed one of the high-

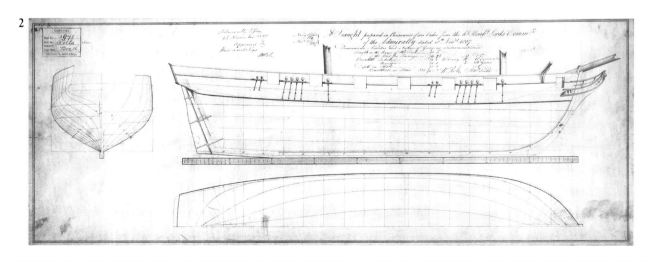

est ratios of firepower to tonnage of any warship type; their crews were relatively small in number, a factor of great importance to an expanding navy with over-stretched resources; they also possessed both speed and seakeeping (although they were far from comfortable ships for long service), and were relatively shallow draught so could be used inshore where the war was increasingly fought – at first in anti-invasion actions, and then enforcing the blockade in every creek, inlet and island where Napoleon's Continental System was supposed to hold sway.

Brigs were already the Navy's maids-of-all-work by 1806, but thereafter the huge programmes of 18-gun *Cruizer* (1) and 10-gun *Cherokee* (2) classes made the brig sloop the largest single type in the Navy List.

Year	No in Sea Service	No in Ordinary or Repairing
1794	18	2
1797	33	3
1799	37	0
1801	45	0
1804	33	0
1808	103	2
1810	169	0
1812	144	1
1814	155	3

More than any other ship type, the brig sloop reflects the Navy's mushrooming commitments. After 1806 the conflict became increasingly an economic war of attrition; most of the coastline of mainland Europe came under the influence of Napoleon's Continental System of trade exclusion, and the British in retaliation declared the whole continent blockaded. International law as understood at the time required a blockade to be enforced if it was to be legally binding on neutrals, so every small port required a British force to monitor its activities – and more often than not the force was one or more brigs. Denmark, whose fleet was neutralised in 1807, carried on the war with gunboats and small craft, and many a hard action was fought in the narrow waters of the Norwegian fjords and Baltic skerries between these experienced and resourceful squadrons and British mosquito fleets of brig sloops and the smaller gunbrigs. Similarly, the indented and island-strewn coasts of Greece and Italy (3) required numerous small squadrons, which saw much more action than the larger warships, thanks to the successful blockade of the French main fleets and the sea control established by squadrons of British frigates. The British army's campaign in the Peninsula after 1808 was largely supplied from the sea, and this added further to the Navy's escort and inshore support duties, while cam-

3

paigns from the West Indies to Indonesia, and the Indian Ocean to the Baltic all employed brig sloops in large numbers.

Standardisation can mean mediocrity, but in contrast for example to the 'Surveyors of the Navy' class 74s, the *Cruizer* class was a decided success. A single prototype was built in 1797 and not repeated until 1802, but by then the ship had a superb reputation – 'for she sails like the devil', as one correspondent to the *Naval Chronicle*

4

expressed it. The huge class that followed were generally regarded as satisfactory in all their multifarious roles, and their small crews made them very cost effective. They could also claim a high ratio of firepower to tonnage: although in some cases the calibre was reduced to 24-pounders, they were usually armed with sixteen 32-pounder carronades, with two long 6-pounder chase guns, a potent armament at close range, their speed being seen as sufficient safeguard should they wish to avoid action with more powerful opponents. Their later reputation suffered as a result of defeats in the War of 1812, although much of the criticism was misdirected. There were some clear cases of poorly trained and ill-lead crews, reflecting the dilution of quality brought about by the Navy's vast expansion, but every brig sloop was lost to a larger American ship rigged vessel. Even the greater firepower and larger crews of the American sloops were not always the decisive factor, but the distinct advantage in battle of three masts over two can be seen in most of the actions: USS *Wasp* could still manoeuvre after the loss of her main topmast, mizzen topgallant and gaff, whereas the already storm-damaged *Frolic* was completely disabled when her gaff was shot away; similarly, USS *Peacock* survived the loss of her fore mast sails in the fight with *Espeigle*, damage which would have crippled a brig.

Because a number of them actually sank in action or had to be destroyed afterwards, the *Cruizers* were also criticised for their light scantling, but this was central to the design rationale of the class. Light construction meant

ease and cheapness of construction, and contributed to the sailing qualities of these brigs. And they *were* fast and weatherly, despite many occasions when privateer schooners were able to escape them – this was not a matter of what modern yachtsmen call boat-speed, but usually resulted from the inherent ability of the fore-and-aft rig to get nearer the wind than the square rig. This was an advantage when fleeing a more powerful enemy, but the ability to back square sails endowed brigs with better manoeuvrability in battle, making them superior fighting ships to schooners (4). Even so, the chasing performance of brig sloops like the *Sophie* in the Chesapeake during 1813 gained them a lot of respect from would-be blockade-runners. The issue was simply another manifestation of the old argument between quality and quantity: the prime British requirement was the latter, and in general terms the *Cruizers* gave good value for money. Those who complained of their occasional vulnerability to more powerful ships might well have argued that because American ship sloops were captured by frigates, they too were a poor investment: in fact, they were ideal for the commerce-raiding which was their principal *raison d'etre*.

Even the economical *Cruizer* class could not be manned in sufficient numbers to meet all the Navy's commitments, so the smaller *Cherokee* class was introduced. These were less highly regarded and quickly became known as 'coffin brigs', owing to the large number that were wrecked or foundered. A close analysis of the circumstances of these losses suggests no obvious design fault, but they were probably too small for the go-anywhere duties required of them. This is supported by the opinion of Lieutenant William Bowers, who had twelve years in *Helicon* and *Leveret*, and felt the class had been 'unduly vituperated'. He agreed that they were wet and cramped, but was convinced that 'when properly handled' they were as safe as any flush-decked vessel in the Navy. James says that they were dull sailers, but the fact that the class continued to be built for fifteen years after the end of the war – and many served as packets, where speed was of the essence – suggests that at worst this lack of performance was relative (5). Indeed, Bowers describes how *Helicon* became a crack sailer once her very sharp hold had been properly restowed. His own reservation about the 10-gun brigs was their lack of 'warlike capabilities', and he especially objected to their rating: 'Rated as sloops of war, we but risk our national reputation, and undermine the prestige of our power at sea, by risking a collision with the larger vessels of a like rate of other nations.' With the sobering lessons of the American war in mind, he concluded, 'Assuredly such a craft would be but a morsel for any of brother Jonathan's brig sloops.'

1. Sheer draught of the *Scout*, one of the numerous 18-gun brig sloops of the *Cruizer* class. The fine hull form is evident.
NMM neg DR3177

2. Sheer draught for the small 10-gun brig sloops of the *Cherokee* class.
NMM neg DR3971

3. 'H.M. Brig *Wizard* off the Island of Maritimo', watercolour by Lt William Innes Pocock, no date but about 1811. *Wizard*, of 16 guns and 283 tons, was midway between the *Cruizers* and *Cherokees* in size.
NMM ref PAF0052

4. 'HM Sloop *Sparrowhawk*', watercolour by William Smythe, 1822-23. A *Cruizer* class brig.
NMM ref PAF5966

5. 'HM Brig *Nautilus*', lithograph by John Ward, no date. One of the post-war additions to the *Cherokee* class, built in 1830.
NMM neg A341

5

Warrington and the *Peacock*

THE LAST of the *Frolic* class sloops to sail, USS *Peacock*, was to be the most successful of all. Escaping the attentions of the New York blockading squadron in March 1814, she sailed south under the command of Master Commandant Lewis Warrington (1), an experienced officer who had served in the Tripolitan War and later in the frigates *Essex*, *Congress* and *United States*. He had been promoted in July 1813 and appointed to stand by the *Peacock* during her construction, so she was fitted out as closely as possible to his requirements.

Having first delivered a cargo of military stores to St Mary's, Georgia, in April Warrington took his sloop to cruise in the narrow channel between Florida and the Bahamas, through which much of the Caribbean trade passed. However, so well organised was the British convoy system by this date that during the course of a week only one neutral and two privateers were encountered. Moving north proved more fruitful and off Cape Canaveral on 29 April *Peacock* spotted a small convoy of three merchantmen escorted by a brig sloop, HMS *Epervier* (Commander Richard Wales), yet another of the numer-

ous *Cruizer* class. Ordering the convoy to separate, the brig bore down to defend her charges – but with no more success than in any other clash with American ship sloops (2). After about 45 minutes, the brig surrendered, having suffered 8 dead and 15 wounded; only two of the *Peacock*'s crew were wounded.

As in so many of the ship versus brig actions of this war, the *Espeigle* was quickly disabled by the loss of her main topmast and damage to the fore mast (3), but her real problem appears to have been the mountings of her carronades, which either overset or drew their fighting bolts. Whatever the reason, the difference in efficiency was substantial, although it is also clear that *Espeigle* was not fought with the same tenacity as others of her class. Edward Codrington, a senior Royal Navy officer then serving as Captain of the Fleet to the local commander-in-chief, advanced a suggestion in a letter to his wife:

It is said that that fellow ————-'s [Wales] people showed no spirit until he was wounded and carried below. Something of the same sort attaches to the name of Captain ———— [Carden, of *Macedonian*],

1

2

3

whose ship did not do as well as her *reputed* discipline promised. This is the case with many of our *crack ships*, where the people, from being tyrannically treated, would rejoice in being captured by the Americans, from whom they would receive every encouragement. I have heard many shocking stories of cruelty and misconduct witnessed by the relators, now officers in this ship; and I hope the punishments will be more strictly examined into than they are now, by the late regulation of quarterly returns.

To emphasis the point, the *Espeigle*, did not sink like *Avon* or the original *Peacock*, nor need to be destroyed like *Reindeer* or *Penguin*; Warrington was able to bring his prize, although badly damaged, into Savannah.

More significant in its effect on the war was his next

cruise, which ranged from the Grand Banks, across to the Azores, and up to the Irish coast – 'in smelling distance of coal fires', as the journal of one of her midshipmen proudly recorded – and as far north as Shetland and the Faroes, before retracing her route, and across the Bay of Biscay and down the Portuguese coast. In all she took fourteen prizes, twelve of which were burned and the other two sent as cartels with the prisoners to England, returning to New York via the West Indies on 30 October after a voyage of 147 days.

Peacock's final operation was as part of the squadron with *Hornet* intended to raid British trade and possessions in the East Indies. Although separated during their initial breakout from New York at the end of January 1814, the two sloops and their supporting store vessels rendezvoused at Tristan da Cunha (as related in the section on *Hornet*). They were again separated on 28 April in the Indian Ocean when *Cornwallis*, 74 guns, preferred to pursue *Hornet* rather than *Peacock*, which sailed on to Java. Pickings were surprisingly slim – just three small ships – and, rather more disturbing for officers looking for prize money and promotion, news of a peace. First intimations were gleaned from the British *Venus* taken on 22 June, confirmed on the 28th by the prize *Brio de Mais*, which informed them that hostilities were to continue until the treaty was formally ratified by the President. The Americans were not impressed by the proposed terms, and Midshipman Rodgers confided to his journal, 'if such is the case, we are the last ship East of the Cape & so will make the most of our time.'

Off Anjer on 1 July *Peacock* was approached by a British brig, which sent over two of her officers in a boat along with the local master attendant. They were bundled below, and the sloop ranged up ominously alongside the brig (4). The commander of the latter hailed that peace had been signed, but when Warrington's peremptory demand to strike his colours was refused, *Peacock* fired a broadside which quickly secured compliance. What Midshipman Rodgers jocularly called 'a salute of 17 guns' killed 6 and wounded 8, including the brig's commander and lieutenant. She was the *Nautilus* of 16 guns belonging to the East India Company's Bombay Marine, carrying $30,000 in specie and copper worth $100,000. However, the master attendant was able to produce printed proof of the ratification of the treaty, so the brig had to be returned – 'thus are our bright prospects blighted' noted Rodgers of the loss of the substantial prize money involved, but it was probably the sentiment of many naval officers on both sides faced with peace and unemployment.

As a commerce-raiding venture, *Peacock*'s final cruise was not an obvious success, but it proved that the US Navy could operate globally, and that there was no sea in which even a great naval power's interests could not be threatened.

1. 'Lewis Warrington Esqr of the United States Navy, engraved for the Analectic Magazine', stipple engraving by Gonbrede after an original by Jarvis, published by M Thomas, 2 October 1815.
Beverley R Robinson collection ref BRR51.7.732.58

2. 'Peacock and l'Epervier', brown aquatint engraved by William Strickland after an original by Thomas Birch, no date.
NMM ref PAD5849

3. 'Epervier and Peacock, 29 April 1814', watercolour by Irwin Bevan (1852-1940), no date.
Beverley R Robinson collection ref BRR51.7.494.18

4. 'Peacock and Nautilus, 30 June 1815', watercolour by Irwin Bevan (1852-1940), no date.
Mariners' Museum, Newport News ref QW416

4

Constitution's last victory

1

THE LAST wartime commander of 'Old Ironsides' was to be Captain Charles Stewart (1), transferred from the blockaded *Constellation* at Norfolk where he had done good work in the defence of the area. He was a fine seaman, but these talents were largely wasted while he was unable to escape the watching British forces; he had ably protected his ship, but the occupation of the Chesapeake meant that there was now little chance of getting her to sea, so in May 1813 Stewart was sent to Boston, which was almost impossible to blockade in winter.

Although he was ordered to sea in September, it was the turn of the year before *Constitution* could get away, but her three-month cruise in the Caribbean proved very disappointing. The British convoy system was both rigorous and well organised, leaving as easy prey only insignificant coasting vessels. She did chase the frigate *Pique*, 36, in a rather half-hearted fashion and captured

the naval schooner *Pictou*, but missed the convoy she had been escorting. As a result Stewart could report only four prizes before he was forced to return home by the lack of stores and the need to make port before the reimposition of the close blockade in the spring. On this latter point, however, he miscalculated, running into HM frigates *Junon* and *Tenedos* (both 18-pounder ships rated 38s) and was ignominiously chased into Marblehead (2). The ship had to be lightened in order to regain safe haven in Boston.

Despite Stewart's best endeavours, here the *Constitution* was immured until winter gales blew the blockading squadron off station in the last days of 1814. This time Stewart took the ship across the Atlantic, and about midday on 20 February 1815 when about 200 miles east-northeast of Madeira he sighted first one and, an hour later, a second sail. They were both British cruisers, the *Cyane* and *Levant*. The former was a small frigate-built

2

3

ship, of a type usually described as a corvette in most navies but in Royal Navy parlance a Sixth Rate 'post ship', rated 22 but actually carrying twenty-two 32-pounder and ten 18-pounder carronades, plus two long 9-pounder chase guns. The *Levant* was a flush-decked ship sloop of the type built to match the American *Frolic* class and armed with eighteen 32-pounder carronades and two long 9s. Although the British had a slightly larger aggregate weight of metal at short range, in the absence of any modern 'command and control' systems, it would be impossible to co-ordinate any simultaneous attack that could turn that superiority to practical advantage. The *Constitution*'s 24-pounder main battery could defeat either ship with great ease, and Stewart's only problem was how to take both.

By about 5.45pm the two British ships had formed a line ahead on the starboard tack, with *Levant*, the senior officer's ship, leading by about three ship-lengths. *Constitution* held the weather gage and by 6pm in the gathering twilight was abreast the *Cyane*, opening fire at about the extreme range for the latter's carronades (3). After a punishing quarter of an hour, *Cyane*'s fire fell way, and *Constitution* sailed on to give *Levant* the benefit of a broadside. *Cyane* took the opportunity to try to rake, but as she luffed up, Stewart had the after sail backed and dropped astern to meet the threat with his own broadside. *Levant* meantime had decided to run downwind and *Constitution* had to make sail to catch her, turning across her stern and loosing two raking broadsides from the port battery, before returning her attention to the other British ship. *Cyane* was in the act of wearing, but although *Constitution* was a much longer ship she was able to wear short round before *Cyane*, raking her from astern with her starboard

guns in the process. After one more broadside in reply, the British ship had suffered enough and at about 6.50pm struck her colours.

After putting a prize crew aboard and effecting the most important repairs to his ship's rigging, Stewart sailed off in pursuit of *Levant*. Despite being vastly out-gunned, the sloop returned to the battle, but a couple of broadsides persuaded her of the hopelessness of her cause. She turned to escape, but she had left it too late and was overhauled about 10pm and promptly surrendered. In what were, in effect, two simultaneous one-sided battles, the casualties were relatively light: *Constitution* lost 4 killed and 14 wounded, *Cyane* 6 dead and 29 wounded, and what Mahan called the 'plucky little ship' *Levant* 6 killed and 16 wounded. Damage was rather less equal, with the British ships badly knocked about, especially in their lower masts; the *Constitution*, on the other hand, was hit often enough in the hull, but having fought at extreme range for carronades the shot simply did not penetrate.

American single-ship victories seldom relied solely on the individual superiority of their ships, a consistent feature being the consummate skill with which they were handled during the battle. There is no finer example than Stewart's defeat of these two ships, in which he used his advantages to maximum effect, so it is doubly regrettable that his report emphasised the enemy's 'divided and more active force, as also their superiority in the weight and numbers of his guns' rather than pointing to his considerable tactical feat in taking both. Every victorious officer in any navy was inclined to present his achievement in the most favourable light, but this claim is tactical nonsense, a point made – albeit with 'the

4

5

6

1. Charles Stuart Esqr of the United States Navy, engraved for the Analectic Magazine', stipple engraving by Goodman after an original by Wood, published by M Thomas, no date.
Beverley R Robinson collection ref BRR51.7.732.19

2. 'Escape of *Constitution*, 3 April 1814', watercolour by Irwin Bevan (1852-1940), no date.
Mariners' Museum, Newport News ref QW361

3. 'Capture of HM Ships *Cyane & Levant*, by the US Frigate *Constitution*', lithograph by James Queen after an original by Thomas Birch, published by P S Duval, Philadelphia, no date.
Beverley R Robinson collection ref BRR51.7.535

4. 'Escape of *Constitution*, 12 March 1815', watercolour by Irwin Bevan (1852-1940), no date.
Mariners' Museum, Newport News ref QW409

5. 'USS *Constitution* towing the HBM Ship *Cyane* captured February 28th 1815', painted by Edward Mueller, lithograph published by Max Williams, New York, no date.
Beverley R Robinson collection ref BRR76.55.1

6. '*Constitution* at Table Bay, Cape of Good Hope', oil painting by Ambroise Louis Garneray (1783-1857). With a diameter of only 3⅛ inches, it is one of a pair of remarkable miniatures of the ship (the other being of the *Guerriere* action reproduced on p42); this probably represents the ship during her 1844 round the world voyage.
Beverley R Robinson collection ref BRR80.26.13

utmost diffidence' – by the great American historian A T Mahan.

The *Constitution*'s reputation as a 'most fortunate ship' was enhanced a few weeks later, when she was surprised at anchor off Porto Praya in the Cape Verde islands by a strong British squadron looming up out of the fog. Commanded by Sir George Collier, this force had crossed the Atlantic in pursuit of the *Constitution*: it comprised the *Newcastle* and *Leander*, ships built specifically to match the US Navy's spar-decked frigates, and the large 18-pounder frigate *Acasta*. They were fast and powerful, and with the very weatherly *Acasta* working up to windward, *Constitution* faced the greatest peril of her career (4). But in a moment the danger was over: thanks to misunderstandings and confusion in the British squadron, the *Acasta* was ordered to tack in pursuit of the *Levant* and the

other ships followed suit. *Levant* was retaken, but *Constitution* and *Cyane* were allowed to escape. Despite having to tow the slow-sailing *Cyane* (5), *Constitution* and her prize reached New York in safety, the war being long over and the blockade withdrawn.

The unique status of the big frigate in the affections of both the navy and the nation was already established. The *National Intelligencer* suggested:

> Let us keep 'old Iron Sides' at home. She has, literally, become a *Nation's* Ship, and should be preserved. Not as a 'Sheer hulk, in ordinary' (for she is no *ordinary* vessel); but, in honorable pomp as a glorious Monument of her own, and our other Naval Victories.

A later age might attempt to tear her tatter'd ensign down, but in 1815 it would have been sacrilege (6).

Part II

WAR ON THE GREAT LAKES

IT was by means of invasions across their northern border into Upper Canada (modern day Ontario) and Lower Canada (Quebec) that the Americans planned to make war against Britain most aggressively. Confidence was high in Washington that weak British garrisons would be unable to withstand military thrusts at several points simultaneously and that the sparse population of Upper Canada in particular would soon abandon its loyalty to King George and welcome the republican liberators from the south. 'The acquisition of Canada this year, as far as the neighbourhood of Quebec, will be a mere matter of marching,' wrote Thomas Jefferson in August 1812, 'and will give us experience for the attack on Halifax the next, and the final expulsion of England from the American continent.'

Although pre-war preparations in the United States had been debated for months prior to the declaration, President James Madison and his cabinet failed to appreciate the effects that reductions in the army and navy, instituted primarily during Jefferson's terms as president (1801-1808), would have on the achievement of their objectives in Canada. Less than two weeks after Jefferson made his bold prediction, reality struck. The Army of the Northwest, headed by a worn-out veteran of the War of Independence, Brigadier General William Hull, surrendered his invasion force at Detroit (16 August) to Major General Isaac

A stylised representation of the American attack and repulse at Queenston Heights, 13 October 1812. Only ten of the thirteen American boats actually reached the Canadian shore, but their troops captured the 1-gun battery halfway up the heights and succeeded in killing Major General Brock when he led a charge to recapture the gun and mortally wounded Brock's aide-de-camp, Lieutenant Colonel John Macdonell when he tried to regain the gun, also unsuccessfully. A party of native warriors pinned the Americans down on the heights until Major General Roger Hale Sheaffe organised all available regulars and militia to attack and capture the American army late in the afternoon. Estimates of American casualties ranged between 100 and 500, with nearly 1000 being captured. Coloured lithograph by James B Dennis (fl 1812-1843).
National Archives of Canada, Ottawa ref C276

Brock and a brigade of British regulars, militia and Indians. On 13 October 1812 a second blow followed, when Major General Stephen Van Rensselaer, a politician from New York with a militia command but no military training, watched in dismay as the army he was supposed to have led across the Niagara River, was beaten back at the cost of more than 1000 men after gaining little more than a brief toe-hold at Queenston. Again, British regulars joined with citizens and native warriors to protect sovereign territory (their key leader, Brock, was killed early in the fighting, which greatly deflated the victory celebrations). A later effort to cross the Niagara River also failed miserably, and the thrust toward Montreal by the well-trodden Lake Champlain-Richelieu River route barely started before retiring into winter camp.

One of the reasons why the British were able to stop the American invasions was that they held naval control of the Great Lakes when hostilities commenced. The region around the lakes was essentially a trackless wilderness with only a few dozen villages, towns and forts strung together by a poorly developed road system. The most effective mode of transportation among the communities was by shallow-draught schooner or sloop or the countless smaller craft that plied the lakes and rivers. Britain's mastery on the lakes depended on its colonial naval force, known formally as the Provincial Marine, which operated under the supervision of the Quartermaster General's Department of the British Army at Quebec. Two small ships and two schooners sailed on Lake Ontario and as far as 70 miles down the St Lawrence River where rapids blocked navigation; their home port was the naval establishment at Kingston. A second squadron, including a ship, a brig, a schooner and converted merchantmen, was situated at the dockyard at Amherstburg near the mouth of the Detroit River. It cruised on Lake Erie, above the obstacle posed by Niagara Falls, while low water marks in the passage from Lake Erie to Lake Huron prevented the ship from sailing further up the system.

The Provincial Marine had evolved from a Royal Navy detachment that had fought the French on Lake Ontario in the Seven Years War (1756-1763). During the intervening decades, the force, though still armed, assumed the role

A contemporary view of Montreal and the St Lawrence, about 1811. Its capture was a major object of American strategy, but in practice the city was never seriously threatened throughout the war.   NMM ref PAI0311

of a transport service for the army and the government, its officers and crews being mainly residents of the provinces. Early in 1812, Brock, with the support of Sir George Prevost, the commander-in-chief of British forces in Canada and governor-in-chief of civil affairs, attempted to bolster the ranks of the Provincial Marine crews by enlisting more seamen and embarking companies of the Royal Newfoundland Fencible Regiment to act as marines. Such efforts did nothing to change the fact that the squadrons had no wartime experience. That deficit was revealed in July 1812 when the Lake Ontario squadron under its senior officer, Master and Commander Hugh Earl, made a half-hearted attempt to attack the fledgling US naval base at Sackets Harbor, 35 miles south of Kingston, and failed completely to do any damage. Thereafter, the Provincial Marine resumed its largely passive role, which suited the defensive strategies that Prevost favoured.

Awakened by the shocking defeat at Detroit, President Madison and his ministers began a new initiative in the north, even before Van Rensselaer's disaster at Queenston Heights, by ordering a naval detachment north to win control of Lakes Ontario and Erie. This strategy had been discussed prior to the declaration with

regard to Hull's campaign across the Detroit River, but no effort had been made to provide naval support for him. Only two vessels flew the Stars and Stripes on the lakes, an army transport, the brig *Adams*, stationed at Detroit, and the navy brig *Oneida* on Lake Ontario. The former was captured by Brock and renamed the *Detroit* in honour of his victory, but burned by the British during an American attempt to recapture it in October. That left the *Oneida* at Sackets Harbor as the only American warship on the lakes. The brig had been constructed in 1808-9 to enforce customs laws and was commanded by an energetic officer, Lieutenant Melancthon Woolsey, USN, who seized the tiny British schooner *Lord Nelson* for trade violations just before war broke out. Upon receiving word of the declaration, Woolsey reinforced the small battlement at Sackets Harbor and began converting the *Nelson* and another commercial laker, the *Julia*, which he had purchased, for use as gunboats.

As August ended, Paul Hamilton, the American Secretary of the Navy, appointed 40-year-old Captain Isaac Chauncey to establish squadrons on Lakes Ontario and Erie, using Sackets Harbor and Buffalo as his bases. The intervention of the US Navy was to change the

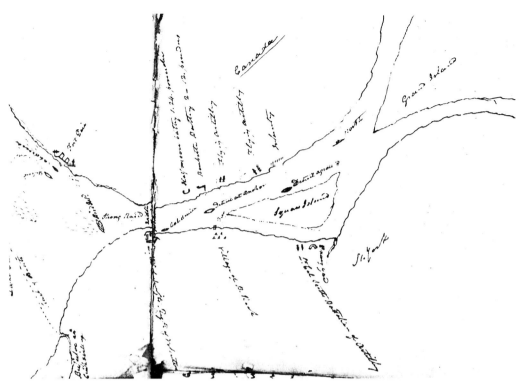

A daring attack by Lieutenant Jesse Elliott, USN on 8 October 1812 succeeded in cutting out the Provincial Marine's Detroit *and* Caledonia *from under the guns of Fort Erie. This is Elliott's own diagram of the attack, showing where the* Detroit *grounded and was burned, but he succeeded in bringing off the smaller vessel.*
National Archives, Washington DC

nature of the war on the lakes. Chauncey ranked among the leading officers of the service and had lately been commandant of the naval yard at New York. His knowledge of its facilities helped him to mobilise a supply train of ordnance, equipment, stores and personnel, including about 600 seamen, 100 US Marines and 140 shipwrights, to the lakes in September and October. Owing to difficulties in delivering the men and materiel to Lake Erie, Chauncey focused his attention on Lake Ontario. Using the *Oneida* as his flagship, he sailed with six converted lakers on 8 November and, two days later, pursued Commander Earl's flagship, the *Royal George*, into the harbour at Kingston. Chauncey's vessels pressed their attack, but the *Royal George*'s broadsides and the bombardment from shore batteries forced them to withdraw. The next day they narrowly missed capturing a merchant vessel as it slipped into Kingston, and on 14 November the Provincial Marine *Earl of Moira* just managed to elude their grasp. Chauncey's aggressive actions prompted the British to curtail their shipping for the season, leaving the two armed schooners, *Prince Regent* and *Duke of Gloucester*, at York, the province's capital, located 150 miles west of Kingston. As

wintry gales forced Chauncey to anchor his squadron at Sackets, he proudly informed a military colleague: 'I am happy to have it in my power to inform you that I have now the command of Lake Ontario.'

Chauncey's success greatly alarmed Prevost, who requested officials in England and at Halifax to send detachments from the Royal Navy to take over the Provincial Marine squadrons. While the despatches were in transit, Prevost approved the building of a 30-gun frigate at York and two corvettes to match the lines of the *Royal George*, one at Kingston and the other at Amherstburg. Upon receiving Prevost's appeals at Bermuda late in February, Admiral Sir John Borlase Warren, commanding the North America and West Indies stations, ordered three commanders, six lieutenants and two gunners to the lakes along with some ordnance and fittings for the new ships. About the same time a force of 465 men was being assembled in England to journey to Canada under the command of Commodore Sir James Lucas Yeo.

During the winter the Americans strengthened their forces also. Chauncey had placed the shipyard at Sackets Harbor in the hands of the

renowned master shipwright from New York, Henry Eckford, who showed his talents by launching the corvette *Madison*, 24 guns, in November. As snow began to fall Eckford set to work on a schooner, the *Lady of the Lake* (1 gun), while plans and materials for a larger vessel were prepared. This project eventually became a sturdy little frigate, made to carry twenty-six long 24-pounders, which Eckford laid down early in April 1813. In December Chauncey had travelled overland to find a suitable establishment for the squadron on Lake Erie. He visited Erie, Pennsylvania where Sailing Master Daniel Dobbins, USN, a local mariner had begun building gunboats and approved the protected, though shallow, anchorage as the best available location for a shipyard; work soon started there on two 20-gun brigs. In February, the Navy Department, at Chauncey's request, appointed Master Commandant Oliver Hazard Perry to the lakes, ostensibly to take over as senior officer on Lake Erie.

Secretary of the Navy Hamilton was replaced in January by William Jones shortly after William Eustis was superseded by John Armstrong as Secretary of War. Along with President Madison and other cabinet officials, the new ministers developed a loose strategy for resuming war in the spring. Although Armstrong and others had long championed a concentrated attack on the St Lawrence River just above Montreal in order to cut off supplies to British posts on the lakes, a plan was devised to renew invasion attempts on Lakes Ontario and Erie simultaneously. Reasons behind that decision included a shortage of capital to finance a major drive against Montreal, the need to protect American settlements south and west of Lake Erie and a belief that conquering the western portions of Upper Canada would prompt the Indian tribes to abandon their British allies. Perry's squadron was intended to serve the latter two purposes by gaining control of the upper lake, transporting an army to invade the Detroit River vicinity of Upper Canada and then sailing up to Lake Huron and Georgian Bay to capture British fur trading centres. William Jones strongly advocated this priority to Commodore Chauncey, who intended to assume command of the Lake Erie squadron once he had gained supremacy on the lower lake. Through the early spring he kept his force on alert at Sackets, expecting an attack from the British, while he planned a combined attack on Kingston with Major General Henry Dearborn. When political pressure was exerted on them to win a victory by the end of April in order to garner support for the Republican Party (led by Madison and New York Governor Daniel Tompkins) in an upcoming election in New York State, Chauncey and Dearborn switched their target to York, which they knew would be free of ice at that time. Chauncey also hoped to capture two warships he had heard were under construction there.

On 25 April 1813 Chauncey set sail from Sackets Harbor with 1700 soldiers crowded aboard his new flagship the *Madison*, the *Oneida*, *Lady of the Lake* and ten converted lakers. They landed the army under the direct command of Brigadier General Zebulon Pike a mile and a half west of the garrison at York on 27 April. Only 360 regulars, 300 militia and a body of native warriors, commanded by Major General Sir Roger Hale Sheaffe, were present to oppose the Americans, which proved to be an inadequate force, and after taking more than 130 casualties, Sheaffe retreated toward Kingston with his regulars. The garrison and town were captured, but not before the detonation of the grand magazine killed and injured 260 of the invaders (Pike suffered a mortal wound) and the single frigate (already named the *Sir Isaac Brock* to honour the fallen general) on the stocks in the dockyard was burned at Sheaffe's instructions. Plunder from the attack included ordnance and naval supplies and the dismantled *Duke of Gloucester*; the *Prince Regent* had sailed to Kingston just days before. Because of poor discipline in both American services, soldiers and sailors ran amok in the town, even after terms of surrender had been negotiated. The British were later to justify their sack of Washington as a reprisal for this outrage. A week of inclement weather kept the crowded warships at the anchorage to the detriment of all aboard, and it was a greatly weakened army that was finally returned to the American shore near Fort Niagara on 8 May.

Chauncey and Dearborn's original plan had been to reduce York and then dart across the lake to capture Fort George, opposite Fort Niagara at the mouth of the Niagara River, while a British column marched, theoretically, to relieve York. The assault on Fort George was delayed, however, as the army recovered its health, and Chauncey returned to Sackets Harbor to bring up reinforcements. A bombardment of Fort George and the adjacent town of Niagara began on 25 May and was followed two days later by a combined operation, which met its objectives, but allowed British Brigadier General John Vincent to escape to Burlington with most of his army intact. The victory gave the Americans a base of operations in Upper Canada, and plans were being made by Dearborn and Chauncey to pursue Vincent when news reached Niagara that the British had attacked Sackets Harbor.

Commander Robert Barclay and the officers from Admiral Warren's Fleet reached Kingston around 1 May and took over the Provincial Marine vessels, superseding their officers, most of whom quit the service. On 15 May Commodore Yeo arrived at Kingston, replacing Barclay's people with his own officers and reassigning Barclay to become senior officer on Lake Erie; Commander Daniel Pring, who had been in Barclay's party, was soon ordered to assume command of the force on Lake Champlain. On 27 May Yeo embarked 800 soldiers in his squadron and set out for Sackets

Harbor to destroy the frigate under construction there and to divert American attention away from the Niagara Peninsula. Adverse weather forced the postponement of the attack the next day, but at dawn on the 29th the troops landed under the command of Colonel Edward Baynes, Prevost's adjutant general. While a lack of wind prevented the squadron from using its few long guns in support of the assault, 1500 American regulars and militia defended their position tenaciously, inflicting 200 casualties among the British. After four hours of fighting, Baynes, with Prevost's full approval, called off the attack. Reluctantly, the troops and seamen withdrew to the squadron, muttering their disappointment and disbelief at leaving what they considered was a nearly-beaten foe. The unsuccessful affair left resentment in its wake, as one midshipman, David Wingfield, recalled: 'The murmurs against Sir George were deep, not loud . . . [T]his disgraceful affair . . . caused a coolness between the Governor and Commodore, and at length broke out into an open rupture.'

Fires had been lit mistakenly in the shipyard by the American naval commander, Lieutenant Wolcott Chauncey, the commodore's

A contemporary view of Lake Erie, about 1811.   NMM neg 8143

brother, which made the British think that one of their goals had been achieved, but the new frigate escaped damage and was launched in June and named the *General Pike*. While it was being outfitted Commodore Chauncey remained at Sackets to guard against further attacks. This deprived Dearborn's army at Niagara of his support and allowed Yeo free rein to provision Vincent's army at Burlington and to harass American shipping and communities along the south shore of the lake throughout June. In July the land war on the Niagara Peninsula stagnated as everyone waited for the two commodores to battle for control of the lake. Chauncey used the time to revise his squadron and add the *Pike*'s guns to his line, while Yeo launched a brig, giving him six vessels, mounting 97 guns to the American 112.

The first face-to-face meeting between the adversaries occurred just north of the Niagara River on 7 August, but the commodores both sought to gain the weather gage amid light airs and failed to engage. That night a tremendously violent gale upset the American schooners *Hamilton*, 9, and *Scourge*, 10, drowning all but sixteen of their crew members. Through the 8th and 9th the wind was fitful, and the squadrons remained apart, but on 10 August a steady breeze propelled Chauncey down upon Yeo, who lay becalmed close to the shore of the Niagara Peninsula. Abruptly, the wind veered around and gave Yeo the weather gage, which he used to pursue Chauncey who attempted to lure him close to the *Pike* by positioning a column of his schooners to windward of his flagship. The ploy almost worked, but a pair of schooners suddenly tacked out of formation and into Yeo's hands. Unable to interest the British in a full battle, Chauncey herded his remaining vessels together and sailed away. Later in the month Chauncey withdrew to Sackets to wait for Eckford's latest project, the schooner *Sylph*, 10 (re-rigged as a brig with 18 guns in 1814) to be readied for action.

The menacing presence of Commodore Yeo's effective squadron had prevented Chauncey from going to Lake Erie to achieve the campaign objectives in that quarter. Commandant Perry had managed the situation well, however, and by the end of July his squadron of two brigs, four newly-built gunboats and several converted merchantmen was ready to challenge the British. Although Robert Barclay had

taken over the British squadron in June, he received only a handful of reinforcements from Yeo, so that his crews were composed almost completely of Provincial Marine personnel and soldiers. After Perry sailed from Erie, he withdrew to Amherstburg to wait for the launch of the corvette *Detroit*, which would increase his force to two ships, a brig, two schooners and a sloop. With Perry on the lake the supply line from the Niagara Peninsula was cut, and shortages soon threatened the army, Indians and citizens at Amherstburg with starvation. After consulting Major General Henry Procter, the military commander of the region, Barclay decided to confront the Americans. He sailed on 9 September and the next day met Perry near Put-in Bay on South Bass Island in the western reaches of the lake. After a hard-pitched battle lasting three hours, during which the commanders and first officers on five of the British ships were wounded or killed, the British surrendered, and Perry scribbled his famous (though not quite accurate) summary of the engagement: 'We have met the enemy and they are ours: Two Ships, two Brigs one schooner & one Sloop.' Two weeks later Perry transported an American army to invade southwestern Upper Canada, but it was too late in the season for an expedition to head into Lake Huron. To Chauncey's dismay, the Navy Department soon allowed Perry to resign his position, which was taken over in 1814 by Captain Arthur Sinclair. Sinclair conducted the campaign on the upper lakes during the summer, attempting to recapture the strategically important fur trading fort on Mackinac Island, which Chauncey and Perry had both intended to do in 1813. His expedition failed, and the Upper Lakes remained in British hands.

By comparison, little had happened on Lake Champlain, which lay in the middle of the virtually unexploited route from Montreal to New York. Lieutenant Thomas Macdonough, USN, took command of two ageing gunboats in October 1812 at Whitehall, New York, to which he added three converted merchantmen. In June 1813 the British captured two of the latter sloops when the Americans tried to raid the British naval base at Isle aux Noix on the Richelieu River. These vessels were then used, along with three gunboats and a flotilla of bateaux, in British attacks against Plattsburgh, New York and Burlington, Vermont that seized

large amounts of supplies and several prizes and gave control of the lake to the British.

September nearly brought the resolution of the mastery issue on Lake Ontario. On the 11th, after manoeuvring around each other for several days, Chauncey caught Yeo in a lull near the mouth of the Genesee River, midway between Niagara and Oswego, and pounded him at long range with his heavy ordnance. This incident might have been the end of Yeo had another fortuitous breeze not sprung up, which he rode to safety at Kingston, easily outsailing Chauncey who was kept behind by the sluggish *Oneida* and the over-burdened lakers. A closer call for the British occurred on 28 September about 12 miles south of York when Chauncey got close enough to Yeo to blast the *Wolfe*'s main and mizzen topmasts over the side. He was kept from making the killing stroke by Yeo's second in command, Commander William Mulcaster, who charged up in the *Royal George* to engage Chauncey, giving the *Wolfe* time to recover and race away before the wind. A mad scramble and pursuit ensued, but, as a gale strengthened out of the east, Chauncey was unable to catch the British, who anchored at Burlington, while the Americans turned away to avoid the lee shore. A week later, just southeast of Kingston, Chauncey captured a convoy of transports that Yeo had failed to protect adequately.

Following these unsuccessful encounters, the British squadron retired to Kingston for the season, while the Americans helped transport elements of an army to Sackets Harbor for a major offensive down the St Lawrence River to Montreal. Chauncey had been led to believe the attack would be made on Kingston and, once the true goal of the campaign was revealed to him, concluded that his squadron had been misused as a mere transport service to the army. Having covered the army's movement into the river, Chauncey left it to proceed down the river on its own as a detachment from Yeo's squadron joined an army brigade that harassed the American army and later helped defeat it at Crysler's Farm on 11 November. The attack on Montreal was cancelled, and the year's fighting ended with the Americans withdrawing from British territory east of Lake Erie.

At both Lake Ontario naval bases the winter was spent building bigger and stronger ships.

The British constructed two frigates and began work on a First Rate, while the Americans, after some delay, built two brigs and two frigates. Naval reinforcements arrived at Kingston from Quebec and Halifax to man the new ships, and at several American ports blockaded warships were stripped of their crews who were then marched north to join Chauncey. Yeo's frigates were ready for service first, and his enlarged squadron carried 550 soldiers, plus 400 Royal Marines, to attack Chauncey's supply depot at Oswego on 6 May 1814. Only a half dozen or so guns, meant to arm Chauncey's new ships, were captured along with some fittings and provisions at the cost of 90 casualties. Yeo then anchored off Sackets to blockade the American supply line directly, but after more than 200 of his men were captured by the Americans in an attempt to seize a convoy of boats loaded with ordnance at Sandy Creek on 30 May, he lifted his blockade and returned to Kingston. Although a reinforcement of 900 Royal Navy officers and men from England soon reached Kingston, Yeo remained there throughout the summer waiting for his First Rate to be completed. He detached four of his smaller vessels to the Niagara River where the army had regained control and was resisting an American army that had crossed over from Buffalo.

The American strategy for the campaign of 1814 was not fully devised until the first week of June. Chauncey was supposed to gain control of Lake Ontario while Major General Jacob Brown invaded the Niagara Peninsula. Chauncey did not set sail from Sackets until the end of July because of supply delays and his own indisposition due to illness. Choosing to seek a battle with Yeo, Chauncey refused to lend Brown any support, for which he was widely criticised; Brown accused Chauncey of acting as if 'the fleet on Lake Ontario was your private property, over which the government has not control.' Yeo was similarly chastised by his military colleagues for not carrying reinforcements and provisions up to the scene of fighting at Niagara, but he remained in port until mid-October when HMS *St Lawrence*, 104, was ready for service. As Yeo led his largest warships to Niagara and back, Chauncey anchored at Sackets Harbor and prepared for an attack. It did not come, and the war ended with the commodores laying down two First Rate battleships each to continue the contest in 1815.

A more decisive culmination came on Lake Champlain in 1814. After a busy winter and spring of conversions and shipbuilding, the American squadron comprised a ship, a brig, a schooner, two sloops and ten gunboats, compared to the British force, which had grown into one ship, one brig, three sloops and thirteen gunboats. The arrival of more than 10,000 veterans from the battlefields of Europe prompted Prevost to commence an invasion along the Richelieu/Lake Champlain route late in the summer. On 6 September he was ready to capture Plattsburgh, but waited for the squadron to overcome the American warships anchored in its bay. Due to the late launch of the frigate *Confiance*, 37, and its hectic preparation for battle, Captain George Downie, who Yeo had just sent to Isle aux Noix to assume control of the squadron, was prevented from confronting Macdonough's force until 11 September. Downie attacked even though it meant beating into the wind, which retarded his progress and prevented his battle plan from being executed properly. The fighting lasted about two hours and ended with a victory for Macdonough and the loss of all the British warships, except some gunboats which escaped. Downie was killed, as were 56 others in his squadron, along with 76 wounded; American losses were 52 killed and 58 wounded. Prevost was supposed to have launched his land assault in concert with Downie's action, but, shocked by the sudden loss of the squadron, Prevost reversed his instructions and ordered a withdrawal to Canada. Criticism raged against his management of the campaign, and Commodore Yeo alleged that Downie had been goaded into action by Prevost. Yeo's protest led to the request for a court martial to investigate Prevost's conduct, for which both men were recalled to England. Prevost died in January 1816, just weeks before the court was to have been convened.

The naval war on the Great Lakes ended with the Americans in possession of Lakes Champlain and Erie, while the British began work to reclaim Champlain and to establish a naval base on Georgian Bay. The unresolved naval contest on Lake Ontario meant that the third year of fighting concluded in the same way as the previous years with neither side having made any significant gains over the other. Control of Lake Ontario and the St Lawrence

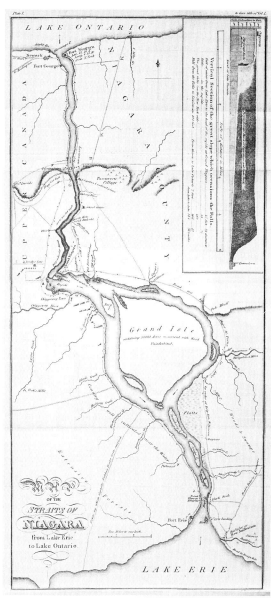

A map of the Niagara Peninsula, from William James, Military Occurrences . . . (London 1818). The area was to see much fighting during 1814, including small-scale but hard-fought pitched battles at Chippewa and Lundy's Lane, but naval activity was generally confined to either end of the river. Chatham collection

River had proven to be more strategically important than the contests fought on the peripheral waterways, and as the peace treaty was signed in Ghent ambitious escalations were underway at Kingston and Sackets Harbor in order to continue the struggle into the new year. When news of peace reached the lakes, most of the dockyard activity was stopped, and the Rush-Bagot Agreement on naval disarmament in 1817 doomed the warships to be sold or laid up to rot; the age of fighting sail on the Great Lakes had come to an end.

1

2

3

4

Lake Ontario, 1813

WITHIN weeks of taking command of the US Navy establishment at Sackets Harbor, New York in October 1812, Commodore Isaac Chauncey (1) employed the US brig *Oneida* and six converted merchantmen to chase two of the four warships of the British Provincial Marine squadron into their winter moorings at Kingston (2). His mastery on Lake Ontario lasted into the following spring when he landed the army of Henry Dearborn and covered its attacks on the British garrisons at the towns of York (3) on 27 April, and Niagara on 27 May. Not only were the public buildings of York burned by the invaders, but the defenders set fire to the incomplete *Sir Isaac Brock* to avoid capture (4). Chauncey's fire support was very effective during the assault on Fort George at Niagara (5), and the temporary occupation of the Niagara Peninsula allowed American reinforcements to pass Fort Erie and join Perry's squadron at Presque Isle. The next step in Chauncey's plan was to send part of his squadron to blockade Kingston (6) while he went to Lake Erie to conduct the campaign there. This scheme was dashed, however, by the arrival at Kingston of Sir James Lucas Yeo (7) and more than 460 officers and men of the Royal Navy, who had been ordered to Canada to assume control of the Provincial Marine squadrons.

Almost immediately, Yeo demonstrated the importance of having a competent force at Kingston by con-veying 800 soldiers under the command of Colonel Edward Baynes to Sackets on 29 May to destroy Chauncey's shipyard. Baynes, with Prevost's approval, withdrew his force from the field when the fighting grew too costly, and the shipyard was saved from destruction, although a fire mistakenly set by the Americans

5

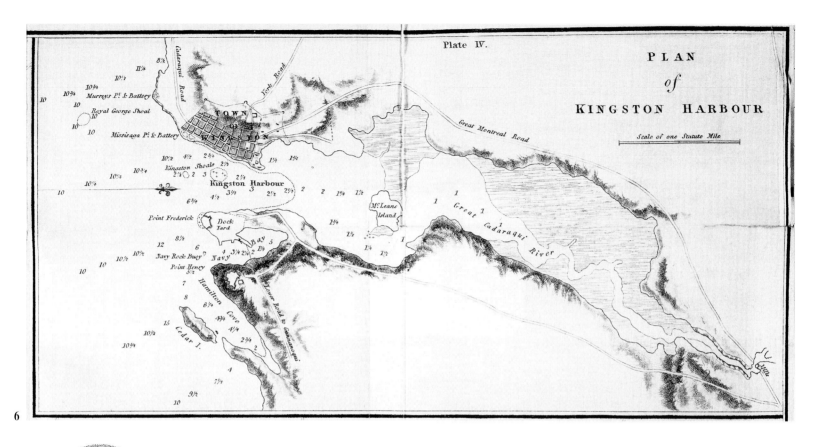

6

7

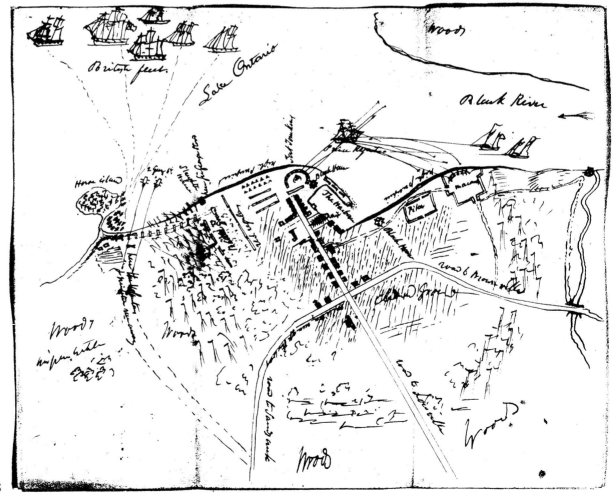

8

9

10

destroyed several buildings and most of the naval stores taken at York (8). The assault made Chauncey less willing to leave Sackets unless it was thoroughly protected by the army, especially when he had a new ship under construction. The frigate *General Pike* had narrowly escaped fire damage, so Chauncey remained at Sackets until late in July when it was ready for service. During most of that period Yeo cruised the lake unhindered, supporting the British army at Burlington, which halted Dearborn's advance and pushed the Americans back toward Niagara (9). He also raided shipping and settlements along the south shore, interrupting the American supply line, proving once again how mastery of the lake could influence campaigns on land.

After Yeo's arrival in May, everyone expected a climactic naval battle to occur, as Prevost explained to Lord Bathurst: 'It is scarcely possible that a decisive naval action can be avoided, and I therefore humbly hope that His Royal Majesty the Prince Regent will approve of its being courted by us.' In July both commodores were instructed by their superiors to focus on that goal, and during the first week of August they finally approached each other in the waters off Niagara.

The opposing forces differed from each other in a number of significant factors. Chauncey's squadron consisted of two ships, the *General Pike*, 26, and *Madison*, 24, the *Oneida*, 18, and ten converted lakers, which carried in total 66 long guns and 46 carronades. Yeo had two ships, the *Wolfe*, 23, and *Royal George*, 20, two brigs, the *Earl of*

Moira, 16, and the *Lord Melville*, 14, and two schooners, the *Lord Beresford*, 12 and *Sir Sidney Smith*, 12, but most of their ordnance was composed of carronades (78 in number) with only 19 long guns to contend with the long-range capability of the Americans. This diversity in armament dictated the commodores' tactical alternatives. '[T]he object of Sir James,' noted one of his officers, '. . . was to engage them at close quarters and board . . . [which depended on] having the wind so in our favour, as to be enabled to maintain a distance, or come to close action.' Chauncey's goal was to remain out of reach of the British carronades while pounding away at his enemy with his long guns, especially the 24-pounders in the *Pike*. His evasive manoeuvres were hampered, however, by the converted lakers, made unwieldy by their heavy ordnance, some of which he frequently towed behind the *Pike*, *Madison* and *Oneida*. Chauncey would have gladly left them in port, except that he hoped that one of the calms that typified summer conditions on the lake would allow his gunboats to sweep close enough to Yeo's line to bombard it with their long 32-pounders.

Success came first for the British when the *Hamilton*, 9, and *Scourge*, 10 (both carrying only small calibre guns and carronades) upset in a storm during the night of 7 August. The next day one of the many calms that fell upon the lake during that hot and sultry summer gave Chauncey a chance to order his schooners to sweep up to the British. As happened repeatedly, though, a breeze sprang up and the lakers were soon fleeing for safety. On 10 August Chauncey again thought he was enticing Yeo within easy range of the *Pike* by using his lakers as bait in a line to windward when two of his commanders suddenly took it into their heads to ignore his orders and

turned back as if to attack Yeo's leeward side (10). The schooners *Julia*, 2, and the *Growler*, 5, were quickly snapped up, while Chauncey, concerned about shepherding his other ill-sailing schooners, abandoned the disobedient pair to their fate. Yeo added the prizes to his line, but only briefly, for he found them to be such a drag on his manoeuvres that he relegated them to transport duty, renamed *Confiance* and *Hamilton* respectively.

On 11 September Yeo's squadron was becalmed along the American shore near the mouth of the Genesee River while a faint breeze still propelled the Americans. The *Pike* inched close enough to wound the British, but the schooners could not get up in time to use their long guns, and a providential breeze saved Yeo again (11).

Yeo suffered a closer shave on 28 September between York and Niagara. After shadowing one another for several days, the two squadrons were proceeding on roughly parallel southward course before a strong easterly breeze when Yeo realised that Chauncey was on a line to cut off his rear. To prevent this, he tacked the squadron and headed due north, whereupon Chauncey altered course and steered to intercept the *Wolfe*. The *Wolfe* fired two or more relatively ineffective broadsides before Chauncey hauled up and let his 24-pounders loose (12). 'In ten minutes from the time I commenced my fire,' wrote Chauncey's flag captain, Arthur Sinclair, 'he was a wreck. His main and mizzen topmasts with the yards topgallant masts and all their appendages were down among his guns.' Seeing his commodore in peril, Commander William Mulcaster raced his *Royal George*

1. Captain Isaac Chauncey, USN, after a painting by J Woods. From Benson J Lossing, *The Pictorial Field-Book of the War of 1812* (New York 1868).
Chatham collection

2. Pursuit of the *Royal George* into Kingston by Chauncey's squadron, 9 November 1812. Pen and ink and watercolour by Owen Staples, dated 10 November 1912; an illustration for C H J Snider's *In the Wake of the Eighteen-Twelvers* (London 1913).
Metropolitan Toronto Reference Library ref T15239

3. 'York Barracks, Lake Ontario, Upper Canada, 13 May 1804', watercolour, pen and ink with white gouache over pencil by Sepronius Stretton (1781-1842).
National Archives of Canada ref C14905

4. The *Sir Isaac Brock* on the stocks at York, April 1813; the dismantled *Duke of Gloucester* is in the background. Pen and ink and watercolour by Owen Staples, about 1913.
Metropolitan Toronto Reference Library ref T15211

5. Chauncey's fleet supporting the attack on Fort George in May 1813: USS *Madison* is in the foreground. Engraving by unknown artist, published in *The Port Folio*, Vol 4 (Philadelphia 1817).
Archives of Ontario ref S1439

6. 'Plan of Kingston Harbour', Plate IV from William James, *Military Occurrences . . .* (London 1818). It is based on the 1816 surveys of Captain W F W Owen, RN.
Chatham collection

7. Captain Sir James Lucas Yeo, RN. Stipple engraving by H R Cook after an original by A Buck; published by Joyce Gold, 1810.
NMM ref PAD3283

8. Eyewitness sketch of the Battle of Sackets Harbor, May 1813. Origin unknown.
Library of Congress ref 400434

9. 'The Fort of Old Niagara, taken from Navy Hall, with the Embouchure of the Strait into Lake Ontario', watercolour by Edward Walsh, 1804. The viewpoint is the Canadian side of the river.
Clements Library, University of Michigan

11

12

10. Capture of *Julia* and *Growler*. 'A View of the night action of one hour and 43 minutes between Part of U. States Fleet Under Command of Comdr Isaac Chauncey, And the British fleet Commanded by Sir James L. Yeo, On Lake Ontario the 10th of August 1813.' Tinted drawing by Acting Midshipman Peter W Spicer, who served aboard USS *Oneida* during this action.
Naval Historical Center, Washington, DC ref NH 75733

11. Night action of 11 September 1813 near the Duck Islands. 'A View of the Running Fight of 3 hour s & 40 m., between the U. S. Fleet Under Command of Comdr Isaac Chauncey, and the British Fleet of a Superior Force commanded by Sir James L. Yeo, On Lake Ontario, the 11th of September 1813.' Tinted drawing by Acting Midshipman Peter W Spicer, who served aboard USS *Sylph* during this action.
Naval Historical Center, Washington, DC ref NH 75734KN

12. 'A Scene on Lake Ontario. United States Sloop of War *Gen. Pike*, Commodore Chauncey and the British Sloop of War *Wolf*, sir James Yeo, Preparing for Action Sept. 28th 1813,' coloured line engraving by Ralph Rawdon, published by Shelton & Kensett, Cheshire, Connecticut, 1 November 1813.
Beverley R Robinson collection ref 80.26.18.

13. 'Burlington Races'. 28 September 1813; the dismasted *Wolfe* is defended by *Royal George* from the approaching *Pike*. Pen and ink, watercolour and gouache by Owen Staples, dated 1912.
Metropolitan Toronto Reference Library ref T15238

into the gap between the *Pike* and *Wolfe*, hove to and blasted the *Pike* to a standstill while Yeo recovered and, setting every scrap of fabric on the fore mast, raced away westward (13). A chase and pell-mell action ensued – the 'Burlington Races' – during which the *Pike* was damaged and several of the British vessels narrowly missed being taken. As the lee shore of Burlington Bay loomed, Chauncey broke off the pursuit (his squadron was scattered by the gale conditions) in order to preserve his vessels.

Yeo anchored near Burlington and made quick repairs before going in search of the Americans on 2 October. No contact was made, though Chauncey hurried eastward late on 4 October thinking the British had given him the slip and succeeded in capturing five transports, which Yeo had left unprotected. The next week Yeo returned to Kingston, where the squadron remained for the season, while Chauncey continued to support the army on the first leg of a major (but ill-fated) campaign down the St Lawrence River. The two commodores never met again in a ship to ship action, though the operation of their squadrons continued to alternately support and frustrate the campaigns fought near the Lake Ontario shores.

13

1

British shipbuilding on the Lakes

LONG before war erupted in 1812 the British had established two freshwater shipyards, one at Kingston on Lake Ontario and the other at Amherstburg on the Detroit River, that were the home bases for the Provincial Marine squadrons operating below and above the obstacle to navigation posed by the

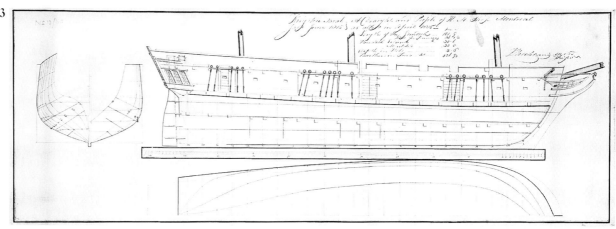

2

3

famous falls on the Niagara River. At Kingston, a master shipwright named John Dennis had been constructing vessels since 1802, while his counterpart at Amherstburg, William Bell, had been launching warships for use on Lake Erie and the Upper Lakes since 1799. Down their slipways had gone gunboats, schooners, snows, brigs and ships, half of which had been lost to decay and accident by the time of the American declaration of war. Over the years officials had proposed other places (York, Georgian Bay and Long Point on Lake Erie) as preferable sites for naval establishments, but the plans had not been put into effect, and Kingston and Amherstburg remained the key centres.

Situated where Lake Ontario emptied in the St Lawrence River, Kingston had developed into the primary transhipment port for cargo passing up from, or down to, Montreal. On the eve of war about 1000 people lived in the town, their livelihoods largely dependent upon

1. The naval facilities, including the dockyard at Point Frederick, Kingston about 1815, watercolour by Hugh Irvine (fl 1812-1817).
National Archives of Canada ref C145247

2. Figurehead design for the *Earl of Moira*, watercolour, pen and black ink by François Baillarge (1759-1830), Quebec, 1803.
National Archives of Canada ref C15227

3. Sheer and profile draught of the corvette *Montreal*, ex-*Wolfe*, dated June 1815. Originally intended to be called *Sir George Prevost*, the ship was renamed in April 1813 and again in 1814; later she was converted into a troopship with the addition of a spar deck.
NMM neg DR6413

the maritime commerce conducted on the wharves along the town's front on the western shore of the mouth of the Cataraqui River. The Provincial Marine establishment stood across the river on a low-lying peninsula named Point Frederick, on the other side of which was Navy Bay, a deep inlet suitable for launches and moorings (1). The dockyard comprised several store-houses and shops, a slipway, a wharf and a mast pond, all protected by a weakly-manned garrison and a battery on the end of the point. While John Dennis was the resident master shipwright, the dockyard was actually run by officers from the Quartermaster General's Department of the Army at Quebec. Early in 1812 four principal vessels, the corvette *Royal George*, 20, the ship rigged *Earl of Moira*, 14, the schooners *Prince Regent*, 12, and *Duke of Gloucester*, 6, and a derelict, the snow *Duke of Kent*, were stationed at Kingston. They exemplified the characteristics of pre-war armed vessels on the lakes, namely shallow draught, lightweight ordnance, and rapid decay.

Though launched only in 1807, the *Duke of Gloucester*, which had been reserved for the use of the provincial government, was so riddled with rot by 1811 that a replacement (the *Prince Regent*) was ordered. Attempts had been made over the years to accrue stocks of seasoned timber that could be used to build longer lasting ships, but they had all resulted in failure. Oak appears to have been the most common material employed in

4

building, with red cedar being considered the best wood, but hard to come by in sufficient quantity. A preservation experiment was conducted on the *Earl of Moira* (2) by packing salt between and around the frames before her launch in 1805, which seemed to be working when the

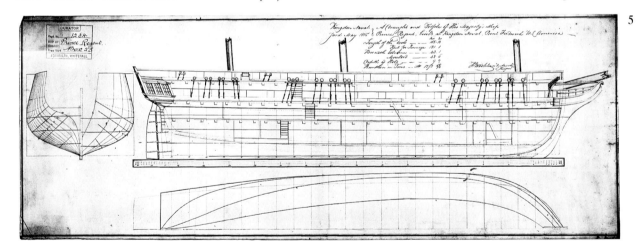

5

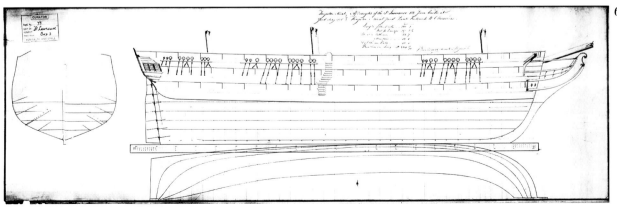

6

4. A watercolour portrait of *Prince Regent*, 1814 by her commanding officer, Captain Henry Davies, RN. *National Archives of Canada, ref C138986*

5. Sheer and profile draught of *Prince Regent*, dated May 1815. *NMM neg DR1284*

6. Sheer and profile draught of *St Lawrence*, dated May 1815. *NMM neg DR73*

7

was 13ft 11ins, which greatly limited her activities close inshore and provoked criticism of the design. Just prior to the war, a suggestion was made that schooners like the *Prince Regent* were the most practical type of armed vessel for the Provincial Marine's use, since they could carry ordnance, but still enter most harbours around the lake.

The outbreak of war, and the failure of the Provincial Marine squadron on Lake Ontario to change magically from its traditional role as a transport service to an efficient fighting force, signalled the end of such concerns for peacetime practicalities. Late in 1812 Sir George Prevost ordered the building of two corvettes (3) similar to the *Royal George* (the *Wolfe*, 22, at Kingston; the *Detroit*, 20, at Amherstburg) and a 32-gun frigate, and appealed for help from the Royal Navy. Prevost also approved the removal of some senior Provincial Marine officials on land, including John Dennis, who was replaced by a reputedly experienced shipwright from Quebec named Thomas Plucknett. At the same time, a decision was made to transfer the marine establishment to York (in order to remove it further from the American shore), where Plucknett began by laying down a frigate, to be named the *Sir Isaac Brock*. However, Plucknett proved to be so incompetent (at Kingston two new master shipwrights were also fired) that the military officers recalled John Dennis to push the frigate ahead, though his efforts came to naught when the Americans attacked in April and the incomplete ship was burned to prevent capture.

Point Frederick remained as the key naval establishment, and when Commodore Yeo arrived in May 1813 he brought order to the dockyard, launched a new brig, the *Lord Melville*, 14 (gundeck 72ft 10ins; extreme breadth 24ft 3ins; draught 9ft 6ins), and recommended the construction of frigates. In the fall work began on the *Princess Charlotte*, 40 (gundeck 126ft 9ins; extreme breadth 37ft 4ins; draught 16ft 4ins), and the 56-gun *Prince Regent* (4, 5), (gundeck 160ft 9ins; extreme breadth 43ft; draught 17ft); the 1812 schooner of the same name had by then been

ship was inspected in 1811, though a closer look several months later revealed extensive decay.

Being unusually small for carrying a three-masted ship rig, the *Moira* (gundeck 73ft; breadth 23ft 8ins) was refitted as a brig during the winter of 1813. She had been built to draw only 8ft 6ins of water even when loaded in order to pass over the bars that obstructed most of the rivers and creeks feeding into Lake Ontario. Consequentially, the vessel and others like her (the slightly smaller *Prince Regent* drew 9ft 4ins) had little space in their holds, were very leewardly, and had to be armed with carronades that would not compromise their stability or crowd their cramped decks. When a trade dispute with Britain prompted the US Navy to build the brig *Oneida* at Oswego in 1808, the British responded by laying down the largest warship seen to that date on the lakes, the corvette *Royal George* (gundeck 101ft; extreme breadth 27ft 7ins), armed with twenty 32-pounder carronades. Unfortunately, the ship's loaded draught aft

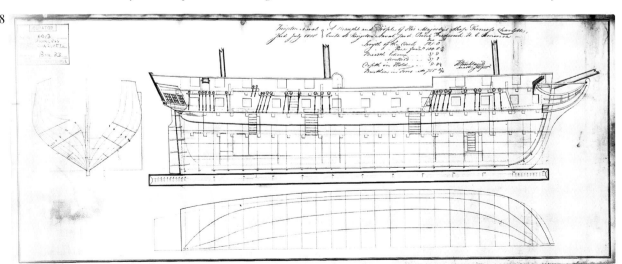

8

7. Launch of HMS *St Lawrence*, 10 September 1814, anonymous watercolour. It conforms so closely to the draught that it is probably an eyewitness view.
Royal Ontario Museum ref 74 CAN 258. 967.106.1

8. Sheer and profile draught of *Princess Charlotte*, dated July 1815.
NMM neg DR6013

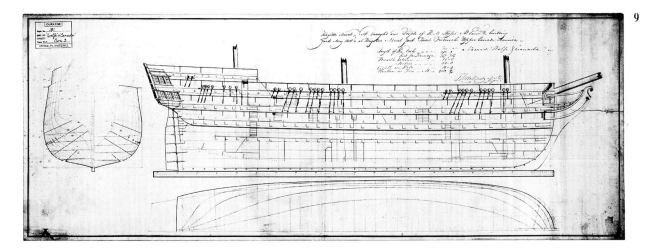

9

re-named the *Lord Beresford*. Though a private contractor built the former ship, which caused labour problems among the publicly-paid artificers, construction progressed smoothly, and the frigates were launched in April 1814, about the time that the keel pieces were laid down at Point Frederick for the *St Lawrence*, 104 (gundeck 194ft 2ins; extreme breadth 52ft 7ins; draught 20ft). William Bell, who had launched the *Detroit* and then escaped from Amherstburg before the American invasion, designed the unique First Rate and oversaw most of its construction, although it appears that Thomas Strickland, a master shipwright sent from England, was in charge of shipbuilding when the *St Lawrence* was launched in September 1814 (6, 7) and proceeded to construct the fir frigate *Psyche* (gundeck 130ft; extreme breadth 36ft 7ins; light draught 9ft 8ins).

When the war was over Strickland made an extensive survey of all the warships at Kingston, producing draughts that were despatched to the Admiralty for filing. Although designed and built by a number of different individuals, the ships exhibited definite similarities. Once the concern about access to lake ports was lifted, the vessels were designed to carry an increasing weight of ordnance and given deeper draughts, but not to the dimensions of their saltwater cousins, since they did not need to carry drinking water or months of provisions. 'The lake frigates,' noted Howard Chapelle, 'had their capacity much reduced by means of a great deadrise, intended to make them fast and weatherly. The *Princess Charlotte* was extreme in this case' (8). Some innovative construction techniques were practised at Point Frederick, and presumably at William Bell's shipyard at Amherstburg. Strickland's records show that Bell built the *St Lawrence*, for instance, with very few knees, which appears to have caused some of his labourers to predict that the ships would break its back upon launch. No such accident occurred, and after his first voyage up and down the lake in his new flagship, Commodore Yeo declared: 'The *Saint Lawrence* has completely gained Naval ascen-

dancy on the Lake and I am happy to say she sails very superior to anything on it.'

The Royal Navy establishment remained at Kingston until its dispersal in the 1830s. Two new First Rates, to be called *Wolfe* and *Canada*, were under construction in 1815 as the war ended (9, 10). Efforts were also underway to build vessels on the Welland River, a tributary of the Niagara, and on the Nottawasaga River in southern Georgian Bay, but these shipyards were later transferred to the mouth of the Grand River on Lake Erie and Penetanguishene Harbour on Georgian Bay. Along with the reduced facilities at Amherstburg and Kingston, they became little more than supply depots following the Rush-Bagot Agreement in 1817 and graveyards for the warships with which Britain had intended to secure mastery of the inland seas.

9. Sheer and profile draught of 'Ships No 1 and 2' (*Wolfe* and *Canada*), dated May 1815. Unlike the *St Lawrence*, they have a poop, which probably implies flag officer's accommodation. *NMM neg DR131*

10. Point Frederick Royal Navy Dockyard, Kingston in 1815, watercolour by Emeric Essex Vidal. It shows the framed but incomplete hulls of the *Canada* and *Wolfe* in the background. *Royal Military College, Kingston*

10

Perry on Lake Erie

1

2

MASTER Commandant Oliver Hazard Perry (1) reached Erie, Pennsylvania on 27 March 1813 and found four schooners and two brigs under construction in the navy yard that had been cleared on the shore of Presque Isle Bay the previous fall. Sailing Master Daniel Dobbins, a local resident, had supervised the projects until Noah Brown, a shipwright from New York, arrived to take over early in March. Perry approved of the work accomplished to date and then hurried south to Pittsburgh to arrange for ordnance and fittings to be sent to the lake. With 300 axemen and shipwrights working at Erie and a continuous supply train streaming north from Pittsburgh, the schooners were launched during the third week of May, followed two weeks later by the brigs. At the same time Perry was sailing five lakers (a brig, three schooners and a sloop) up from Buffalo for conversion into warships. Only men and armament were needed for the US Navy to stake its claim on Lake Erie.

Ordered to the Lakes by Admiral Warren, Commander Robert Barclay (2) was superseded at Kingston by Commodore Yeo and then assigned by him to take over the Provincial Marine squadron on Lake Erie. To make matters worse, Yeo allowed him only two dozen officers and men from Kingston, though it was well known that the Lake Erie squadron was sparsely manned by locals and soldiers. It consisted of the ship *Queen Charlotte*, 18, the schooner *Lady Prevost*, 12, the brig *General Hunter*, 6, and two converted schooners and a sloop, all lightly armed. In the naval base, located at the village of Amherstburg near the mouth of the Detroit River, a 20-gun corvette, destined to become HMS *Detroit*, was rising slowly on the stocks, but Barclay despaired of receiving the ordnance and stores needed to fight the ship, all of which had to come from Kingston, more than 400 miles away.

Barclay's main task was to keep the supply line open between Amherstburg (3) and Long Point, the depot near the eastern end of the lake. Not only did his squadron and dockyard suffer shortages, but so did the army garrisoned at nearby Fort Malden (4) as well as the citizens of the region and the thousands of native allies who had gathered in the vicinity. The squadron patrolled the lake regularly during June and July, narrowly missing Perry, due to fog, when he sailed the five lakers up from Buffalo. Furthermore, on 4 August, as Perry was moving his lightened brigs over the bar at the mouth of Presque Isle Bay, Barclay hove into view, but inexplicably failed to realise the opportunity that lay before him to damage the vulnerable enemy squadron and turned back to Long Point. Shortly thereafter Barclay retired to Amherstburg to await the completion of the *Detroit* and the much-hoped for reinforcements from Lake Ontario. Well supplied with men, ammunition and provisions, Perry took control of the lake during the first week of August and effectively cut off the British supply line.

Perry's mission was to win control of the lake and then transport an army under Brigadier General William Henry Harrison from its camps near Sandusky to invade southwestern Upper Canada. To achieve his first goal, he cruised off the mouth of the Detroit River a couple of times, inviting Barclay to battle, but the bait was not taken. The threat of starvation at Amherstburg pressed the point, however, and Barclay, after conferring with Major General Henry Procter, sailed from Amherstburg on 9 September to fight Perry for mastery of the lake. He had received only 38 more officers and men from Yeo, so that 60 per cent of his crews were composed of regulars from Procter's ranks. The *Detroit* had been armed with a hotchpotch of weaponry, 19 guns and carronades of six different calibres.

From his anchorage in Put-in Bay at South Bass Island,

3

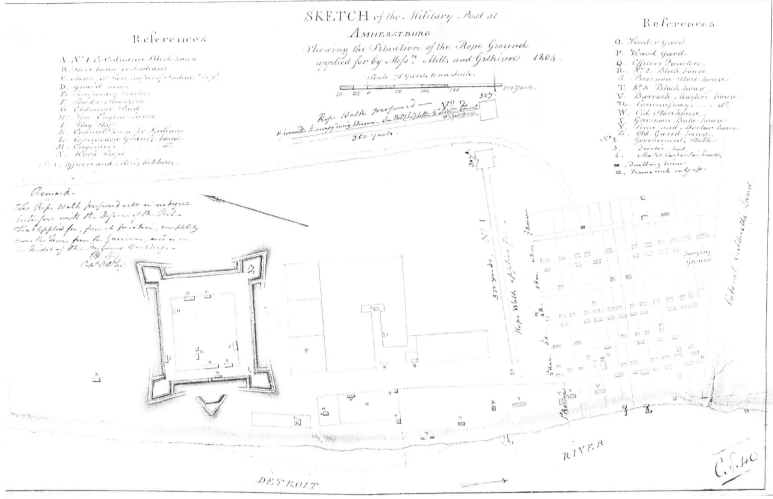

SKETCH *of the Military Post at*
AMHERSTBURG
Shewing the Situation of the Rope Ground
applied for by Messrs. Mills and Gilkison 1804.

4

Perry saw Barclay approaching before a light, southwesterly breeze that favoured the British, but he did not shy away from the challenge. He commanded nine vessels, mounting 15 long guns and 39 carronades, with his flagship, *Lawrence*, 20 and her twin, the *Niagara*, 20 forming the main strength. Barclay's line included six vessels, carrying 35 long guns and 28 carronades, though their smaller calibres meant that they were outmatched by the weight of metal in Perry's broadsides. Just before the action commenced at 11.45am, the wind shifted to the southeast, giving Perry his first stroke of luck. To encourage his men, Perry had raised a battle flag stitched with the slogan 'Don't Give Up the Ship' – the words used by the fatally wounded Captain James Lawrence of the USS *Chesapeake* during her epic fight with HMS *Shannon* the previous June.

5

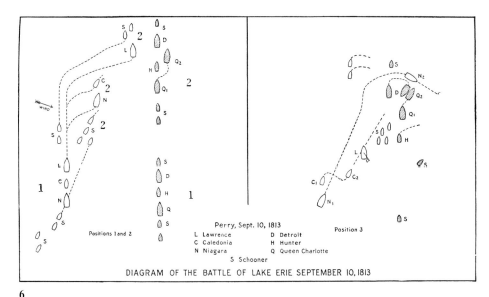

6

tained considerable damage and casualties, but the most telling injury was that the commander and first officer of each of these vessels had been killed or wounded. His thigh ripped open by a splinter early in the engagement, Barclay's shoulder blade was shattered by a grape shot around 2.30pm, and he was carried below to the surgeon. The first lieutenant having been killed, command devolved on to Lieutenant George Inglis, RN. As Perry's schooners closed in to pelt their prey with their 24- and 32-pounder long guns, Perry steered the *Niagara* to cut the British line, firing both of her batteries at once (8). The *Detroit* and *Charlotte* collided while attempting to wear, and in minutes the surrender was signalled. 'We have met the enemy and they are ours,' Perry hurriedly scribbled to General Harrison as his crews seized all six British vessels (9).

The British lost 41 killed and 94 wounded, while the Americans had 27 killed and 96 wounded (10). Barclay survived and was absolved of blame for the defeat in a court martial the next year since it was shown that his squadron had been inadequately manned and outfitted. Perry gained great notoriety and instant promotion to the rank of captain. On 27 September he landed Harrison's army in Upper Canada where it soon routed Procter's force, but an expedition to Lake Huron and beyond was postponed due to the lateness of the season. Perry's victory was sullied by a controversy that soon erupted over Elliott's conduct during the battle. Perry tried to downplay the matter, but it was still being warmly discussed in 1819 when he died of yellow fever while on duty in the West Indies.

The action commenced with a furious duel between the *Detroit* and the *Lawrence*, which crept ahead of her consorts and was soon drawing fire from the *Queen Charlotte* as well (5, 6). Perry had instructed his second-in-command, Master Commandant Jesse Elliott, to take the third place in line in the *Niagara*, behind the slow sailing *Caledonia*, which Elliott resented, but faithfully obeyed, to the detriment of the *Lawrence*, for she was soon battered into a wreck with nearly 60 per cent of the crew killed or wounded. Miraculously, Perry escaped injury and finally decided to leave the *Lawrence* in a small boat (7) and take command of the *Niagara*, which was relatively unscathed, sending Elliott to hurry up the schooners.

The *Detroit, Queen Charlotte. Hunter* and *Prevost* had sus-

7

1. Captain Oliver Hazard Perry, USN, anonymous nineteenth-century oil painting.
US Naval Academy Museum, ref 69.1.11

2. Commander Robert Barclay, RN. Anonymous watercolour, 1814.
Metropolitan Toronto Reference Library ref T15259

3. Amherstburg from the south-southeast, 1821. Watercolour over pencil by Major John Elliott Woolford (1778-1866). The naval establishment is to the left.
Metropolitan Toronto Reference Library ref T14508

4. 'Sketch of the Military Post at Amherstburg', 1804. Fort Malden is on the left.
National Archives of Canada ref C52252

8

9

10

5. 'This representation of the Battle on Lake Erie is respectfully inscribed to Commodore Perry and his Officers and gallant Crews, By their humble Servant, James Webster', drawn by Sully & Kearney and engraved by Draper, Fairman & Co, and published by James Webster, Philadelphia. First stage.
NMM neg A4315

6. Diagram of the battle, from A T Mahan, *Sea Power in its Relation to the War of 1812* (London 1905).
Chatham collection

7. Perry leaving his flagship for the *Niagara* during the Battle of Put-in Bay. Engraving by Phillibrown after an original by W H Powell, published by Johnson Fry & Co, New York, 1858.
NMM neg A3327

8. 'This representation of the Battle on Lake Erie is respectfully inscribed to Commodore Perry and his Officers and gallant Crews, By their humble Servant, James Webster', drawn by Sully & Kearney and engraved by Draper, Fairman & Co, and published by James Webster, Philadelphia. Second stage.
NMM ref PAH8142

9. The aftermath of Perry's victory, left to right, the damaged *Queen Charlotte*, *Niagara*, *Detroit* (dismasted), and *Lawrence*. Watercolour by Lieutenant Robert Irvine of the Provincial Marine, who was the second lieutenant of HMS *Queen Charlotte* during the battle.
Royal Ontario Museum ref 90 Can 42, 990.49.8

10. Funeral procession for those killed at the Battle of Put-in Bay, South Bass Island.
Erie County Historical Society

1

The shipbuilders' war and the attack on Oswego

1. 'Attack on Fort Oswego, on
Lake Ontario, North America,
May 6th 1814', engraving by
Robert Havell & son after an
original by Captain William
Steele, published by R Havell,
London, 8 April 1817.
NMM ref PAG9085

HIS ENCOUNTERS with Chauncey during the summer of 1813 showed Commodore Yeo that he needed to improve his squadron by equipping it with more heavy-calibre long guns. To this end, in October 1813 Yeo began the construction of two frigates at Kingston, the *Prince Regent* and the *Princess Charlotte*, that could challenge the Americans more forcibly for control of Lake Ontario. The *Regent* was designed to carry thirty 24-pounder guns on her gundeck and a battery of twenty 32-pounder carronades and six 68-pounder carronades above; while the *Charlotte* mounted twenty-four 24-pounder long guns below and sixteen 32-pounder carronades topside. As work proceeded on these ships and several large gunboats, rumours reached Kingston that Chauncey was significantly improving his squadron, which led to the approval for construction of a three-decker, with the firepower of a sea-going First Rate, to

be built at Kingston. Work on the giant new ship began around 1 April 1814.

Because of uncertainty in Washington regarding campaign plans for 1814, the decision to increase Commodore Chauncey's squadron was delayed. A pair of brigs, meant to be armed with eighteen 42-pounder carronades and three long guns, were started in January and shortly thereafter a frigate about the size of the *Prince Regent* was laid down, although it would carry thirty 32-pounder long guns on its gundeck, making it far more powerful than its British counterpart. A second frigate, similar in dimensions and ordnance to the *Princess Charlotte*, was started in April.

As the opening of navigation neared in the spring, Yeo was eager to attack Sackets Harbor. With Lieutenant General Gordon Drummond, the recently appointed commander-in-chief of forces in Upper Canada, he planned an ambitious, combined operation against the American shipyard, but Sir George Prevost rejected the idea as too risky. Instead, he encouraged Yeo and Drummond to find other ways to frustrate Chauncey's building programme, which they did by formulating an attack on Oswego, the key transhipment point in Chauncey's supply route. Yeo's frigates were launched in mid-April and manned by reinforcements sent from Halifax and Quebec and by members of the Second Battalion of the Royal Marines. The naval force had also been reorganised by order of the Admiralty, which took over control of the squadrons from the army, renaming vessels from 1813 so that they would conform with the Admiralty list. Unwittingly, the new names, *Montreal* (*Wolfe*), *Niagara* (*Royal George*), *Charwell* (*Earl of Moira*), *Star* (*Lord Melville*), *Netley* (*Beresford*), *Magnet* (*Sir Sidney Smith*), managed to confound subsequent study of British shipping on the lakes.

With his squadron greatly strengthened, Yeo embarked Drummond and 550 army regulars and set out for Oswego on 4 May. After postponing a landing the next day due to bad weather, the British squadron returned to Oswego on the 6th and deployed for the attack (1). While the *Prince Regent* and *Princess Charlotte* anchored offshore, the smaller vessels sailed in to bombard the village (located to the west of the river's wide mouth) and the fort, which was situated atop a bluff on the east side of the river (2). The main body of troops included 400 Royal Marines under Lieutenant Colonel James Malcolm, members of De Watteville's Regiment, and the Glengarry Light Infantry. Supported by two brigs and several gunboats, it landed east of the fort about 2pm just as a detachment of 200 seamen under William Mulcaster (now a post captain) approached the fort from the west. Three hundred American regulars, commanded by Lieutenant Colonel George Mitchell, who had arrived at

2. 'Attack on Fort Oswego, on Lake Ontario, North America, May 6th 1814: Noon', engraving by R Havell & son after an original by Captain William Steele, published by R Havell, London, 8 April 1817.
NMM neg A3914

3. 'Storming Fort Oswego, by 2nd Battalion Royal Marines and a party of Seamen, 15m past Twelve at noon', engraving by R Havell & son after an original by Captain William Steele, published by R Havell, London, 8 April 1817.
NMM neg A3915

4

Oswego only a few days before to man the ageing fortification, put up a stiff resistance, but the two-pronged British attack and the naval bombardment soon forced them to withdraw (3). A small company of seamen under Master Commandant Melancthon Woolsey (he had been promoted in July 1813) also retreated, having waited until too late to remove or destroy all the naval gear that had been brought forward to the village. The British found seven or more heavy guns, some rigging and cables, a stockpile of provisions and two small schooners, a prize that cost them more than 90 casualties (4); Mulcaster was badly wounded and was later invalided home. Commodore Yeo exaggerated when he reported that 'the Forts and Town of Oswego . . .[were] the most formidable I have seen in Upper Canada,' although the expedition demonstrated how difficult it was to execute a combined operation against even a lightly armed position, let alone Chauncey's well-defended post at Sackets Harbor (5).

Yeo next moved to blockade Sackets and keep a close eye on the coastal traffic, still hopeful that Prevost would approve a full-scale attack on Chauncey's base. The American commodore responded by transporting most of his stores overland from the Mohawk River, except for the long 24s and 32s for his frigates. These could only be moved by water, so he collected them at points further up the Oswego River, waiting for an opportunity to run the gauntlet of the British blockade. Woolsey was in charge of the guns and arranged for a detachment of soldiers and Oneida Indians to escort his boats when he made his dash, with nineteen boats carrying thirty-one pieces of ordnance, late on 28 May. When one of his boats went missing in the night Woolsey sought shelter two miles up the winding course of Sandy Creek, 20 miles northeast of Oswego, to where reinforcements hurried overland from Sackets that night. Yeo's lookouts spotted the wayward boat, which was quickly captured, and Captain Stephen Popham, RN, set out with 225 seamen and marines in search of Woolsey's flotilla. Despite Yeo's warning about probing unfamiliar territory, Popham took his gunboats up Sandy Creek early on 30 May and into an ambush. He and all his men were captured or killed, while Chauncey's guns were saved and later delivered to Sackets.

Stricken by the loss of so many men, Yeo broke off his blockade. The first division of a 900-man Royal Navy reinforcement from England reached the lake in June, but Yeo anchored his frigates and corvettes at Kingston (6) to wait for his First Rate to be finished, while he sent his smaller vessels to support the army on the Niagara Peninsula. Led by Commander Alexander Dobbs, the detachment participated with the army in the land actions around Fort Erie. On 12 August Dobbs's party

5

6

carried a gig and five bateaux eight miles overland from the Niagara river to a point west of the American-held fort. After dark they attacked three American armed vessels, the *Porcupine*, *Somers* and *Ohio*, lying close to the fort, carrying the latter two after a brief, but bloody fight (7). Lieutenant Charles Radcliffe, RN and one seaman were killed and four other Britons wounded, while the American loss was one killed and eight wounded. The prizes were sailed down the Niagara River to the British encampment at Chippewa.

The American squadron was supposed to have sailed early in July to secure command of the lake and co-operate with the American army that had invaded the Niagara Peninsula. Equipment shortages caused a delay, and then Chauncey fell seriously ill for two weeks, which prevented him from sailing until 1 August. He chose to search out Yeo rather than help the army and was widely criticised for that decision. About the same time Lieutenant General Drummond and Prevost were appealing to Yeo to transport men and provisions to Niagara aboard his frigates, but he refused, explaining that Chauncey's enhanced squadron would outgun him and that it would be wiser to wait until his First Rate was ready. That ship, HMS *St Lawrence*, 104, was not launched until 10 September and finally sailed a month later with the frigates and corvettes to relieve Drummond. By that time Chauncey had returned to Sackets to prepare for an attack that did not come as Yeo made two supply trips to Niagara and then went into port for the winter.

Both commodores then initiated work on two First Rates each, with the approval of their superiors, intending to pursue the contest for control of the lake into 1815. News of a peace treaty terminated the work and left a pair of massive skeletons bleaching in the sun at Kingston for decades, long after one of the American First Rates had been sold for scrap; the other, the USS *New Orleans*, 106, towered over the tranquil anchorage at Sackets Harbor until it was pulled down in the 1880s.

6. 'Kingston dockyard and citadel from the town, Ontario, 1816-17', watercolour, pen and coloured inks, from the sketchbook of Francis Hall, 1833.
National Archives of Canada ref C3236

7. The cutting out of the American schooners *Ohio* and *Somers* in the Niagara River off Fort Erie, 12 August 1814. Pen and ink, watercolour and gouache by Owen Staples, about 1913. After capture they were renamed *Sauk* and *Huron* respectively.
Metropolitan Toronto Reference Library ref T15221

7

Ships-in-frame: the fir frigates

LITTLE WAS known in England about the naval war on the Great Lakes until November of 1813 when the British press reported Perry's capture of Barclay's entire squadron on Lake Erie. Although *The Times* wrongly asserted that Barclay's ships had been 'wholly manned and equipped by the inhabitants of the Province [of Upper Canada]' and falsely condemned Perry's 'disgraceful conduct' of leaving his flagship, after he had surrendered it, to take command of the brig *Niagara*, the defeat was not shrugged of as an inconsequential event. Government officials soon reassessed the state of the American war and made plans to bolster the Royal Navy force (and the army) significantly.

Originally, Commodore Yeo had been instructed to

1

create one establishment for all the ships and men at Kingston and to operate under the supervision of Sir George Prevost. In January 1814 the Admiralty assumed control of the Great Lakes squadrons, directing Yeo to revise his organisation along traditional naval lines with an establishment in each vessel. All the vessels were reclassified, renamed and added to the Admiralty's list, and officials were assigned to run the dockyards. Furthermore, the Admiralty chose Captain George Downie and three other newly-promoted post captains to lead a force of nearly 900 officers and men to join Yeo on the lakes (between the summer of 1813 and the following winter about 800 men had already been sent from Halifax, Quebec and Britain to augment Yeo's 465-man detachment).

The Lords of the Admiralty also concluded that a lack of proper shipping had contributed to the Navy's inability to overcome the Americans and they initiated a project designed to remedy that situation; namely, fashioning the components for warships in English yards and transporting them, complete with fittings and armaments, across the ocean for assembly on the lakes. This idea had first been proposed in December 1812 by Sir Howard Douglas, the inspector-general of instruction at the Royal Military College, who had spent time in Canada during the 1790s and had heard of the use of prefabricated vessels on Lake Champlain during the War of Independence. Douglas suggested to the government that the parts for warships could probably be transported to Kingston as early as 1 June, where they could be readily assembled. A copy of Douglas's plan was forwarded early in 1813 to Sir George Prevost who rejected it outright as totally impractical, but later in the year the Admiralty considered the scheme again, having heard from at least two other advisers. One of the proponents, a citizen of Quebec, recommended that components for twelve xebec-frigates, designed to carry 23-guns apiece and drawing only 3½ft of water, be sent to Canada where '[t]hey may be put together in a month or six weeks at the farthest [and] . . . master the Lakes and keep them for ever in possession of the British Empire.' (1) Admiral Sir John B Warren had also advocated the use of ships-in-frame, demonstrating his lack of knowledge about the rugged topography of the Canadian wilderness, by advising that they could be forwarded to new shipyards on Lake Erie and Georgian Bay.

Early in January 1814 the Admiralty approved the preparation of vessels-in-frame for Canada. They included two frigates, the *Psyche*, and the *Prompte*, Fifth Rates to be crewed by 300 men and to carry thirty 24-pounder

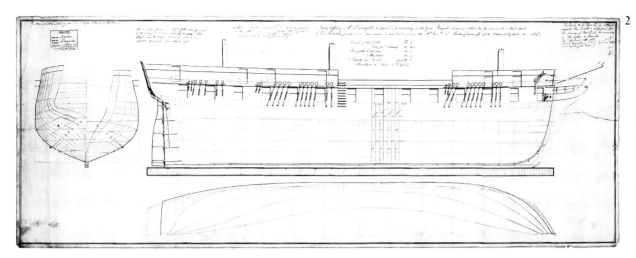

1. Xebec design proposed to the Admiralty, from the Melville Papers. Its wilder innovations include hinged iron gratings with spikes in the end, designed to be let down on boats attempting to board.
Clements Library, University of Michigan

2. Sheer draught of *Psyche* and *Prompte*, dated 21 December 1813. Annotations on the draught note the lowering of the decks by 1ft 9ins, and describe the proposed battery as 'short 24-pounders'. Mid way in size, weight and power between a carronade and a genuine long gun, there were two patterns of these, designs by Congreve and Blomefield, although neither is specified. The later modification to incorporate a spar deck is also noted.
NMM neg DR2409

3. 'John Bull making a new Batch of Ships to send to the Lakes', drawn, engraved and published by William Charles, Philadelphia, 1814. The punning reference to 'Mac Do-enough' [Macdonough] puts the date after Plattsburgh in September; the joke about the Fox relates to the capture of the ordnance transport *Stranger* by the American privateer *Fox*.
*Beverley R Robinson collection
ref BRR94.9.1*

long guns and eight 32-pounder carronades (2), and two brig sloops, the *Goshawk* and the *Colibri*, with crews of 140 and batteries of eight 24-pounder long guns, two 12-pounder long guns and eight 24-pounder carronades. Chatham Dockyard had finished work on the components (fashioned out of fir) for the four vessels by 22 February while their rigging and ordnance were collected for shipment in a convoy in March, and Captain Downie and his colleagues mustered their crews for the trans-Atlantic voyage.

News of the 'fir frigates' reached Quebec early in April, whereupon Prevost immediately convened a board of officers to evaluate the scheme and sought the reaction of Commodore Yeo. Everyone agreed that the idea was unrealistic, given the demands already placed not only on the shipwrights at Kingston, but on the St Lawrence River supply train, which was nearly overwhelmed by the current needs of the army and navy. The report was despatched to England shortly before the transports began arriving at Montreal in June. Having received no orders to cancel the project, Prevost had the components surveyed and landed, and the pieces of the *Psyche* were selected for carriage to Kingston, a private contractor named William Forbes being hired to do the job. Through the summer and early fall Forbes's crews hauled the heavy pieces up the St Lawrence in bateaux and by wagons over the portages that skirted several stretches of boisterous rapids. When the dockyard at Kingston had finished with HMS *St Lawrence*, the shipwrights turned their attention to the new frigate, fitting its prefabricated parts together to form the frame of the hull and then, apparently, planking it with wood from the yard's stockpile. Captain Sir Robert Hall, the new commissioner lately arrived from England, decided to close in the ship's upper deck, thereby increasing her strength to 56 guns. HMS *Psyche* was launched on 25 December 1814, the day after American and British representatives signed the peace treaty at Ghent.

The report about the ships-in-frame written by Prevost's board reached England in July 1814 and prompted the Admiralty to cancel the whole project, somewhat belatedly, and order all the components to be sent to Halifax. A later investigation revealed that nearly £58,000 had been spent on the venture. Information about the project inevitably leaked out, and an American cartoon of late 1814 makes reference to 'new-baked' ships (3).

When Commodore Sir Edward Owen arrived at Kingston in March 1815 to replace Yeo, he raised his broad pendant in the *Psyche*. The ship was rigged and employed on two voyages to Niagara carrying supplies and troops, but by June her sailing career was over. She was soon placed in ordinary where she remained, gradually decaying until the Royal Navy establishment at Kingston was closed in the 1830s and the ship, along with her sisters, was broken up or scuttled in a nearby bay.

JOHN BULL making a new BATCH of SHIPS to send to the LAKES

The Battle of Plattsburgh, 11 September 1814

1

THOMAS Macdonough (1) began his service on Lake Champlain during the fall of 1812 by taking charge of a pair of leaky gunboats that had been launched in 1809 to help enforce customs regulations. Although he converted a number of merchant vessels into warships the next year, during which he was promoted to master commandant, Macdonough's most ambitious undertakings occurred in 1814 when he greatly improved the squadron on the lake. On Otter Creek at Vergennes, Vermont, the base he established during the winter, he supervised the building of the sloop *Saratoga*, 26, and six 75ft row-galleys, and the conversion of a merchant vessel on the stocks into the schooner *Ticonderoga*,

17. The design and construction of the new shipping was conducted in astonishingly little time by Adam and Noah Brown, who had worked with Perry at Erie the previous year; the *Saratoga* had gone from keel to launch in 40 days.

On 14 May the British squadron appeared off Otter Creek, having come up the lake from Isle-aux-Noix (2). Commanded by Commander Daniel Pring, it consisted of a newly built brig, the *Linnet*, 16, two armed sloops, seven gunboats and two lakers. Pring's plan was to bombard the Americans and then land an assault party, but the determined opposition put up by Macdonough's gunboats and a land battery, caused Pring to haul off and

2

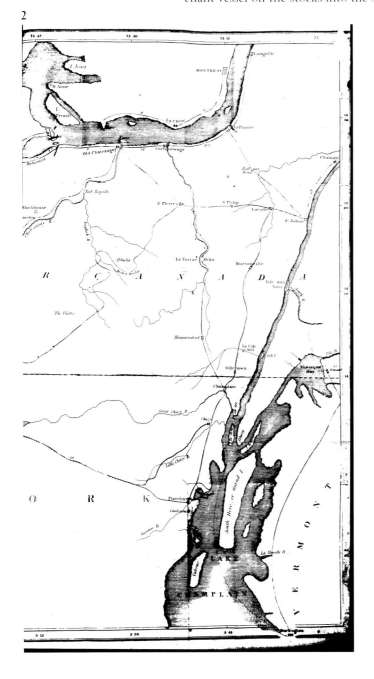

3

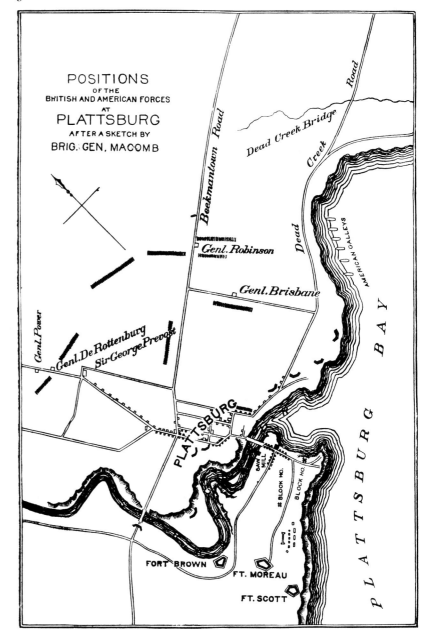

return to his base. There, a frigate, the *Confiance*, 37, was laid down in June just about the time that Captain Peter Fisher arrived from Kingston to supersede Pring, who remained as second in command. Hearing that the British were building a frigate, Macdonough obtained permission from Washington to construct a brig, the *Surprise*, 20 (soon renamed *Eagle*), which was launched on 11 August.

Delayed for want of supplies, the *Confiance* was not launched until 25 August. Sir George Prevost was anxious for it to be readied for duty because he was planning a large scale invasion of New York State, employing thousands of troops who had been transported to Canada from the Napoleonic battlefields. Preparations at Isle aux Noix were set back on 2 September when Captain George Downie suddenly arrived to replace Fisher, who had fallen out of favour with Commodore Yeo. Meanwhile, Prevost had crossed the border, reaching Plattsburgh on 6 September and writing to Downie to bring his squadron there to fight off Macdonough's squadron, which was anchored in a line across the bay, so that he could attack the American land force (3). Unfamiliar with his new station and its unfinished flagship, Downie answered Prevost with 'it is my duty not to hazard the Squadron before an Enemy who will be superior in

4

Force.' Nevertheless, he had the ship towed away from the dockyard on 9 September and early on the 11th he rounded Cumberland Head at Plattsburgh to challenge Macdonough; another note from Prevost had insulted Downie with its snide remark that 'the unfortunate change of wind' had caused Prevost the disappointment of not seeing the Navy sooner. Shortly after dawn on 11 September Downie went in a small boat to inspect the American squadron, which consisted of the *Eagle*, *Saratoga*, *Ticonderoga* and sloop *Preble* anchored on a north-northeast heading, flanked on the landward side by ten large gunboats. Macdonough flew a battle flag bearing

5

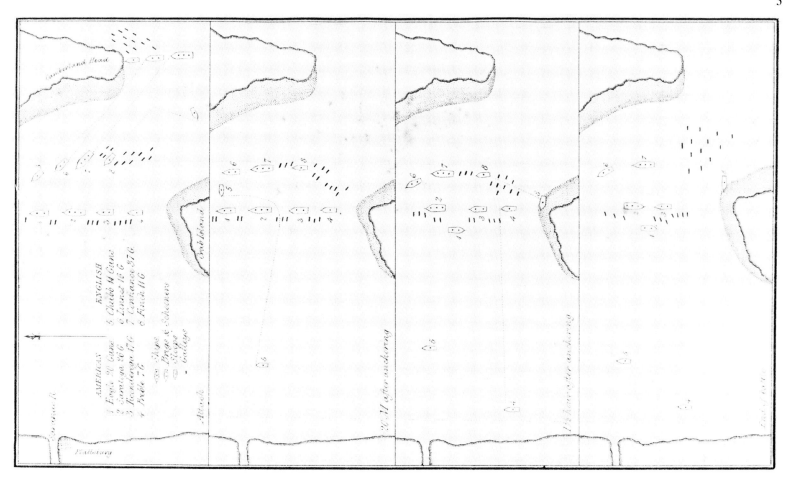

6

1. Commodore Thomas Macdonough, USN, published by D Appleton & Co, New York. *NMM ref PAD3377*

2. The country between Montreal and Lake Champlain, part of a contemporary map reproduced in Sir Charles P Lucas, *The Canadian War of 1812*. *Chatham collection*

3. 'Positions of the British and American Forces at Plattsburg, after a sketch by Brig. Gen. Macomb' (the American commander), from Henry Adams, *History of the United States*, Vol 8 (New York 1891). *Chatham collection*

4. 'Macdonough's Victory on Lake Champlain and defeat of the British Army at Plattsburg by Gen. Macomb', engraving by B Tanner after an original by H Reinagle, published by B Tanner, Philadelphia, 4 July 1816. *NMM neg 5354*

5. 'The Battle of Plattsburg Bay', published by R Bentley, London 1837. *NMM ref PAD5853*

6. 'Com. Macdonough's Victory on Lake Champlain Sepr. 11th 1814', engraved by W Hoigland after an original by M Corné, published by A Bowen, 25 November 1815. *NMM neg A3920*

7. Key to (6). *NMM ref PAD5854*

the slogan 'Impressed seamen call on every man to do his duty.' Downie expected that Prevost would support the squadron by launching his land attack at the same time and capturing the American batteries beside the bay.

The American squadron carried 86 long guns and carronades, compared to about 92 pieces of British ordnance in the *Confiance*, *Linnet*, two sloops (the *Chub* and *Finch*), and thirteen gunboats. Besides carronades, the frigate boasted twenty-seven 24-pounder long guns, which alone could have pounded the Americans into submission from a safe distance, but Downie decided to assault the enemy line, assigning his commanders to run up to specific adversaries, while the gunboats concentrated on the *Ticonderoga*. This plan required the British to sail into a faint northerly breeze and allowed Macdonough's crew ample opportunity to fire at their opponents as they approached (4).

The first shots came around 9am with the action becoming general about half an hour later. Only the *Linnet* reached her prescribed location, with the *Eagle* as her target. Downie soon abandoned his plan and anchored roughly opposite the *Saratoga* at a range of 300

yards. The flagships blazed away at each other with dreadful effect; aboard the *Confiance* a 24-pounder upset and crushed Downie to death minutes after the fighting grew intense. The lack of experience in the flagship's crew revealed itself when the elevation of the guns was not altered for the reduced range, and their shot were soon shredding the American rigging with little impact on the crew. The *Chub* was battered by the heavy-calibre carronades on the *Eagle* and surrendered while the *Finch*, after a few rounds, drifted out of control and went aground, and the lieutenant commanding the gunboats lost his nerve and fled with most of the boats. The broadsides of the *Confiance* gradually diminished, leaving only the *Linnet*, captained by Daniel Pring, still engaged until just after 11am when he finally surrendered (5). The butcher's bill was 52 Americans killed and 58 wounded, while the British suffered 54 killed and 116 wounded. Macdonough was honoured for his decisive victory with promotion to a full captaincy.

Prevost watched the battle for an hour or so before signalling his troops to advance on the American defences (6, 7). As the broadsides diminished, and the ensigns fluttered down, Prevost cancelled the assault, to the amazement of his European veterans, and shortly afterward ordered a return to Canada. Exchanged within a week of the battle, Pring reported Prevost's 'goading' of Downie and his lack of support during the battle, which Yeo relayed to the Admiralty. The criticisms were turned into charges against Prevost, who was recalled, along with Yeo, to prepare for a court martial but died before proceedings could be convened. During the winter the British began new ships at Isle-aux-Noix with the full intention of regaining control of the lake in 1815, though, as elsewhere, the dockyard soon fell silent.

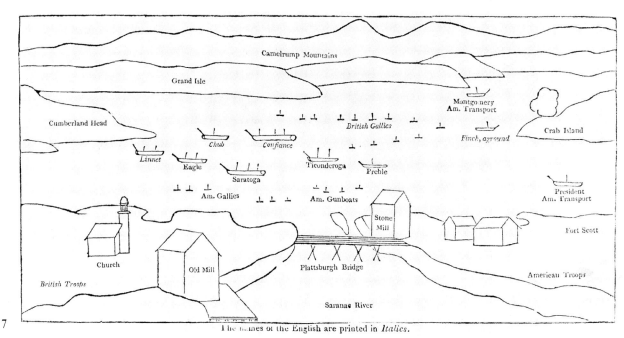

7

The names of the English are printed in *Italics*.

American shipbuilding on the Lakes

THE first US Navy ship built on the Great Lakes was the brig *Oneida*, which was ordered in 1808 to help enforce the customs restrictions imposed under the Embargo Act that Thomas Jefferson had introduced the previous year in response to French and British interference with American trade on the high seas. The embargo backfired on Jefferson by provoking so much illegal commerce with Canada that customs officials needed protection, and a 'gunboat' was required on Lake Ontario. Plans for the gunboat expanded, turning into a powerful little brig, measuring 85ft on the gundeck, and equipped with sixteen 24-pounder carronades and a pivot-mounted 32-pounder long gun on the forecastle (1). Designed by a master shipwright from New York named Christian Bergh, it was built by his partner, Henry Eckford, between the fall of 1808 and the spring of 1809 on the shore of the bay at Oswego. Timber of various types was cut from the forest for use, and salt from the works that flourished in the vicinity was packed between the frames on the assumption that it would forestall rot. All equipment, rigging and ordnance for the brig had to be hauled from New York via the Hudson and Mohawk Rivers and the lesser streams and short canal that linked Oswego to the bustling seaport.

By the time the *Oneida* slid into the bay at Oswego in March 1809, Jefferson's Embargo had been repealed, and the brig became redundant. She sat idle for two years until international tensions tightened again, and Lieutenant Melancthon Woolsey, USN, who had overseen the construction, returned to the lake with a small party of men to commission the vessel. The water level on the bar that enclosed the Oswego River dropped to six or seven feet during the summer dry spells, causing Woolsey to empty the *Oneida* and lift her over the bar by means of a pair of camels (large scows that were sunk alongside the brig and secured to the hull before being

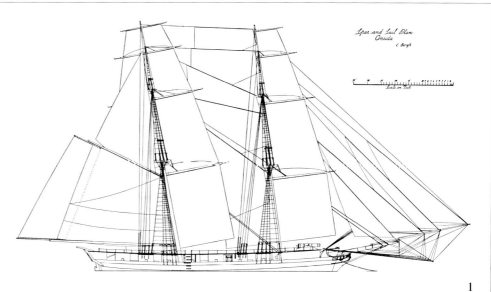

1

1. Spar and sail plan of the *Oneida* as reconstructed by Howard Chapelle.
By courtesy of the Smithsonian Institution, NMAH/Transportation

2. Plan of the brigs *Lawrence* and *Niagara* as reconstructed by Howard Chapelle.
By courtesy of the Smithsonian Institution, NMAH/Transportation

2

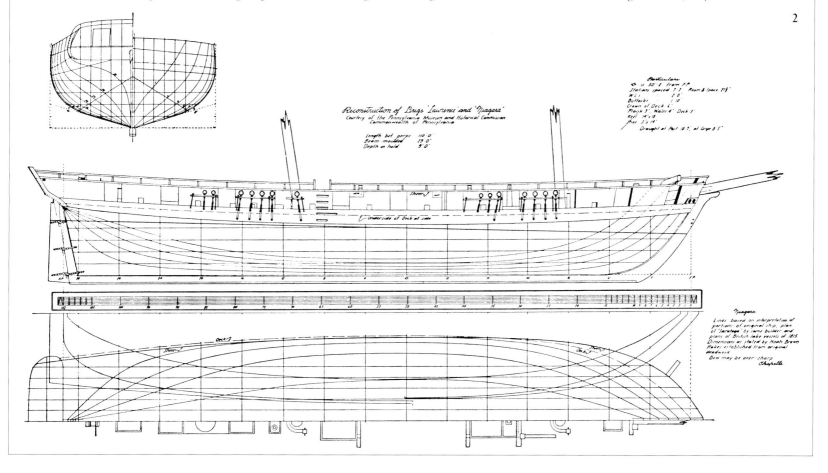

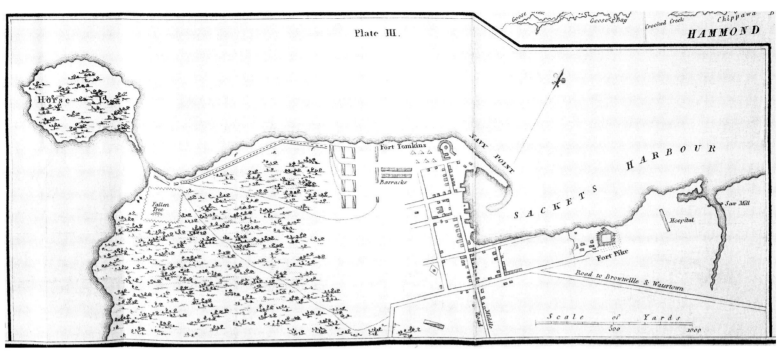

Plate III.

HAMMOND

SACKETS HARBOUR

3

None of Eckford's original draughts have come to
light, but an archaeological study of the brig *Jefferson*, the
hull of which was uncovered beneath a marina at Sackets
in the 1980s, revealed much about his construction techniques. He employed white oak (green and rotten within four years of launch) for the main structural components, wrought-iron bolts and spikes for fastenings and
required high standards for quality in the finishing and
fitting of pieces. To save time and reduce weight, Eckford
installed no wooden knees, bracing the hull with diago-
nally situated rider timbers instead. The *Jefferson* had a
sharp and shallow hull, a lofty rig (making for a speedy
cruiser) and a heavy battery of ordnance (four 24-
pounder long guns and sixteen 42-pounder carronades),
which almost led to the vessel's loss near Niagara in
September 1814 when a gale knocked the brig on her
beam ends twice, forcing half her armament to be jettisoned in order to prevent capsizing. Eckford's vessels
were considered to be greatly successful by his contemporaries and helped to test building techniques that lay
the foundation for the era of the clipper ship. Howard
Chapelle considered him a 'genius as a designer and
builder, as an organiser and manager, and as a master of
the art of high-speed production of ships.'

The other main America shipyard on the Great Lakes
was at Erie, Pennsylvania. A site at Black Rock, on the
Niagara River near Buffalo, had been considered late in
1812, but it was open to attack from British guns near
Fort Erie. Like Sackets Harbor, a peninsula enclosed a
spacious bay at Erie, although its opening was sharply
restricted by a bar, forcing Perry to use camels when
moving his larger vessels onto the lake. Late in 1812 a
shipwright named Ebenezer Crosby began work on four

pumped out). Although *Oneida*'s draught is not recorded, her hold was only 8ft deep, so the lack of water clearly ruled out Oswego as the site of any new US Navy base.
Bergh had given the brig a shallow draught so that she
could cruise inshore, but by doing so he created a vessel
that sailed so poorly that one mariner remarked that she
was 'as dull as a transport . . . [and] would not travel to
windward.' Furthermore, the long 32-pounder over-
burdened her bow to such an extent that Woolsey
removed it and was forced to rely on carronades alone
for firepower. Built to navigate the lake's bar-choked
streams, the dozen or so merchant schooners and sloops
that Commodore Chauncey eventually added to his
squadron suffered similar problems: they wallowed
beneath their heavy ordnance and could maintain their
stations in the line of battle under only the best
conditions.

Woolsey selected Sackets Harbor (3) as the only place
suitable for the navy, a decision that Chauncey confirmed after he arrived on the lake. The harbour itself
was a 30-acre sheet of deep water, partially enclosed by a
narrow peninsula, but not closed by a bar. Henry Eckford
(4) mapped out a dockyard on its gently sloping shore in
October 1812 and went to work on a corvette measuring
112ft on the keel and 32½ft in breadth that would mount
twenty-four 32-pounder carronades. Named the *Madison*,
the corvette was launched only 45 days after the keel was
laid, setting a pattern that Eckford repeated throughout
the war as he converted lakers for Chauncey's use and
built a schooner (the *Lady of the Lake*, 1), three brigs (the
Sylph, 18, *Jones*, 21 and *Jefferson*, 20), the corvette *General Pike*,
26 (5), two frigates (*Superior*, 58 and *Mohawk*, 42) and began
work on a First Rate (the *New Orleans*, 106).

3. 'Plan of Sackets Harbor', Plate
III from William James, *Military
Occurrences . . .* (London 1818). It
also shows the military
movements of the forces during
the abortive British attack in May
1813.
Chatham collection

4. Henry Eckford, Chauncey's
shipbuilder. Photogravure by W
Sartain, published New York.
*Naval Historical Center, Washington,
DC ref NH66615*

4

gunboat-schooners (the *Tigress, Porcupine, Ariel* and *Scorpion*) under the direction of Sailing Master Daniel Dobbins. When Chauncey visited the dockyard on the eve of the new year he ordered two of the gunboats extended and later directed that two brigs be laid down. There is some uncertainty as to whether the draughts of the brigs (2) were drawn by Eckford or by Noah Brown, a master shipwright from New York. Brown eventually took over supervision of the Erie dockyard, and the brigs rose under his watchful eye to stand 110ft long and 34ft in breadth; drawing 9ft of water, the hull showed a flatter bilge than Eckford's *Jefferson* and *Jones*. Pressured by Perry to launch the brigs (the *Lawrence* and *Niagara*) and gunboats as soon as possible, Brown seems to have used whatever timber came to hand (though he appears to have installed dagger knees), and not worrying too much about decoration and finishing. 'Plain work , is all we want,' he is reputed to have said: 'They are only required for one battle; if we win, that is all that will be wanted of them. If the enemy are victorious, the work is good enough to be captured.' The brigs and gunboats served their purpose successfully, but their duty did not end so easily. The *Lawrence, Niagara, Tigress* and *Scorpion* were employed in Commodore Sinclair's expedition to the Upper Lakes in 1814, where the schooners were captured. While supporting the army on the Niagara Peninsula late in the season, the *Lawrence* and *Niagara* were almost lost in a gale, prompting Sinclair to complain that the shallow draught and lack of space for ballast combined with the lofty rig and heavy armament to make the brigs roll heavily in a high sea. Brown's brother, Adam, employed the same methods when he built the brig *Eagle* on Lake Champlain, although the nineteen days taken to complete the work meant that there was no time to fashion and install knees.

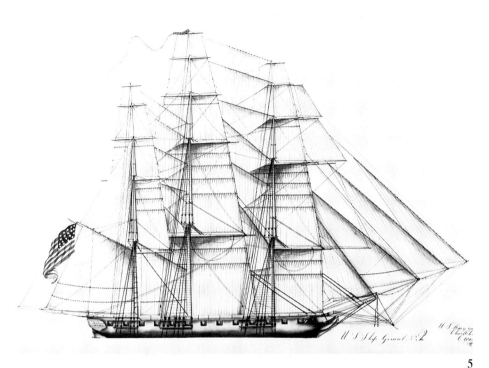

5

Following the war Perry's and Macdonough's squadrons were deliberately scuttled so that immersion in the cold water would retard the decay caused by alternate soaking and drying (6). As a result the hull of the *Eagle* survives to the present, and the hulk of the *Niagara* was retrieved in 1913 for centennial celebrations of Perry's victory; restored and preserved, it exists today as part of the modern *Niagara*, Pennsylvania's official 'tall ship'. Commodore Chauncey recommended that his ships be scuttled, but they were sold or scrapped instead. Only Eckford's *Jefferson* escaped oblivion, sinking at Sackets and lying there still as a treasure chest of marine architectural secrets from the days of Chauncey and Eckford.

5. Spar plan of *General Pike*, by Charles Ware, Boston Navy Yard about 1840.
US National Archives ref NH57006

6. A post-war view of Sackets Harbor, showing vessels laid up alongside the mole.
NMM neg 8144

6

Mackinac and the struggle for the Upper Lakes

ONE OF the most significant events in the war occurred on 17 July 1812 at a place far removed from the focus of action when a weak company of British regulars, supported by nearly 200 fur traders and twice that number of Indians, captured the American post on Mackinac Island (1). The island, located at the confluence of Lakes Huron and Michigan and

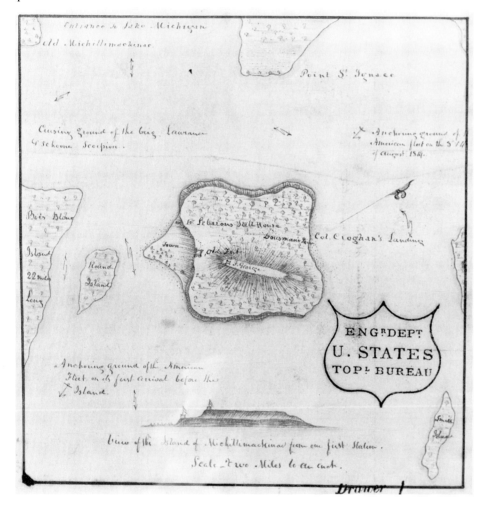

1

2

near the entrances to Lake Superior and Georgian Bay, lay on the trading route to the western regions and was the rival of the British post at St Joseph Island, 50 miles to the northeast. Around the time of the declaration of hostilities, Major General Isaac Brock sent Captain Charles Roberts, the commander at St Joseph, several conflicting despatches, which prompted Roberts to undertake his expedition even though it contravened Sir George Prevost's defence-dominated policy. Fearing that the seizure would ignite indignation among the Americans whose early support of the war was luke-warm, Prevost was less than enthusiastic about its success, though he later admitted: 'the Island and Fort of Michilimackinac [as it was also known] is of the first importance . . . , its geographical position is admirable; its influence extends and is felt amongst the Indian tribes to New Orleans and the Pacific Ocean.'

No attempt was made by the Americans in 1812 to regain Mackinac, but formation of their campaign goals for 1813 was influenced by the British possession of the post. When William Jones replaced Paul Hamilton as Secretary of the Navy, he promoted recapture of the island as a priority, pointing out to Commodore Chauncey that 'this commanding position . . . gives to the Enemy the absolute controul of the Indians.' The importance of Mackinac also rested on its role as a fur trading centre, especially since the government funded the campaign of 1813 in part with a loan from several financiers, including John Jacob Astor, who had lost a valuable shipment of furs when the British seized the post. The development of Perry's squadron on Lake Erie and Harrison's invasion of southwestern Upper Canada were the first steps in a plan to achieve supremacy on the Upper Lakes, which Chauncey intended to complete until Yeo's arrival at Kingston altered his priorities. Perry's victory at Put-in Bay came too late in the season for an expedition to be launched into Lake Huron, and his departure from that station inconvenienced preparations for a prompt start in the new year.

Early in June 1814, President Madison's cabinet finally set its objectives for the summer campaign, among which were the recapture of Mackinac and the destruction of a Royal Navy base said to be under construction on Georgian Bay. Arthur Sinclair, who had been the flag captain aboard Chauncey's *General Pike* the previous year, took over command of the squadron at Erie and by mid-July sailed on to Lake Huron with 1000 soldiers crowded aboard the brigs *Lawrence*, *Niagara* and *Caledonia* and the schooners *Tigress* and *Scorpion*. The initial target of the task force was Machedash Bay, the rumoured location of the naval yard on Georgian Bay, but a lack of knowledgeable pilots prevented Sinclair from finding it. He turned back, burned the abandoned British fortress on St Joseph (2), captured a pair of small lakers and then steered for Mackinac, arriving there on 26 July.

Fort Mackinac (3), standing on a rocky cliff towering over a hundred feet above the anchorage, posed a difficult challenge to the Americans although it was defended by only 300 British regulars and militia, under Lieutenant Colonel Robert McDouall, and several hundred Indians. Sinclair was surprised to find an agent at the post making arrangements, apparently with diplomatic immunity, on behalf of John Jacob Astor to retrieve the latter's captured property; Sinclair complained to Secretary Jones about the matter, but received no satisfactory answer. Intent on fulfilling their mission, Sinclair and his military colleague, Lieutenant Colonel George Groghan, landed their force on the opposite side of the island, hoping to force McDouall to march out to do battle, which he did with about 150 of his troops, supported by the native allies. The dense forest made tactics difficult, and a portion of Groghan's men ran into an Indian ambush while trying to outflank McDouall, suffering heavy casualties. After some brief, but deadly exchanges, the Americans retreated and the attack on Mackinac ended.

Sending the *Lawrence* and *Caledonia* back to Lake Erie with the 70 casualties suffered in the fighting, Sinclair returned to Georgian Bay in search of another fur trading vessel, the schooner *Nancy*. He succeeded in navigating to the southern rim of the bay and found the *Nancy* in the Nottawasaga River where Lieutenant Miller Worsely, RN, and about twenty seamen, who had been operating the schooner for several weeks, had attempted to hide it. When Sinclair and Groghan launched an assault on the schooner on 13 August Worsely and his men offered some resistance, but finally retreated as the Americans plundered the *Nancy* and burned her.

Rightly concluding that no Royal Navy base existed on Georgian Bay, Sinclair headed back for Erie in the *Niagara*, leaving the *Scorpion* and *Tigress* to blockade the approaches to Mackinac. Worsely's party returned to the Nottawasaga and set out on 18 August in two bateaux and a canoe, with assistance from several voyageurs and a handful of Indians, to carry the few supplies they had preserved to their comrades at Mackinac. Six days later they reached St Joseph, barely escaping the notice of the two American schooners that were cruising nearby. Worsely next headed for Mackinac in the canoe with some of his men, reporting to McDouall on 30 August and suggesting that an attempt might be made to capture one of the schooners. McDouall approved of the idea, gave him four boats and fifty men from the Royal

3

Newfoundland Fencible Regiment, commanded by Lieutenant A H Bulger, and Worsely hurried back toward St Joseph on 1 September. The next day they spotted the *Tigress*, which they attacked after dark on 3 September, capturing her in a fierce hand-to-hand combat. Two days later the *Scorpion* came into view and anchored two miles away; the following morning, 6 September, Worsely calmly sailed the *Tigress* down to her sister ship, fired the 24-pounder long gun at her unsuspecting crew and then sent his men swarming aboard. The second schooner was carried in minutes, thereby ending American plans to starve out the garrison at Mackinac and interfere with the fur trade on the Upper Lakes.

In December the crew of HMS *Niagara* (*Royal George*) anchored at York and began the ambitious project of carrying ordnance and equipment northward overland to the Nottawasaga River where a frigate was to be built during the winter. News of peace terminated these plans, but the British went on to establish a base at Penetanguishene, which remained in operation until the 1830s (4).

1. A US map of Mackinac by Charles Gratiot, 1814.
National Archives, Washington DC

2. 'A View of the Post of St Joseph at the Head of Lake Huron (the last Garrison in British North America) taken July 12 1804', watercolour by Edward Walsh.
Clements Library, University of Michigan

3. Mackinac Island in 1842. The fort on the bluff above the township is much as it was in 1812.
Library of Congress

4. Sheer and profile draught of the schooners *Newash* and *Tecumseh*, built in 1815 for service on Lake Huron. At 166 tons, they were somewhat larger but were otherwise similar in form and layout to the schooners that fought on the Upper Lakes during the war.
NMM neg DR4362

4

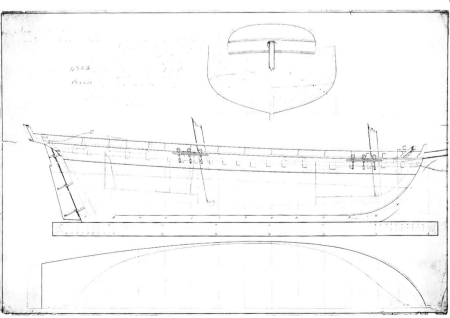

Part III   THE WAR ON THE COASTS

IN THE first few months Britain was reluctant to accept that war with the United States was irreversible, but when the revocation of the Orders in Council produced no softening of the American position, British measures were gradually stepped up. The order for general reprisals was delayed until 13 October, but thereafter an ever-increasing pressure was to be exerted on the coasts of the United States. The strategy employed was the classic approach of a dominant maritime power, namely blockade, which had been the foundation of British naval successes against all the seapowers of Europe over the previous twenty years. There were two distinct, but overlapping aspects to this: firstly, the enemy main fleets were confined to their ports wherever possible, allowing the Royal Navy the freedom of the seas, to pursue other tactical goals like the capture of colonies, while relieving the pressure on forces assigned to trade protection; the second was the commercial blockade, whereby the enemy's trade was curtailed as much as possible, even when carried in neutral ships (this was successful enough to be one of the causes of the war with America).

From the beginning the British North America squadron had sought to confine the US Navy's few warships to port, but on 27 November 1812 a selected commercial blockade was also announced. This was to be 'the most complete and vigorous blockade of the ports and harbours of the Bay of the Chesapeake and of the river Delaware'. The British Government realised that the war was unpopular in the eastern states, and it felt that pressure might be most effectively directed at the warlike southern states who were also best placed to influence policy in Washington. It also suited the British to continue licensed trading, particularly in corn for Wellington's Peninsular army, from the northern states; while a further consideration was the relative ease of maintaining blockading squadrons inside the Chesapeake and Delaware compared with the difficulties of standing off ports further north and east.

Thus grew up a dichotomy in the British treatment of different areas of the union. The blockade was notified to neutrals on 26 December, but because of winter weather Admiral Warren did not have ships on station until February 1813. Because he had signally failed to take or destroy any of the American big frigates, Warren had to be reinforced with ships of the line, in order that the smaller blockade craft might operate in safety. Much to the Admiralty's irritation, the battleships could only be withdrawn from Europe, where what they considered the 'real' war was reaching a climax. Although it thereafter became increasingly difficult for the big frigates to get to sea, they proved the soundness of their basic concept by tying down far more powerful ships that should have been employed on strategically far more important duties. The Admiralty was forced to take specific measures against them, including sending a few battleships that had no poops, in the hope they might be mistaken for frigates and engaged by a '44'. They went on to cut down small battleships as *rasées*, and eventually to build specific ships to counter them.

As one British officer had complained about the Brest blockade, the term was often considered the equivalent of putting a cork in a bottle whereas the practicalities of wind and weather meant that there were often conditions under which a few fast ships might escape and occasionally circumstances where whole fleets could not be intercepted. This was especially true of privateers on the American coasts, but when Warren complained of 'swarms' and asked for additional ships, he was told in no uncertain terms

... my Lords [of the Admiralty] never doubted that the privateers of the enemy would become extremely numerous, as most, if not all, of their commercial marine would probably be diverted into privateering; but they were convinced of the impracticality of the remedy for this evil which you seem to propose, namely, the meeting them with an equal number of ships. The only measures with any attention to economy, and any reasonable prospect of success can be opposed to the enemy's privateering system, are those of blockading their ports, and of not permitting our trade to proceed without protection; and for the execution of these purposes the force under your command will, no doubt, by judicious arrangement be found adequate.

On 13 March the area under blockade was extended to take in New York, Charleston, Port Royal, Savannah, and the entrance to the Mississippi, the Admiralty underlining its instructions: 'we do not intend this as a mere paper blockade, but as a complete stop to all trade & intercourse by sea with those ports...' At this time Warren proposed to dispose his forces as following:

Blockade of the Chesapeake – two 74s, three frigates, two smaller
Blockade of the Delaware – one 74, one frigate, one smaller
Off New York – one 74
Off Nantucket Shoal, Block Island, Montuck Point – two frigates
In the Bay of Fundy – three sloops, two schooners
For the protection of Nova Scotia – three frigates
Off Charleston, Beaufort, Ocracoke & Roanoke – one frigate, one sloop
Savannah & St Augustine – one sloop
Relief forces for the Chesapeake and Delaware – two 74s, two frigates, two smaller.

In truth, this was not overwhelming force for the area to be covered, and Warren pointed out that in spring he would need an additional squadron to watch Boston and its surroundings.

132

However, reinforcements did reach Warren during the course of the year, and the strategy bore its first real fruit on 1 June when a potentially destructive force under Decatur, comprising the frigates *United States* and *Macedonian*, accompanied by the sloop *Hornet*, was intercepted in Long Island Sound and compelled to take refuge in New London. Only *Hornet* made any further contribution to the war, the frigates being trapped for the duration. However, the existence of a naval force in New London led the British to extend the blockade in November to include Long Island Sound, leaving only the coast from Narragansett Bay northwards exempt. After the defeat of Napoleon, in May 1814 the blockade was finally completed by formally taking in New England, although in practice the coast was already feeling the effects of restriction.

Ocean-going commerce had been quickly reduced to a trickle, but as the blockade became tighter and British attitudes hardened, the coastal trade also became a target. In a country heavily indented by rivers and bays, with few roads or internal communications, the coastal traffic was crucial. The aggregate tonnage of vessels in the coasting trade had doubled each decade from 1790 to 1810 when it stood at 405,000 tons, but so effective was its destruction in the last year of the war that the immediately post-war shipbuilding boom – in 1815-1817 an average of 1282 vessels per year were launched – was predominantly coastal.

The only alternative was slow and expensive land carriage by wagon, and substantial trains of vehicles became a feature of American life. For once-busy seaports, especially in Federalist areas that opposed the war, these developments were an affront. They were palpable symbols of the failure of government policy, and as such ripe for satire. Newspapers like the *Salem Gazette*, with little to fill its Ship News columns, from 1813 began to replace genuine notification of movements with articles headed 'Terrapin Ship News' or 'Horse Marine'. The tone of these can be gauged from a couple of examples:

Yesterday a fleet of Jefferson's land ships passed by in ballast from New Haven, having discharged their cargoes at the port of Boston. The headmost was a first rate Pennsylvania built vessel moved by the power of five full fed, stout bodied horses.

Monday, August 11, cleared and sailed at 3 p.m. with all canvas spread, Adm. Todd's eight horse ship *Dreadnought*, Capt. Boynton, for New York, cargo vitriol and cream o' tartar to order.

The siege of the American coast was possible because its defences were incomplete or inadequate. A partial pre-war programme of fortification had secured a few of the major ports, like New York, against all but determined attack, whereas others like Boston depended entirely on the navigational difficulties of approach to keep the enemy out. For most of the estuaries and harbours, the sole defence was a few Jeffersonian gunboats, which as the advocates of a blue-water navy had predicted before the war, were simply inadequate to the task. In theory they should have possessed tactical advantages over sea-going ships, especially in confined waters and windless conditions, but in practice they always proved vulnerable to attack by ships' boats. The US Navy made plain its disappointment with them during the war, by decommissioning most of them and drafting the crews to more useful employment.

By land the situation was no better, there being few regular infantry and fewer artillerymen, most towns depending on their own militia for last-ditch defence. Most lacked experience of being shot at and could be stampeded by concerted attack. The low level of resistance met by some of the Royal Navy's first landing parties gave the British every encouragement when they came to adopt a more aggressive policy towards American communities from 1813. The arrival of Rear Admiral George Cockburn at the beginning of the year was the harbinger of this new offensive strategy. The blow was to fall on the Chesapeake area, partly in retaliation for the depredations of its privateers, and partly because it was strongly in

'Map of the American Coast from Lynhaven Bay to Narraganset Bay, by John Mellish', engraved by H S Tanner, published by John Mellish, Philadelphia, June 1813. The features of the coast make it clear why the initial British blockading effort centred on the Chesapeake and Delaware, and later New York and Long Island Sound, where there was shelter and opportunities for resupply. Chatham collection

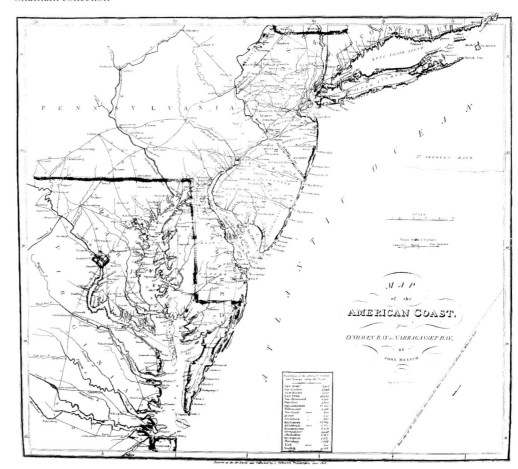

A watercolour portrait of Courageux, *74, from the journal of Lt Samuel Walters,* RN. *A line of battle ship without a poop, she was originally intended for the North American station, where it was hoped her deceptive appearance might fool* Constitution *or her sisters into a one-sided battle. In the event, she was retained at home, but the* Plantagenet *of the same form saw much American service.*   National Museums & Galleries on Merseyside ref N98.0286

favour of the war, so it was argued that, being close to the capital, any change in its attitude might be quickly conveyed to those in government. The ambition of the British Cabinet went further, however, and it was hoped that a substantial military force would form a diversion in favour of the hard-pressed Canadians. For this they provided 2400 men, the most effective being two battalions of Royal Marines, but also including 300 highly dubious 'Chasseurs Britanniques' formed from French prisoners.

Although he failed to take Craney Island and destroy the frigate *Constellation*, most of Cockburn's raids in the spring and summer of 1813 were spectacularly successful. They were also sensationally controversial, Cockburn being held responsible for every conceivable atrocity. The worst incident was the capture of Hampton, where looting, assault and murder did occur, but it was the work of the Chasseurs, who were sent back to the fleet in disgrace and never employed again. There were more minor incidents of looting – one midshipman claimed that no 'power on earth could possibly restrain the hungry stomachs of midshipmen and their numerous boats' crews', but British forces were under strict orders not to plunder.

Many British naval officers regarded this form of 'punitive war' as ignoble, but they were equally unimpressed by the habit of American

citizens in taking a few pot-shots at the landing parties before making off. As with so many aspects of this war, the lack of mutual understanding represented a culture-clash between traditional European notions and the more radical American ideas. European armies were essentially professional and operated to established conventions: civilians who did not resist were not to be molested, but in cases where, for example, a besieged city refused terms and was stormed, it was given up to the soldiery to be sacked. Although wide-scale conscription and the French army's habit of living off the land had done much to erode these rather more gentlemanly concepts, the British army in the Peninsula made a virtue of treating the civilians well (they were, after all, allies), supplying its own needs wherever possible, and paying for anything sequestered. Cockburn and his men attempted to work on similar principles. However, the United States is a country where even today it is regarded as every citizen's right to carry arms, and it is a tradition with powerful historical precedents: if the settlers had not fought the native population there could have been no colonies, and if the colonists had not fought colonial authority there could have been no independence. It was inevitable that many civilians would attempt to defend their property, and that the very attempt would

brand them belligerents in the eyes of the British.

Relations between the two sides were not always so strained. Some of the blockading squadrons worked out amicable arrangements with local communities for water and stores, particularly in the northern states, but these tended to deteriorate as the British undertook more and more destructive raids, and the Americans sent unconventional weapons, like Fulton 'torpedoes', against the blockaders. The British themselves had been known to use explosive vessels and the like, so it was not the weapon itself they objected to so much as the means of employment. The booby-trapped schooner *Eagle* which attempted to destroy the *Ramillies*, 74, in June 1813 was a case in point, dismissed by Admiral Warren as 'diabolical and cowardly'. With regard to 'torpedoes' (which at this time were actually a form of sea mine), they were on even shakier moral ground, having been the first to deploy Fulton's inventions in attacks on Napoleon's invasion flotilla in 1805-6. As Fulton discovered, even US Navy officers did not care for his devices, and Captain Abraham Crawford, RN, who had been involved in the Boulogne attacks, probably spoke for most conventional officers when he wrote:

> This species of warfare, unmanly, and I may say assassin-like, I always abhorred. Under cover of the night, to glide with muffled oars beneath the bows of a vessel, and when her crew is least suspicious of impending danger, to affix such an *infernal machine* beneath her bottom, and in a moment to hurl them to destruction, in what does it differ from the midnight attack of the burglar, who steals into your house, and robs his sleeping victim at once of money and life?

But he was aware of the hypocrisy of British objections.

> In a few years afterwards, when similar attempts were made . . . by the Americans on our ships, which were engaged in the blockade of their ports, I well remember what an outcry was raised against such dastardly proceedings, and how much the cowardice and baseness of such a mode of

warfare was railed at and condemned by the English journals. Aware, however, that the example had first been set by England, I, for one, could not join in the outcry.

Americans also vent their fair share of moral outrage on British actions, reserving particular vitriol for Congreve rockets, which they likewise regarded as 'unfair' and 'barbarous'. To those brought up on twentieth-century notions of total war, these attitudes may seem naïve, yet modern armies still pay lip service to the Geneva Convention, and there is currently a very successful campaign under way to ban the indiscriminate use of anti-personnel land mines.

Morality notwithstanding, the war entered its final most destructive phase in 1814. Having lost faith in a combination of blockade and pin-prick raids to push the Americans to the peace table, the British government decided to go on to the offensive. After May they were greatly assisted by the end of the war against Napoleon, when substantial numbers of Wellington's victorious army were available for transatlantic operations. The previous year's raids in the Chesapeake turned into a full-scale assault on Washington and Baltimore, the coast of Maine was occupied, and an advance into New York State from Canada was undertaken.

These offensives met varying degrees of success, but all depended on the flexibility that seapower endowed. The capture of Washington was a perfect example of what an amphibious operation mounted on a relatively modest scale could achieve; the advantages of speed and tactical surprise were squandered before Baltimore and the operation failed, but even then the invading force was withdrawn without significant loss. On the Canadian front the British invasion, which depended on a logistic chain stretching down Lake Champlain, foundered because they lost mastery of the water at the Battle of Plattsburgh; although much criticised then and since, Prevost had little alternative except to retire back into Canada. Part of northern Maine was seized without much opposition, but the British held little more than the coastal towns they garrisoned (which were provided with transports standing by to evacuate the troops should a serious threat develop). By the time the final operation, against New Orleans, had failed –

arguably because the British did not make the best use of the mobility their seapower gave them – there was no further appetite for the war.

Discussions about terms on which the war might be concluded had been under way almost continuously since the declaration of war, but although the British had revoked the Orders in Council they flatly refused to abandon the impressment of British seamen from neutral vessels. An offer of mediation by the Russian Tsar was welcomed by both parties but made no headway, and after the abdication of Napoleon in April 1814 the British looked to some permanent gains from the war. Peace commissioners from both countries gathered at Ghent in the summer, but the British were intransigent on the main issues, looking forward to successes in the field that would further reduce the bargaining power of America. They also made their own claims for the first time, seeking to establish a homeland for the Indians that could act as a buffer state between Canada and the United States, and looking to various rectifications of the border agreed in 1783, including sole British military use of the Great Lakes.

Simultaneously involved in the much more important deliberations of the European Great Powers in Vienna, Britain was careful not to overplay her hand, even after news of the capture of Washington seemed to promise major military gains. While the American envoys were resisting British proposals to base a peace on their present possessions, the victory on

Lake Champlain became known – the importance of this was widely understood, and even the Duke of Wellington, who was then offered the command in Canada, regarded naval superiority on the Lakes as essential to the defence of British North America. He not only turned down the command, but produced such a pessimistic evaluation of the British position that the Prime Minister, Lord Liverpool, decided not to press for major concessions from the United States. The state of negotiations at Vienna and the threat of new upheavals in France were major influences on British thinking, but when the American envoys proposed a peace based on the *status quo ante bellum*, the British were inclined to listen.

American claims on impressment and the law of blockade were rejected by the British (along with American claims for compensation) and promptly abandoned by the Americans, so the proclaimed causes of the war were not addressed. Both sides gave up the small amount of enemy territory they were occupying, and although the Indians were restored to their pre-1811 rights, there was no provision for a separate state. Finally, it was agreed that joint commissions would settle the United States-Canada border to the west, and in deference to British popular agitation, both nations undertook to do their best to promote the abolition of the slave trade.

The Treaty of Ghent was signed on 24 December 1814, but hostilities continued until the American ratification on 17 February 1815.

'New York, from Governor's Island. No. 20 of the Hudson River Port Folio', coloured aquatint and etching by J Hill after an original by W G Wall, published by J Henry, about 1818. Very few American ports had any permanent fortification, New York being an exception. NMM neg 6250

Ships of the Royal Navy: the 80-gun ship

THE TWO-DECKED 80-gun ship was a decidedly foreign type, the first to serve in the Royal Navy being the French *Foudroyant*, captured in 1758, followed by the ex-Spanish *Gibraltar* taken in 1780. Being longer, the 80 carried more guns per deck than the standard 74, and the upper deck calibre was usually heavier to boot; in fact, the French 80 carried more broadside weight of metal than a British three-decker 98. Furthermore, their great waterline length tended to make them fast, and with only two gundecks they were noticeably more weatherly than towering Second Rates. With their long rows of gunports – although not as many as the naïve artist of the *Sans Pareil* (1) depicted – they gave the impression of great size. Cochrane's flagship off the American coast during the War of 1812, *Tonnant* (2) was described by one of her lieutenants as 'this glorious ship of ships . . . I thought her an equal match for any ship afloat, and so she certainly was . . .' Yet despite these obvious advantages only two British-built 80s saw service in the wars of 1793-1815.

Three reasons may be advanced for this apparently illogical state of affairs. The most important is the lack of a clear role – at least in the first decade of the war with France – for what were relatively expensive ships; they had neither the accommodation most admirals required in a flagship, nor did they have the presence of a three-decker in battle, so the British showed a decided preference for 98s. The second is more subtle, and largely invis-

1. 'His Majesty's Ship Sans Pareil shortening sails 1802', watercolour by I. M, no date.
NMM ref PAD6039

2. Sheer and profile draught of *Tonnant* as taken off, dated 15 October 1810. The ship was captured at the Battle of the Nile.
NMM neg DR7499

3. 'Donegal', watercolour by Lt George Pechell Mends, 1840. *Donegal*, ex-French *Hoche*, was taken by Warren's squadron off Ireland in 1798, and lasted long into the post-war years.
NMM neg X244

ible to historians like William James, who was an outspoken advocate of 80-gun two-deckers: the extreme length of these ships made them very vulnerable to hogging, the distortion caused by the less buoyant ends drooping in relation to the midships body. Before the diagonal construction methods of Sir Robert Seppings were perfected in the post-war years, it was difficult to build a two-decked hull of over about 180ft with sufficient girder strength for British requirements. In general, French and Spanish ships made relatively short sorties, but when 80s were exposed to the rigours of almost continuous sea-time in the Royal Navy they became expensive and costly to maintain. The final reason for so little ship-building effort being expended on the 80 must be the significant numbers taken from the enemy: all bar two of the ships listed below were prizes (3).

Year	No in Sea Service	No in Ordinary or Repairing
1793	0	1
1796	5	0
1799	6	1
1801	5	3
1805	4	2
1808	7	0
1811	6	1
1814	1	4

With so few ships in service it is difficult to generalise about their employment, but like all first class ships there was a tendency to allocate them to the Channel or Mediterranean Fleets, the majority being kept in home waters. Here some of the more active flag officers began to discover the advantages of the 80, particularly for winter cruising or inshore blockade duties: as a Vice-Admiral, Cornwallis had the 80-gun *Caesar* in the winter of 1794, before hoisting his flag in the First Rate *Royal Sovereign*, and in the following years *Sans Pareil* wore the flag of Rear-Admiral Seymour, despite the presence of a number of 98s acting as private ships; and *Foudroyant* was chosen by Lord Keith as flagship of the Mediterranean Fleet after the *Queen Charlotte* was destroyed by fire in 1800; the reverse of the medal was represented by the *Gibraltar*, which was a very dull sailer, and nobody's favourite as a flagship.

However, in the 1790s while the French and Spanish still possessed significant fleets-in-being, there was a tendency to assign a three-decker to most detached squadrons – Cornwallis's Retreat would have been unthinkable without the awesome bulk of the *Royal Sovereign* to deter the numerically superior French force. The close blockade instigated by St Vincent demanded the utmost in sailing qualities from the ships employed in the

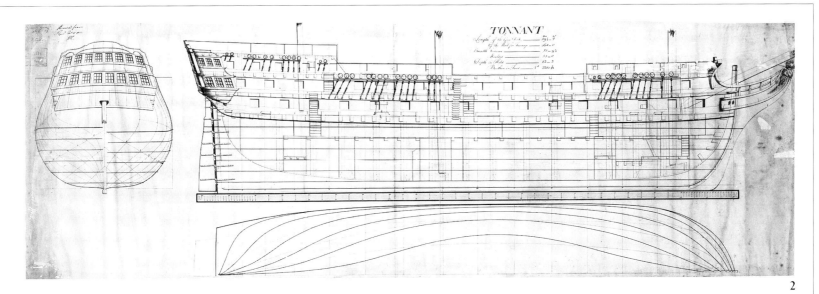

2

inshore squadrons, and so the habit arose of leading such detachments from 80s rather than leewardly three-deckers. Saumarez commanded such a squadron off Brest from the *Caesar* in the first half of 1801 and kept the same ship when transferred to the Cadiz station; thus she was his flagship and fought with distinction in the actions of Algesiras and the Gut of Gibraltar later in the year. As the strategy of blockade became effective, and especially after the heavy French and Spanish losses of 1805, enemy battlefleet activity was largely reduced to the escape of relatively small divisions. The subsequent British pursuit was usually placed in the hands of flying squadrons, but initially these were hampered by the lumbering 98s chosen as flagships – in January 1801, for example, Sir Robert Calder's *Prince of Wales*, 98 led a select detachment of Channel Fleet two-deckers in search of Ganteaume's squadron, which contained no three-deckers. By 1806, when Willaumez's and Leissiègues's divisions slipped out of Brest, the pursuing forces of Sir John Borlase Warren and Sir Richard Strachan were both commanded from 80s (*Foudroyant* and *Caesar* respectively), although they still each had a 98 attached because one French squadron was known to include a three-decker. Ironically, Leissiègues's force – including the 120-gun *Imperial* – was tracked down and destroyed off Dan Domingo by Vice-Admiral Duckworth with a squadron that contained nothing larger than the 80-gun *Canopus*. There was less success against Willaumez, and both Warren and Strachan eventually abandoned their three-deckers: as William James dryly concluded, 'It had by this time been found that a 98-gun ship was no acquisition to a flying squadron.'

Thereafter, detached squadrons were often commanded from 80-gun ships, particularly where fast-sailing might be a significant qualification. Sir Richard Strachan's *Caesar* had led the force that rounded up the Trafalgar stragglers in 1805 and was later the flagship of Rear-Admiral Stopford's division off Rochefort; *Canopus*

was another popular ship, in succession flying the flags of Rear-Admirals Campbell, Louis and Martin between 1803 and 1809; *Foudroyant*, after a spell as Rear-Admiral Graves' flagship in the Channel, led Rear-Admiral de Courcy's South America squadron in 1809. The 80 was also employed on occasion as the flagship of a secondary station, like the *Sans Pareil* at Jamaica in 1801.

In this respect, the 80 finally developed a role, but it was not distinctive enough – large 74s often functioned as flagships on similar missions – to warrant large scale construction. The first British-designed 80 since 1788 was ordered in 1809 (and that from a desire to test the hull form of the captured Danish *Christian VII*), but only one other was laid down before the end of the war, and neither saw service before 1815. Nevertheless, with the coming of Seppings's diagonal construction system longer ships were suddenly feasible, and post-war two-deckers grew to 84 and even 90 guns.

3

The blockade

1

ALTHOUGH INDIVIDUAL British warships were in evidence right from the beginning of the war, it was not until early 1813 that squadron-size forces became a common sight on the American coast. Because the big American '44's were too powerful for British frigates, these squadrons usually paired a 74-gun ship with a frigate (1), sometimes plus some shallow-draught small craft to chase coasters and privateers. In October 1813, for example, the pairings were: *La Hogue* and *Tenedos* off the Grand Banks; *Poictiers* and *Maidstone* off Cape Sable; south of Cape Sable *Ramillies* and *Loire*; *Valiant* and *Acasta* (with sloop *Atalante* and gunbrig *Borer*) at the entrance to Long Island Sound; uniquely, *Plantagenet* was without a frigate consort off New York; and in the Chesapeake *Dragon* was accompanied by two frigates and two sloops. There were also frigate squadrons off the Delaware, and an inshore squadron off Boston that included the *rasée Majestic*, 54.

The whereabouts of the major US warships were known to the British, who were careful not to expose

2

inferior forces to counterattack. A greater concern to the blockaders were the gunboat flotillas, which had been designed specifically for coastal defence duties. In estuaries and bays, with conventional sailing ships either at anchor or restricted in their powers to manoeuvre, they were potentially damaging if handled with daring. In June 1813 fifteen of them attacked the frigate *Junon* off the James River, but because there was enough wind for the ship to get under way, she was able to drive off the gunboats with only slight loss.

The Delaware flotilla faced a tactically more advantageous situation the following month when they discovered the sloop *Martin* aground at the mouth of the bay. The *Junon* was again in evidence, about a mile offshore, and supported the sloop when she was attacked by eight gunboats and two block-sloops (2). A rather ineffectual mutual cannonade went on for nearly two hours, the Americans not closing the range – although they later blamed bad powder for the lack of effect. Throughout the war the British had been dealing with similar gunboat attacks in the Mediterranean, and especially by the very skilful Danes in the Baltic, so had a well-tried response. They manned the boats of the ships and

3

advanced against the nearest gunboat *No 121*, boarding and capturing her after a fierce hand-to-hand battle; the rest of the flotilla then retreated, for which the commanding officer was later censured.

In confined waters for which the British had no reliable charts, the employment of the ships' boats became

4

an important method of extending blue-water seapower into the creeks and rivers of the interior. Hardly a navigable stretch of water was safe, and many a craft which had successfully broken through the seaward blockade was captured while anchored off an apparently safe haven (3).

The blockade could be said to have scored its first strategic success in June 1813, when an intended commerce-raiding mission to the West Indies by Decatur's squadron came to a premature end with *United States* and *Macedonian* being chased into New London by the *Valiant*, 74 and *Acasta*, 40 (4). This brought a permanent blockading force to the area, command falling to the captain of the 74-gun *Ramillies*, Thomas Masterman Hardy, Nelson's famous flag captain at Trafalgar (5). The presence of Decatur's ships was not very welcome in New London, which had so far largely escaped the effects of the war, and soon an amicable *modus vivendi* grew up between the local authorities and the blockaders. It was even said that the locals used blue lights to warn the squadron of attempts by Decatur to escape.

Not all Americans, however, were content to leave the blockaders alone, and encouraged by the 'Torpedo Act' of March 1813 which promised rewards to those that destroyed enemy ships, there were some who were prepared to try unconventional tactics. Noticing that intercepted small craft were usually brought alongside the flagship for inspection, a consortium of New Yorkers prepared the schooner *Eagle* as an explosion vessel, and abandoned her when challenged off New London. However, she was secured to a prize sloop when she blew up killing 11 and wounding a further 3 British seamen. Since the 'projectors' of the scheme were civilians, this attack changed the attitude of the British towards the

coasting trade which had been largely unmolested; now every possible vessel, however small, was chased, and if not captured then burned.

For their part, the British became very nervous of 'torpedo' attack, but even now it is unclear how many operations were genuinely undertaken and how many are just local legends. An attack with a weapon invented by a Mr Ryker of New York was carried out against *La Hogue*, 74 on 25 March 1814, but without success, and in June a semi-submersible 'Turtle Boat' was destroyed in Long Island Sound. Although none of these raids did any damage to blockading warships, they provoked ever harsher British reprisals, like the bombardment of Stonington, which was believed to harbour 'torpedo men'. The Ryker attack also had curious ramifications, for in its aftermath the British captured a suspicious individual alone in a skiff at night. To prove his innocence, he offered to pilot a British expedition up the tricky Connecticut River, which on 7 April was carried out by six boats of the blockading squadron (6). Off Pettipague Point seven privateers, twelve large merchantmen and ten coasters were consigned to the flames.

This and similar raids were the final stage of the blockading policy. As the Baltimore *Niles Register* reported in 1814, 'Having destroyed a great portion of the coasting craft, they seem determined to enter the little outports and villages, and burn everything that floats.' While it was immensely destructive in its own right, it was primarily a psychological tactic intended to bring home the real meaning of the war to the ordinary citizen. In the northern states, always reluctant supporters of the conflict, it was enough to produce a movement for secession; further south, more pressure would be needed, and by spring 1814 the British were ready to apply it.

1. 'British 74 and frigate at anchor, Plate 19 in Collection de Toutes les especes de batiments . . . 2eme Livraision', engraving by Baugean after his own original, published by Jean, 1826
NMM ref PAD7395

2. 'American gunboat flotilla attack on HM sloop *Martin*, 29 July 1813 off Cape May', watercolour by Irwin Bevan (1852-1940), no date.
Mariners' Museum, Newport News ref QW417

3. 'Boarding an enemy vessel from boats', lithograph engraved by Ducote and Stephens after an original by John Christian Schetky, published by Whittaker, 1835.
NMM ref PAF5041

4. 'Action off New London, 1 June 1813, watercolour by Irwin Bevan (1852-1940), no date.
Mariners' Museum, Newport News ref QW326

5. 'Sir Thomas Masterman Hardy, Bart, G.C.B. Vice-Admiral of the Blue, Governor of Greenwich Hospital &c.', stipple engraving by H Robinson after an original by Richard Evans, Published by Fisher, Son & Co, 1846.
NMM ref PAD3487

6. 'Connecticut River attack, 7 April 1814', watercolour by Irwin Bevan (1852-1940), no date.
Mariners' Museum, Newport News ref QW362

6

2

Raiding in the Chesapeake in 1813

IN BRITISH military eyes, Chesapeake Bay in 1813 had particular strategic importance. It was situated on the mid-Atlantic coastline, close to the United States capital, where local public opinion could do most to affect the will of the United States to prosecute war. It was accordingly to be subject to all the pressure that the British navy could bring to bear. Not only was its mouth to be closed by blockade, but its shores were to be controlled, and the trade goods and war manufactures of its hinterland to be destroyed. Local command of the British squadron in the Bay was held by Sir George Cockburn, then at the height of his experience and vigour. A veteran of the Walcheren expedition and the capture of Martinique in 1809, he was still in his early forties and rejoiced in campaigning around the Bay, landing himself wherever possible to establish a regime of destruction, punishment or paternal benevolence according to the economic occupations and hostility of the local inhabitants.

Initially, in March 1813 he did not penetrate far, anchoring in Lynhaven Bay near the entrance to the Chesapeake with the vessels Warren had already stationed there. There the most important target was the frigate *Constellation*, moored in the Elizabeth River below Norfolk. To test American strength in that river, Cockburn moved his three ships of the line, *Marlborough*, *Victorious* and *Dragon* (all 74s), north into Hampton Roads. But the intricate channels of the Elizabeth River, sounded at only three and a half fathoms over its first four miles, were very different to the charts and directions possessed by the British and only resulted in the *Constellation* being run up beyond Norfolk and three merchant ships being sunk to block the river channels by the able commandant of the Gosport Navy Yard, Captain John Cassin (1).

Local inhabitants, fearing similar visits to other rivers entering the bay, came out under flags of truce to make their peace with Cockburn. 'An intelligent merchant of

1

1. 'Capt John Cassin USN', stipple engraving after an original by R G, no date.
NMM ref PAD3380

2. 'Capture of the *Arab, Lynx, Racer* and *Dolphin* in the Rappahannock River, 3 April 1813', watercolour by Irwin Bevan (1852-1940), no date. All four were first class Baltimore letter-of-marque schooners.
Mariners' Museum, Newport News ref QW319

Richmond' told him that the outbreak of the war had been popular in that part of the world, but since then the stagnation of trade had only produced 'lamentations' from those who were now beginning to suffer from the effects of the war. To test for himself the resilience of the Americans, Cockburn took his squadron up the Chesapeake as far as Annapolis, and from there took the *Marlborough*, a 74, two frigates, some brigs and smaller vessels further up the Bay to penetrate each of the tributary rivers in turn.

On 3 April four large armed schooners were chased into the Rappahannock River; boats of the squadron pursued them 15 miles, eventually taking them (2). In the River Patapsco, having driven off a gunboat, the boats again brought out several vessels, though this time bombarded from small guns and field pieces on shore. At a flour depot in the Elk River (an army warehouse), army clothing, cavalry equipment and flour were burnt.

The Americans had taken to building batteries to protect strategic points or buildings. Such batteries tended to attract Cockburn's attention, rather than to deter him. Thus while anchoring off Specucie Island on 2 May, he noticed guns firing and American colours flying from

3

4

3. 'Admiral Cockburn burning & plundering Havre de Grace', print by William Charles (1776-1820). Claiming to be 'done from a sketch taken on the spot at the time', the original is keyed and contains much circumstantial detail, including a rocket-launching frame (No 5) and (No 6) a carriage said to have taken Cockburn's fancy and loaded on to a launch. Charles, however, was a Scottish caricaturist with little affection for the English who had emigrated to America some years previously, and the print is best seen as a piece of clever propaganda.
Anne S K Brown Military Collection, Brown University Library

4. 'Norfolk: from Gosport, Virginia', coloured aquatint engraved by J Hill after an original by J Shaw, published by M Carvey & Son, no date.
NMM ref PA10385

5. 'Pilote-Bot, petit Batiment des Etats-unis, au pluspres. Bateau d'Amerique. Plate 56 in Collection de Toutes les Especes de Batiments . . . 5eme Livraison', engraving by Baugean after his own original, published by Jean, 1826.
NMM ref PAD7420

6. Plan of operations at Craney Island, engraving from Benson J Lossing, *Pictorial Field Book of the War of 1812* (New York 1869).
Chatham collection

a new battery at Havre de Grace, at the entrance to Susquehanna River. Consequently at daylight the following day, launches and rocket-boats closed with the battery, while 150 marines and artillerymen landed and took it. The Americans retreated into the buildings of the town, there maintaining 'a teasing and irritating fire from behind the houses, walls, trees etc' until driven into the woods.

The guerrilla warfare practised by local inhabitants at first seemed dishonourable to Cockburn. He recalled that they 'took every opportunity of firing with their rifles from behind trees or haystacks, or from the windows of their houses upon our boats, whenever rowing along the shore within their reach, or upon our people when employed watering . . . in short, whenever they thought they could get a mischievous shot at any of our people without being seen or exposed to personal risk in return'. He thus repeatedly received reports 'of our poor fellows being killed in this dastardly and provoking manner', and consequently felt justified in adopting and publicising a policy of strict retribution. Those inhabitants who fired on the British 'from behind lurking places on their farms or from their houses' would have their property 'treated as a place of arms' and their persons as military prisoners of war. At Havre de Grace he therefore set fire to the houses that had been deserted by their owners, presuming that they had 'formed part of the militia who fled to the woods'. He aimed to teach them 'what they were liable to bring upon themselves by building batteries and acting towards us with so much useless rancour' (3).

Cockburn also despatched a division of boats up the Susquehanna to take or destroy whatever they found. They returned that evening having destroyed five vessels and a large store of flour. Cockburn himself meanwhile went north with the remaining boats in search of the Cecil or Principic cannon foundry, supposed to be 'one of the most valuable works of the kind of America'. Its destruction took the rest of the day, and included 'the complicated heavy machinery attached to it'. In all 51 guns were destroyed that day.

By 5 May the squadron had entered the Sassafras, 'being the only river or place of shelter for vessels at this upper extremity of the Chesapeake which I had not examined and cleared'. In the evening boats proceeded upstream for Georgetown and Fredericktown, which were warned through local inhabitants against resistance. Although vessels and public property would be seized, provisions or the property of individuals required for the squadron would be paid for in full. Even so, about a mile from the first town, about 400 men opened fire on the British boats with muskets and a field gun. With five men wounded, Cockburn kept his word. All the houses,

5

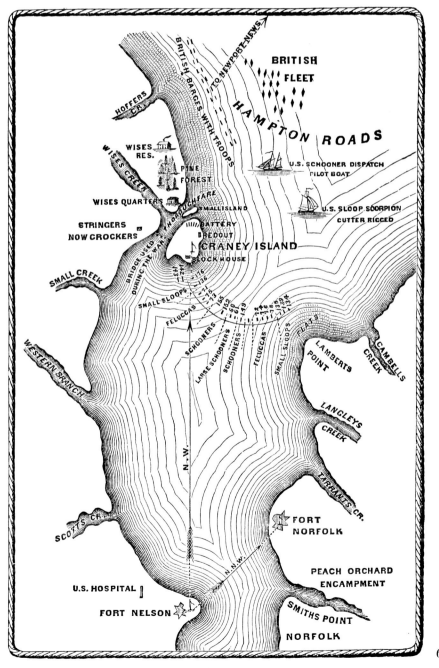

6

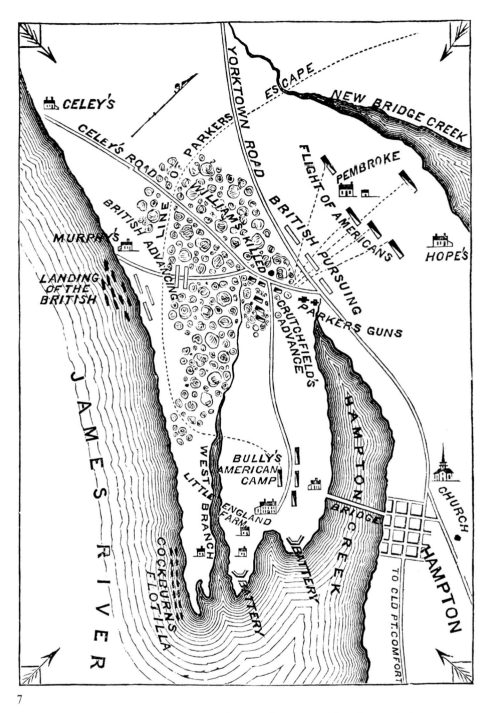

7

7. Plan of operations at Hampton,
engraving from Benson J Lossing,
Pictorial Field Book of the War of 1812 (New
York 1869).
Chatham collection

8. 'Capture of the *Asp*, 14 July 1813',
watercolour by Irwin Bevan (1852-
1940), no date.
*Mariners' Museum, Newport News ref
QW332*

9. 'A View of the Town of St George in
the Bermudas or Summer Islands',
coloured aquatint engraved by Joseph
Constantine Stadler, 1 January 1816.
NMM neg A1907

they too would permit neither guns nor militiamen
there. He was assured, moreover, that all the towns in
the upper part of the Chesapeake had adopted similar
resolutions.

The Commander-in-Chief on the North American
station, Sir John Warren was deeply impressed with the
freedom with which Cockburn was able to operate in the
Chesapeake. Receiving news of the imminent arrival of
the two marine regiments, Warren instructed Cockburn
to set about planning an attack on Norfolk, sheltering
the *Constellation* (4). American defences consisted of a line
of gunboats and small craft, with a pilot schooner and
the cutter *Scorpion* thrown forward for reconnaissance.
(5). The troops arrived on 19 June, commanded by
Colonel Sir Sidney Beckwith; they comprised 2650 men
in all. Within hours preparations were in train for taking
Craney Island at the mouth of the Elizabeth River, which
mounted a battery that commanded the channel up the
river, and the west bank that commanded the island.
Soldiers were put on shore at a place called Pig's Point
and briefly took possession of the nearby bank. However,
an attempted landing on the island proved a fiasco. The
boats carrying marines grounded on mud flats too distant from shore to permit a landing but within range of
the island's battery. Two boats were sunk, the remainder
fell into confusion and were ordered to retire (6). Three
marines were killed, 16 seamen and marines were
wounded, and 62 went missing, presumed drowned.

Three days later Hampton was attacked. The town lay
across the James River from Norfolk and commanded
the latter's communications to the north. Compared to
the earlier debacle, the operation went smoothly and
Hampton was taken (7). Cockburn commanded the
boats and naval contingent. But, at the end of a point
penetrating the Chesapeake, the position was not for
long tenable against American troops and, after the
town's fortifications were destroyed, the troops were re-
embarked. In spite of this success, Warren called off further operations against Norfolk. The British remained in
command of the Bay and its estuaries, and when in July
the US Navy's *Scorpion* and *Asp* were sent to the mouth of
the Potomac on a reconnoitring mission, they were
promptly chased and the latter captured by the boats of
the sloop *Contest* and brig *Mohawk* (8).

The campaigning season in the Bay was coming to an
end with the onset of hot, humid weather, and the
troops were growing sickly in their transports. Islands in
the centre of the Bay had to be occupied upon which to
rest the troops and command the Bay. Nevertheless
Cockburn, who remained in local command until he
withdrew to Bermuda (9) in September, had got the
measure of local forces and defences which he was to
exploit in 1814.

except those still occupied by their inhabitants were
destroyed, along with stores of sugar, timber, leather and
four vessels lying in the river. By contrast, returning
downstream Cockburn visited a small town he had
noticed a little way up a river flowing into the Sassafras.
There, he was pleased to discover, his warnings had had
the desired effect. 'The inhabitants . . . met me at landing,
to say that they had not permitted either guns or militia
to be stationed there and that, whilst there, I should not
meet with any opposition whatever'. After a search for
'warlike stores', the town was left undamaged. Shortly
afterwards Cockburn was to receive a deputation from
Charlestown 'in the North-East River' to assure him that

8

9

Burning Washington

1

THE EXPERIENCE of Rear Admiral Sir George Cockburn (1) in the Chesapeake in 1813 and the early months of 1814 confirmed to him the total inadequacy of local defence. 'The numbers of their militia, their rifles, and the thickness of their woods still I believe constitute their principal, if not their only, strength . . . The country is in general in a horrible state; it only requires a little firm and steady conduct to have it completely at our mercy.' Such assurances had the effect of convincing the new Commander-in-Chief on the North American station, Sir Alexander Cochrane, to direct the first large scale military reinforcements in the direction of the Chesapeake. Cockburn urged him to send them straight up the Bay, 'that the armaments may arrive before the accounts of it', and argued that, for greatest effect, large scale military operations ought to begin 'about the seat of Government and in the upper parts of the Chesapeake.'

Initially Cochrane was unsure whether the troops should be pointed against Philadelphia, Baltimore or Washington. On 17 July 1814 Cockburn committed his opinion to paper, setting out the relative difficulties and advantages for each target, but emphasising his preference for an attack on Washington via Benedict.

It is, I am informed, only 44 or 45 miles from Washington & there is a high road between the two places which tho' hilly is good; it passes through Piscataway, no near to Fort Washington than four miles, which fortification is sixteen miles below the city of Washington, and is the only one the army would have to pass. I therefore most firmly believe that within 48 hours after the arrival in the Patuxent of such a force as you expect, the city of Washington might be possessed without difficulty or opposition of any kind.

He argued that a landing might be made at Benedict, where 'the safety of the ships and the smoothness of the water in the river would render us entirely independent of the weather in all our projected movements', where the army might be 'sure of good quarters in the town of Benedict', and where the rich surrounding country would 'afford the necessary immediate supplies, and as many horses as might be wanted to transport cannon etc, and all without the slightest opposition. The facility and rapidity, after its being first discovered, with which an army by landing at Benedict might possess itself of the capital . . . must strongly, I should think, urge the pro-

2

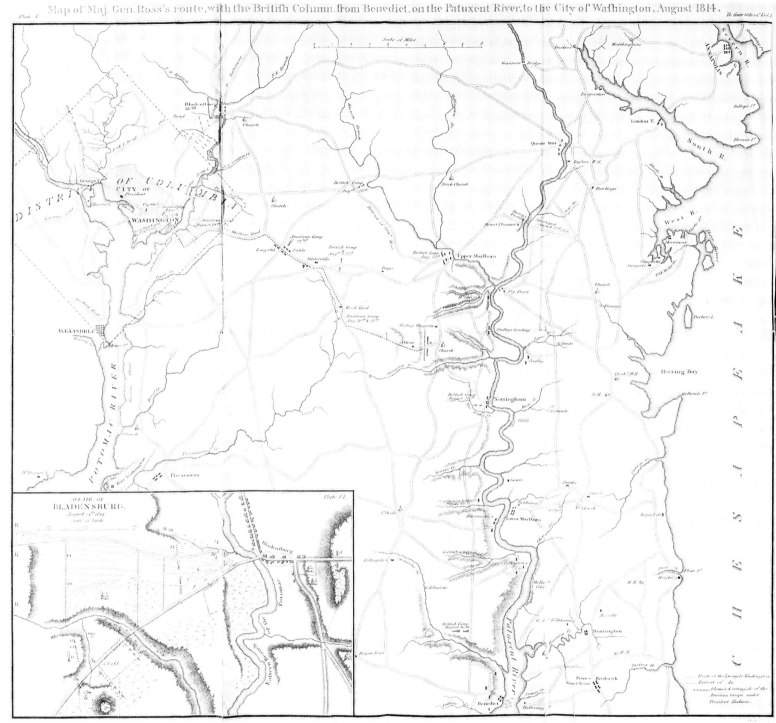

priety of the plan, and the more particularly as the other places you have mentioned will be more likely to fall after the occupation of Washington than that city would be after their capture.'

To allay American fears, Cockburn followed a strategy he had outlined to Cochrane, and temporarily abandoned the Patuxent. Leaving four vessels to maintain a presence in that river, he took the troops that had arrived, with marines from the ships and a division of seamen, into the Potomac. With this force – about 500 men – he began a series of diversionary raids intended to distract immediate attention from the Patuxent. Disembarking first on the Maryland side, then on the Virginian, the country was overrun in places up to ten miles inland. Intent on attracting attention, he caused the greatest havoc possible, destroying military stores, seizing merchandise, obliging the inhabitants 'to furnish him with everything required as the price of his forebearance'. In all nine raids were made in 25 days.

Meanwhile, at Bermuda (2) Cochrane received news

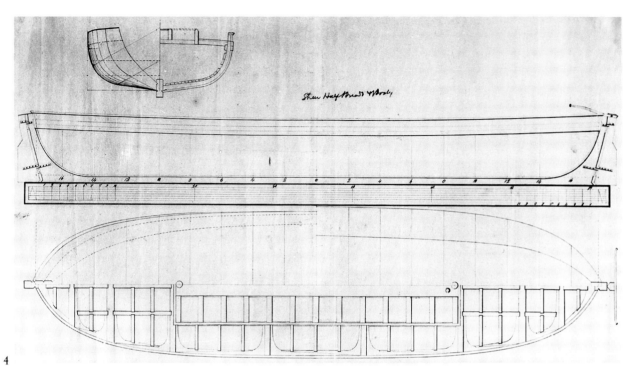

4

5

of American atrocities on the Canadian border. On the 18th he issued orders to all squadron commanders 'to destroy and lay waste' all towns and districts accessible to them from the coast. A week later the first instalment of the main force arrived from Europe in a convoy commanded by Sir Pulteney Malcolm. On 29 July another convoy arrived, bringing the troops available for a campaign to 3700 men. With them came Major General Sir Robert Ross, a 47-year-old veteran of Wellington's Peninsular staff. He had power of veto over deployment of the troops, total command of their operations on shore, and orders cautioning him against 'extended operations at a distance from the coast'. Cochrane's ideas were still not settled but, influenced by Cockburn's despatch of 17 July, he directed the troops towards the Chesapeake.

Cochrane and Ross joined Cockburn in the Potomac on 14 August, in advance of the main convoy. Cockburn immediately went on board the flagship. The meeting was critical. There was disappointment: Ross came with but a quarter of the anticipated troops. Furthermore, neither Cochrane nor Ross was convinced that Washington should be the immediate objective. Ross in particular was determined not to place the army in unjustified danger. Cockburn started afresh, setting out his arguments, convincing those present that an attack on Washington was viable, even with only 4000 men. He cited his own excursions that last month with only one-eighth the force; the defenceless state of the country; the accessibility of Washington from Benedict. Above all, Ross had to be convinced of the state of defence of the country thereabouts. At 5am the following morning

Cockburn therefore landed with Ross and a party of marines, moved inland from the St Mary's river and destroyed a factory several miles from the boats. They returned to the ships 18 hours later without a shot being fired. Ross was impressed. The preliminary steps towards an attack on Washington were agreed. That evening the main convoy of troop transports approached and was directed to press straight on for the Patuxent.

Two small squadrons split off – one up the Potomac, the other towards Baltimore – both to provide diversions, cut communications and, in the case of the first, clear an escape route. On the 18 August, after shifting troops between vessels at the mouth of the river, the frigate transports, brigs and boats began to ascend the Patuxent. Captain Nourse in the *Severn*, having for the last month maintained a presence there, led the way with the only accurate chart. At 2am on the 19th the disembarkation began at Benedict. Landings continued throughout the day, covered by a gunbrig with 32-pounders moored with springs on her cables to command the surrounding land. The last troops were not landed until early on the 20th. Even then they waited. Ross finally appeared about 4pm. Only then did they march, heading north for Nottingham, parallel to the river. Three hours and six miles later they halted for the night. They reached Lower Marlborough about midday and Nottingham towards the close of the 21st (3).

Cockburn meanwhile had organised the naval boat force: a miscellaneous collection of barges, boats, cutters, gigs and captured vessels in three divisions. Moving upstream, he endeavoured to keep the boats and tenders as nearly as possible abreast of the army so that he might communicate with Ross as occasion offered. At Lower Marlborough, while the army rested, Cockburn again met the General, and once more at Nottingham. The ulterior motive for his ascent of the river was an attack on the American flotilla of gunboats (4) that had taken refuge in the Patuxent. At Nottingham he learned that the American flotilla had withdrawn beyond a bend further up the river known as Pig Point. Next morning, after landing marines to encircle the Americans on land, the flotilla was found drawn up in line astern. Aiming for boarding and immediate seizure, the boats pulled hard for the leading vessel, a sloop bearing the broad pendant of Joshua Barney (5), a Revolutionary hero, privateer and experienced naval officer. As they approached, however, the sloop was seen to be on fire, blowing up as they drew near. Behind, moreover, other gunboats too were abandoned and blown up, sixteen in all (6). Only the last, the seventeenth, was left, to be taken prize. Thirteen merchant schooners were also there, sheltering behind the gunboats. Some were taken, some burned.

From Nottingham, Ross with the army started to move away from the river on the road for Upper Marlborough. To maintain contact, that afternoon Cockburn retired downstream with a division of his boats to anchor off Mount Calvert, from there the better 'to confer on our future operations with the major general', who by then had arrived at Upper Marlborough. There, however, Ross took stock. He has been accused of wavering. But to have advanced further would have exposed the army's rear, while intelligence suggested an American force 'collecting in front was very strongly posted'. An army staff conference was obviously split, the weight of opinion inclining towards discreet retirement. At this point Cockburn was collected from the river, only five miles away, by two representative of the minority for advancing. At the conference his comments had the desired effect. Ross decided to press on. Cockburn accompanied him, probably to command seamen and marines brought from the river. Most marines from ships were left in defence of Upper Marlborough. But the marine artillery and seamen provided human haulage for the guns; and the rocket brigade of marine artillery, the 'colonial marines' (former slaves, recruited into the Royal Navy, some from the Chesapeake) and a company of regular marine infantry all played significant parts at the Battle of Bladensburg.

From Upper Marlborough in the afternoon of 23 August, the troops advanced another five miles, an American corps of about 1200 men retiring as they proceeded. Twice that distance was managed next morning, to reach Bladensburg — a bridging point for the eastern branch of the Potomac — about midday. The American army, under the inexperienced command of Brigadier General Winder (7), was discovered in formation commanding the high ground across the river. In spite of considerable fatigue, the British troops coming up were

7

6

1. 'Rear-Admiral Sir George Cockburn', oil painting by John James Halls (*fl*1791-1834). Cockburn is shown in the boots and spurs he wore on land campaigns, with the buildings of Washington burning behind.
NMM ref BHC2619

2. 'A View of the Town of Hamilton, in the Bermudas or Summer Islands', coloured aquatint engraved by Joseph Constantine Stadler, 4 June 1816.
NMM ref PA10286

3. Map of the British advance on Washington in August 1814, with map of the Battle of Bladensburg inset, Plate V of William James, *Military Occurrences of the Late War ...* (London 1818).
Chatham collection

4. Draught of a gun barge, the kind of rowing gunboats used in the defence of American rivers and estuaries during the War of 1812, often replacing the older, less handy sailing gunboats of the Jeffersonian era.
US National Archives ref RG19, 80-10-10

arranged for an immediate attack on both wings and the centre. The Americans were in some strength, estimated at 8000 infantry, 300-400 cavalry and over 200 pieces of artillery. Cockburn reported that only 1500 British troops were involved. The rockets fired by the marine artillery seem to have created alarm if not damage; eventually a flank was turned and the Americans fled. Ross lost 250 men that day, killed and wounded, many of them in the pursuit the soldiers derisively termed 'the Bladensburg Races'. The Americans actually lost fewer men, but it included the capture of a wounded Commodore Barney, whose landed gunboat crews had put up the only effective resistance to the British assault.

A 'broad and straight' road led from the battlefield to Washington. Ross determined to push on with the minimum of rest. The army reached the city's outskirts by 8pm that evening, 24 August. Ross had no time to waste. While the remainder made camp at the end of the turnpike, Ross, Cockburn and about 1500 men immediately pressed on to the Capitol buildings. One of the first

houses sheltered snipers, but there was little further resistance. All but civilians had mainly deserted the city, the flight of Madison's government providing ample fodder for the cartoonists (8). As the British entered, the Americans themselves set fire to their dockyard within which a frigate and sloop also burned. Other government buildings were simply abandoned. Parties of British troops were thus able to tour and burn unopposed the Capitol – including the Senate House and House of Representatives – the Treasury and War Office buildings, 'the President's Palace', the 'Arsenal', two ropewalks, and surviving buildings in the dockyard. Government property valued at $1.5 million was destroyed; in addition over 200 cannon, 500 barrels of powder, and 100,000 musket cartridges were removed (9, 10).

Within 24 hours the British army had begun its withdrawal. Taking the same route by which it came, after a forced march the army made Upper Marlborough late on 26 August. Next day, the seamen, marines and walking wounded went on board the boats and tenders in the

9

Patuxent near Nottingham. Meanwhile the troops marched for Benedict where they began re-embarkation in the evening of 29 August. At 6am on 31 August the squadron weighed anchor and began moving down river. As the officers in the fleet grasped what had been achieved, jubilation reigned. In April 1813 the Americans had symbolically burned the parliament buildings at York, capital of Upper Canada. Now the British had proved the fabric of American government was also open to violation. As John Wilson Croker later wrote to Cockburn, they had achieved 'an exploit which for moral effect both in America and in England has never been excelled.'

10

Gordon's diversion on the Potomac

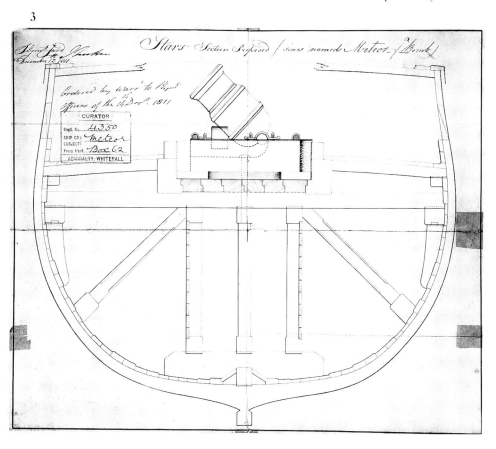

1

2

3

O N 17 AUGUST 1814, as the main expeditionary force under Cochrane and Ross pressed on from the mouth of the Potomac to disembark for the attack on Washington in the Patuxent, two diversionary forces set out, one up the Potomac River to bombard Fort Washington, on the left bank of the river about 14 miles below the federal capital; and the other up the Chesapeake to create a diversion around Baltimore. This latter force, led by Sir Peter Parker (1) of the *Menelaus*, was routed by American militia and Parker and thirteen others killed. Parker was a very popular commander, and the decision to abandon his body provoked a near-mutiny; despite all the difficulties, it was eventually carried back to the ship.

The Potomac force was to be far more successful. Commanded by Captain James Gordon (2) in the 38-gun frigate *Seahorse*, it also comprised the 36-gun frigate *Euryalus* under Captain Charles Napier, the bomb ships *Devastation, Aetna* and *Meteor* (3), the rocket vessel *Erebus* and a small despatch boat. Ascending the river without the aid of pilots, the ships went aground over twenty times, involving guns being shifted and often unloaded into the despatch boat. There were also sudden squalls incurring damage to masts and rigging, demanding immediate repairs where the ships lay close to the banks, vulnerable to American fire and the possibility of board-

ing. The whole ascent took ten days, of which the last five days were spent warping less than 50 miles.

Abreast of Fort Washington on 27 August, the bomb ships immediately began dropping shells into the fort (4). The garrison was first driven out before, that evening, the powder magazine blew up with the destruction of the inner buildings. The fort was occupied next morning and twenty-seven large-calibre guns were destroyed. Meanwhile boats began buoying a channel further up the Potomac, which led to Alexandria. A flag of truce from the common council of the town promptly came down to Gordon, who proceeded to negotiate their surrender (5). Aware from previous experience that American ships would be sunk at their moorings, their equipment removed and cargoes secured elsewhere, Gordon insisted on terms of capitulation that ensured all vessels were afloat, rigged and stowed under the eye of his officers before they were towed out by his squadron.

Following the British retirement from Washington, Gordon's squadron also retired down the Potomac. It was accompanied by twenty-one loaded prize vessels, some of which had been raised and fitted within the space of three days. Inevitably, with much press publicity, the Americans attempted to prevent their progress, which was anyway made more difficult by the necessity to warp against contrary winds. When the *Devastation,* grounded, the Americans attacked with three fire vessels and rowing boats, only to be driven off by the ship's own boats. The rest of the British squadron had by then drawn ahead, and when a second attack was launched on the *Devastation,* boats from the squadron had to row five miles upstream against the current to provide assistance.

Meanwhile, at a shoals downstream the Americans had created several batteries that held up the squadron; these were commanded by three of the US Navy's brightest luminaries, Captains Rodgers, Porter and Perry. Nevertheless, the first of 11 guns was passed on 5 September after the guns of the frigates provided cover for the other vessels; it was eventually destroyed by the fire from the ships. Two more batteries of 14-18 guns on a range of cliffs about a mile in length was cleared with rockets from the *Erebus* and shells from the bomb ships. No further batteries were constructed.

All the vessels that entered the Potomac on 17 August emerged again on 9 September after an expedition of 23 days. Seven men had been killed and 35 wounded, including Captain Charles Napier. The master of the *Seahorse* gained particular credit for finding and buoying the channel up the river which, it was claimed, no ship of similar draught of water had ever before passed with her guns and stores on board.

4

5

1. 'Captain Sir Peter Parker', oil painting by John Hoppner (1758-1810).
NMM ref BHC2934

2. 'Capt James Alexander Gordon, RN', stipple engraving published by Joyce Gold, London, 31 May 1814.
NMM ref PAD3679

3. Midship section of the *Meteor* bomb, showing the 13-inch mortar, dated 12 December 1811.
NMM neg DR4350

4. 'Attack on Fort Washington on Potomac, 17 August 1814', watercolour by Irwin Bevan (1852-1940), no date.
Mariners' Museum, Newport News ref QW384

5. 'Johnny Bull and the Alexandrians', cartoon satirising the pusillanimous capitulation of the citizens, drawn and published by William Charles (1776-1820), Philadelphia, no date. The Bull demands all the local produce, except Porter and Perry (beer and a pear cordial), a punning reference to the victorious American naval officers – 'keep them out of my sight, I've had enough of them already'. In fact, Porter, Perry (as well as Rodgers) unsuccessfully opposed the return passage of the British expedition.
Library of Congress, Washington DC, ref USZ62-349

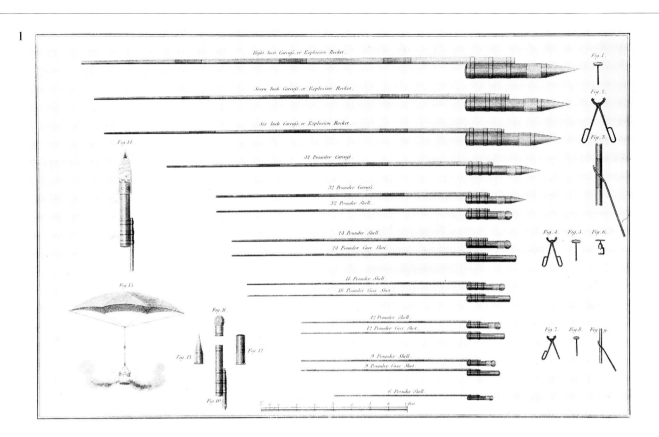

Steam, torpedoes and rockets

URING THE War of 1812 both sides deployed futuristic weapons that were decried by the other as 'unfair', 'underhand' or 'barbarous'. In no case was this conflict the first use of such inventions, but a fierce propaganda battle brought these hitherto secret weapons to a wider public attention.

Since the 'rockets' red glare' is enshrined in the American national anthem, it is probably fair to say that it is this device which is most closely associated with 1812. The war rocket was an ancient Chinese invention, but was much used by the armies of the local princes in India,

where it came to the attention of the British—most recently in their campaigns against Tipu Sahib. Captured examples were examined at Woolwich by one William Congreve, who became convinced that they could be much improved and might eventually substitute for conventional artillery. Although not himself a military man, his father was—indeed, he was both an artillery-man and an innovator, having developed far more efficient methods of manufacturing gunpowder—so the younger Congreve was able to obtain advice, access to facilities, and influential backing. His work concentrated mainly on improving the propellant, for additional range, and on devising effective warheads.

What Congreve was to call his 'rocket system' comprised a variety of sizes, from 6-pounder to 42-pounder payload, carrying explosive shell, incendiary 'carcass', or anti-personnel case shot (or combinations thereof); he even invented a primitive parachute flare (1). These were intended to match field artillery or sea ordnance in range, but there were also heavy rockets designated 6-inch to 8-inch regarded as mortar substitutes. Compared with conventional artillery, the advantages claimed by Congreve for his weapons were: portability, absence of recoil, terror-inducing effects on the enemy, and rapidity of preparation and high rate of fire. They were certainly light and easy to transport, and were fired from a simple ladder-like launcher, which was equally at home on land (2) or in a boat (3).

The disadvantages of the rocket became rapidly obvious when they went into action. First used in the attacks on Napoleon's would-be invasion flotilla in the Channel ports in 1805-6, the weapon proved to be very inaccurate, but also unpredictable and erratic in behaviour. Greater experience also showed that it was liable to misfire or explosion after lengthy transportation, or even long storage, and its manufacture was both slow and dangerous. Nevertheless the British persevered, and discovered its value as a somewhat indiscriminate area-bombardment weapon at Copenhagen in 1807 when some 300 were fired, contributing to the conflagration that destroyed so much of the old city. Its very unpredictability was also a psychological asset, as the Rocket Brigade discovered at the Battle of Leipzig, when it terrified 2500 French infantry into surrendering. If it could demoralise regulars, it was doubly effective against the largely militia forces of the United States, being deployed with great success in the battles on the Canadian border and, notably, at Bladensburg before the fall of Washington. It was said that the capital's building were set on fire using rockets.

The Royal Navy was the first to try the rocket in action and Congreve went so far as to design and fit out special 'rocket ships', which had angled troughs within the hull firing out through miniature gunports in the side. The first of these, *Galgo*, was a converted merchantman, but the rather more elaborate *Erebus* was modified from a purpose-built fireship. As the latter proved before Fort McHenry, they were not very effective in destroying hardened targets, and lacking the maximum range of the largest mortar, they also risked the firing ship. The best use the Navy could put them to was in the kind of raiding warfare Cockburn perfected in the Chesapeake in 1813. A light frame in a ship's launch could provide a weight of covering fire in shallow water otherwise unobtainable, and as long as pinpoint accuracy was not required the mere noise and smoke could be employed to overawe inexperienced defenders.

For the Americans, attacks on their coastal communities only enhanced the need for an antidote to British seapower. In the absence of an opposing battlefleet, British blockaders sat boldly in the estuaries, bays and sounds of the seaboard, offering tempting targets for unconventional warfare. The obvious answer was underwater attack, as practised in primitive form during the Revolution by the likes of David Bushnell. It was given official sanction and encouragement by Congress in March 1813, in the so-called Torpedo Act, which promised anybody who blew up a British ship half the estimated value of the target. Not surprisingly, a number

3

tried, and all failed. The nearest to being successful was Sailing Master Elijah Mix, USN, who made a number of attempts on the 74-gun *Plantagenet* lying in the mouth of the Chesapeake; one explosion was close enough to send a spout of water onto the ship's deck.

His weapon was a Fulton 'torpedo', or floating mine. In Robert Fulton America could claim the world's leading exponent of underwater warfare, although he had first tried to sell his talents abroad. Having failed to interest Napoleon in a submersible, he took his ideas to Britain, where fears of a French invasion led the government to fund and test his explosive devices in action (see, in this series, *The Campaign of Trafalgar* for details and drawings of his weapons). The principle weapon was a pair of explosive canisters joined together by a line and designed

4

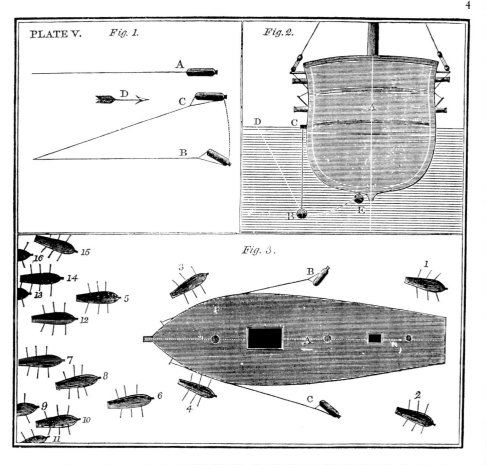

5

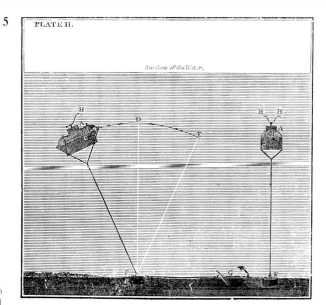

PLATE II.

Surface of the Water.

6

to be floated down on a tide against an anchored ship;
when the line snagged on the anchor cable, the canisters
would be dragged against the ship's side, where a clock-
work time fuse would eventually set them off (4). They
were none too effective, and as the invasion threat
diminished Fulton became disillusioned and returned to
America. In his homeland, at first his ideas were well
received by the Jefferson administration, since Fulton
promised cheap coastal defence which obviated the need
for a navy, and in one demonstration in 1807 he blew up
a brig, repeating a result he had previously achieved in
England. The government did not respond with the
enthusiasm he eternally longed for and Fulton went off
to develop the steamboat for which he is perhaps best
remembered.

In 1810 he made another attempt to sell his ideas to
the government, and on this occasion the US Navy
agreed to provide as a target ship the sloop *Argus*.
However, it was not only British naval officers who
looked askance at weapons likely to put them out of a
job, and Fulton arrived to find *Argus* defended by booms,
netting and grappling hooks, against which he had no
chance. Given time for thought, he later proposed various counter-countermeasures, including an ingenious

netcutter, but as far as the US Navy was concerned, in his
proposal for a ship-attack weapon he had failed.
Unfortunately for America, other more practical ideas
were dismissed at the same time, most importantly an
early version of the moored mine (5) that might have
made areas like Chesapeake Bay no-go areas to the Royal
Navy in the war to come.

Because his name was well known to the British,
Fulton was usually credited with any 'Infernal'
employed against them, but his involvement was confined to supplying the weapons in return for a percentage of the bounty on any destroyed ship. Other inventors
also tried their hand, a Mr Ryker of New York being
responsible for the device which exploded under the
bowsprit of *La Hogue*, 74 on 25 March 1814 off New
London. Fulton was also associated with submersibles, so
was held responsible for the famous 'Turtle Boat',
destroyed in Long Island Sound by the boats of the frigate
Maidstone in the following June. Captain Burdett of the
frigate enclosed a sketch of the semi-submersible hand-
cranked craft in his report and had little doubt it was the
work of Fulton, although a recent biographer disclaims
this, a contemporary report attributing the boat to 'an
ingenious gentleman by the name of Berrian'.

The reason Fulton was not more actively engaged was
his work on another novel weapon, the steam block-
ship he called 'Demologos', or 'Voice of the People'.
Developed out of his experiments with underwater
guns, the new vessel had the advantage of input from
Commodore Decatur, who kept the sometimes vision-
ary inventor in touch with the requirements of naval
warfare. Fulton had more experience of steamboats than
anyone else alive, and what emerged was a perfectly
practical, if limited, warship – the first of its kind in
history. Decatur's patronage helped convince the navy's
officer corps that, far from abolishing their profession
as Fulton's earlier work had threatened, the new tech-
nology would vastly strengthen the US Navy.

The catamaran design was propelled by a paddlewheel
between the stoutly-built hulls, where it could not be
damaged, and the boiler (in one hull) and the engines (in
the other) were both positioned below the waterline.
Some canvas was later added for manoeuvring, but
steam was the principal mode of propulsion. With a powerful battery of 32-pounders, the ship would have made
an assault on New York harbour an extremely risky venture for a conventional warship. Launched as *Fulton the
First* on 29 October 1814 (6), the ship was not completed
until the war was over, but by that stage another was
under construction for the defence of the Chesapeake.
Had the fighting continued for a few extra months, the
war might well have seen the first employment of a
steam warship in combat.

1

Baltimore reprieved

AFTER THE attack on Washington in August 1814, Sir George Cockburn was keen to attack Baltimore, home of the most effective American privateering industry (1): a 'dash against that place' would, he argued, take that city as much by surprise as Washington had been. His Commander-in-Chief, Sir Alexander Cochrane, was less sure, conscious of the strategic plan for assaults elsewhere. However, while the troops rested on Tangier Island in Chesapeake Bay, Cochrane learned that the approaching equinoctial new moon (and its related tides) made it unsafe for some vessels to navigate the mouth of the Bay immediately. Sufficient time had elapsed for Baltimore's defences to be strengthened. Nevertheless, on 7 September it was agreed that an attempt should be made against the city. As against Washington, Cockburn would accompany the expedition in command of a brigade of 600 seamen, a battalion of marines (those from the ships) and the colonial black marines.

Retracing its course, the expedition made the mouth of the River Patapsco on 11 September. Cockburn, in the leading vessel with Major General Sir Robert Ross, chose 'North Point' for the landing (2). That night, troops were ferried up to the vessels close to the landing place, where they disembarked at first light on the 12th. Frigates, sloops, bomb ships and a rocket vessels passed by on their way to bombard the fort commanding the water approach to Baltimore, where Cochrane was to join them later.

There was no opposition to the British army and the naval contingent as they landed, but it was evident the Americans were 'in a state of activity and alarm'. Some light horsemen were cut off, taken by the advancing troops; and some freshly made entrenchments were discovered, just abandoned. About five miles from the landing place, Cockburn and Ross with the advance guard of 50 to 60 men were some way ahead of the main column. Cockburn recalled pointing out to Ross their forces had become separated. On his own excursions in Virginia and Maryland he had always concentrated his force and had skirmishers spread along the flanks of the main column. Within a hundred yards his fears were realised. At a wooded turning in the road, an ambush occurred. Unsupported by the main force, 'there was . . . nothing left for it but to dash forward against them, returning their fire as quickly as possible to induce them to suppose our whole force to be at hand'. The charge had the desired effect, the Americans breaking and running. Ross had turned back to order up more troops when one of the last 'straggling shots' hit him in the arm and

2

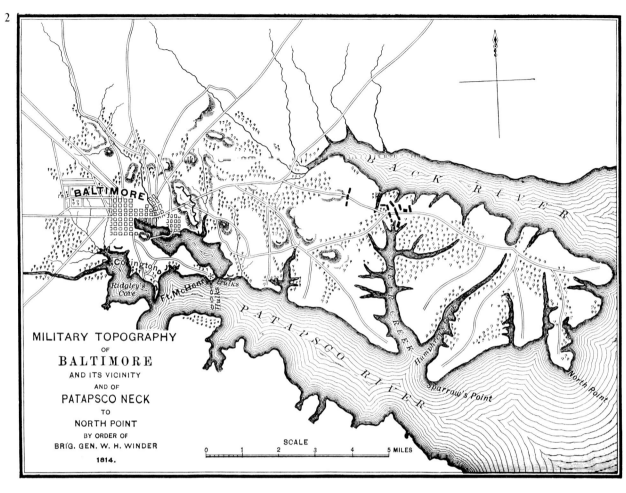

MILITARY TOPOGRAPHY
OF
BALTIMORE
AND ITS VICINITY
AND OF
PATAPSCO NECK
TO
NORTH POINT
BY ORDER OF
BRIG. GEN. W. H. WINDER
1814.

3

entered his chest. He died on a stretcher on the way back to the river.

Colonel Brooke succeeded to command of the army. No further opposition was encountered until within five miles of Baltimore. But there, an estimated 6000 men with six pieces of artillery and some 100 cavalry were drawn up in dense order across the road, partly sheltered by a wood and lining a strong paling fence about chest high that stretched either side at right angles to the road. Both flanks appear to have been protected by creeks and inlets of the Patapsco and Back rivers which approach each other at this point. Brooke made the necessary dispositions under cannon fire, and ordered an immediate advance. Some light troops were ordered to encircle the American left flank. As soon as they came into range, the advancing troops came under heavy musket fire but maintained their impetus, eventually breaking through and over the palings. Within fifteen minutes, as at Bladensburg, the Americans had been routed. Seamen with small arms and the marines formed the whole left flank of the British army. The slaughter was particularly heavy. Brooke estimated American casualties at above 500. British losses were almost as bad: 41 killed, 261 wounded from the army; 14 killed and 92 wounded from the naval contingents.

The army camped that night in the wood from which they had just driven the Americans, around a Meeting House which became the British headquarters. Next morning, 13 September, Brooke and Cockburn took up the advance. American cavalry showed themselves occasionally, hovering about, watching the line of march. About 10am they reached Baltimore's outer defences, about a mile and a half from the city (3). Brooke and Cockburn reconnoitred at leisure. The city was surrounded by a series of hills upon which a string of palisaded redoubts had been constructed all connected by breastworks. Chinkapin Hill, which lay directly in front of the advancing army and over which their road passed, was the most strongly fortified. Overlooking the palisades and double ditches were batteries of artillery from which advancing troops would find little protection, the hill's slopes being clear of any cover. Moreover Chinkapin Hill, so they were informed, was defended by at least 15,000 men, including all the seamen from the ships in Baltimore harbour and militias from Philadelphia and Washington. To Brooke and Cockburn there seemed no immediate likelihood of an attack from the Americans. On the other hand, the only chance of their 4000 men storming the hill was by surprise attack at night. Hoping for diversionary movements from Cochrane, they planned to storm the hill at midnight.

Meanwhile in the Patapsco, Cochrane had himself run into difficulties with the frigates and bomb vessels. That morning of the 13th they opened their bombardment on Fort McHenry that protected the entrance to Baltimore harbour (4). The fort stood on the western point of the entrance and shells from the bomb vessels appeared to land in it. Yet, as well as that fort, a battery set on the eastern point – the Star fort – was also returning their fire. And, even if both forts were silenced, there seemed little prospect of penetrating the harbour, the mouth of which behind a shallow bar was 'entirely obstructed' by a barrier of sunken vessels. Behind them, moreover, was a squadron of gunboats, with the harbour sides fortified, the left one bearing a battery of 'several heavy guns'. The giant American flag was still flying over the fort the following morning, inspiring one eyewitness, a Baltimore lawyer and amateur poet called Francis Scott Key, to pen the words of 'The Star Spangled Banner', eventually to become his country's national anthem.

By the evening Cochrane had abandoned hope of reaching the city, still two miles beyond the harbour mouth, and could offer little hope of help to Brooke and Cockburn. Of this, Cochrane sent Brooke and Cockburn a warning. Furthermore, he explicitly left the decision whether to make a land attack to Brooke, deterring him by reference to the number of American defenders, esti-

mated at 20,000, to the potential waste of British lives, and to the hazard losses to the army would make to the opportunity of going on 'other services'. Before Chinakapin Hill, the rain was just as heavy. Brooke and Cockburn knew that their attack would incur losses, probably heavy ones, and Cochrane's letters made clear 'the onus of preventing other services was to be thrown upon any such loss'. Brooke took the decision to retire immediately. Next morning Cochrane also called off the bombardment of the forts at the harbour mouth.

The retirement was steady and dignified. The first of the British troops began their return march at 1.30 in the morning of 14 September. At the Meeting House, American prisoners were sorted, Brooke taking about 200 'persons of the best families in the city'. After resting through the heat of midday, they marched another three miles late in the afternoon. Re-embarkation began at North Point early on 15 September.

Cockburn regarded the expedition as a military failure. His reminiscences harp repeatedly on the week's delay at Tangier Island. However, Cochrane, Melville and the British government judged it by other standards. Cochrane termed the Baltimore expedition a 'demonstration', and stressed the defeat of the American army near the Meeting House, the alarm and disturbance created throughout the area, and the Americans' destruction of their own shipping, public buildings and ropewalk. Melville compared it to operations in Canada, which he considered much less creditable. Above all, the British government valued the expedition for its impact on the peace negotiations that had been under way at Ghent since early that year.

1. 'Baltimore taken near Whetstone Point', coloured aquatint and etching by W J Bennett after his own original, published by Henry J Megarey, 1831. *NMM ref PA10383*

2. 'Military Topography of Baltimore and its vicinity and of Patapsco Neck to North Point, by order of Brig Gen W H Winder 1814', plate from Henry Adams, *History of the United States*, Vol 8 (New York 1891). *Chatham collection*

3. 'East View of Baltimore, Maryland', coloured aquatint and etching by T Cartwright after an original by G Beck, published by Atkins and Nightingale, 1 January 1802. *NMM ref PA10384*

4. 'A View of the Bombardment of Fort McHenry . . . taken from the Observatory,' engraving by J Bowers, Philadelphia, no date. *Beverley R Robinson collection ref BRR80.59*

4

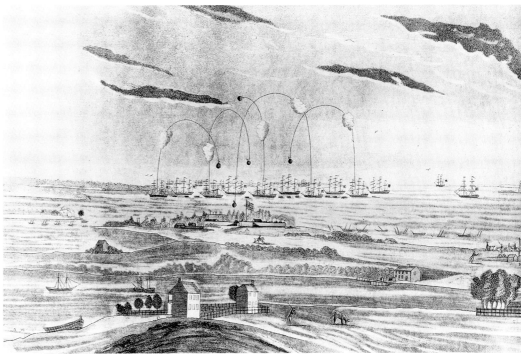

1

Ships of the Royal Navy: big frigates

2

THE VICTORIES of the big American spar-decked frigates provoked the Admiralty into considering more powerful classes than the 18-pounder-armed 38 that had been the standard heavy frigate since its introduction in 1778. However, in 1812 the Royal Navy was not entirely devoid of larger frigates, nor was a 24-pounder main battery a novel idea. Apart from a few French and Dutch prizes, a handful of more powerful ships had been built or converted during the 1790s, but none since.

At the beginning of the French War in 1793, there were persistent rumours about heavily armed 'frigates' cut down from battleships and called in French *rasées*. These were the inspiration for Humphreys' concept for the *Constitution* class, and in 1794 the British also cut down three small 64s: *Anson, Magnanime* and *Indefatigable*, retaining their main batteries of twenty-six 24-pounders. The capture about the same time of the French *Pomone*, with a similar main armament to the British *rasées*, led the Admiralty to a brief flirtation with big frigates. These comprised the 24-pounder-armed *Endymion* (a copy of *Pomone*) and *Cambrian* (1); and *Acasta* and *Lavinia* with thirty 18-pounders on the main deck. Compared with the *Constitution*, of around 1500 tons, these were not large ships at about 1200 tons for the first pair and 1100 tons for the others.

They were, however, very big by British standards and

did not give an entirely satisfactory return on the substantial investment in their construction. The 24-pounder frigates in particular were vulnerable to structural problems, and soon they were all reduced to 18-pounders. Not only did the heavy 24-pounders rack the hull, but they were found difficult to handle on a frigate's relatively lively deck and rate of fire and accuracy suffered as a result. This was one reason why Royal Navy officers who had some knowledge of the American '44's were not particularly deterred by the prospect of meeting them in action, failing to see that the far greater dimensions of the American ships made them steadier gun platforms.

Of all the 'super frigates' of the 1790s, *Endymion* was the star. She was very fast, handled well, was an excellent seaboat, and could if required carry 24-pounders. Indeed, she was so highly regarded that she was still the benchmark for sailing qualities as late as the Experimental Squadrons of the 1830s. The only more powerful frigates to have seen Royal Navy service were the 1400-ton sistership *Forte* and *L'Egyptienne*; the former had been lost too soon for the lines to be taken off, while the latter, captured at the fall of Alexandria in 1801, proved so weakly built that she was confined to harbour service from 1807. Thus in 1812 when the Admiralty cast round for an answer to the big American frigates, it was natural that *Endymion* would come to mind. The ship herself was not immediately available, since she was undergoing a year-long refit, officially described as 'Between a Middling and Large Repair', but when completed in May 1813 she was restored to her 24-pounder armament and dispatched to America. In the meantime, as the one existing satisfactory prototype of her class, she became the model for the first of the new 40-gun frigates.

Although an excellent ship, *Endymion* had only twenty-six ports on the main deck compared to thirty for the American '44's, but being based on a French design, she did not carry guns right forward, so it was possible to contrive fourteen ports a side in the revised draught. Building in pine produced a significantly lighter hull, which could make such ships very stiff, but as in this case it could be turned to advantage by carrying heavier weights. The gundeck of the new class was somewhat crowded as a result, but they suffered no stability problems. Once fine-tuned, they were generally good under sail, if not quite as outstanding as *Endymion* herself. Five ships of this class were on order by the middle of January 1813, all to be built of pitch pine by Sir Robert Wigram's yard, with three contracted to be launched by June. They became the *Forth* class of a nominal 40 guns (2).

Despite the speed of softwood construction, the Admiralty needed an even quicker counter to the US spar-deckers. Reviving the *rasée* concept was an obvious short-term response, and in January Admiral Sir John Borlase Warren, Commander-in-Chief on the North America station, requested 'six or seven good sailing old ships of the line, such as *Canada, Captain, Bellona, Monarch*, cut down and reduced as razies . . .' Having had *Indefatigable* and *Anson* in his squadron in 1795, Warren's interest was predictable, but the Admiralty had the satisfaction of telling him they had foreseen his request and already had the matter in hand. In fact they were acting with great vigour on a suggestion of November 1812 from Captain John Hayes.

His original idea was to convert 64s, but by this time 64-gun ships, with a main battery of twenty-six 24-pounders, were simply too weak, and in any case the Navy Board pointed out that there were no 64s in Ordinary that would make economical conversions. As a result , the Admiralty decided to cut down fast-sailing small 74s instead, three being chosen – *Majestic, Goliath* and *Saturn*, all rescued from the ignominy of conversion to prison ships.

The conversion itself was rather different from the 1794 *rasées*, which were given an open waist and frigate-like topsides. The 74s, on the other hand, were nothing

3

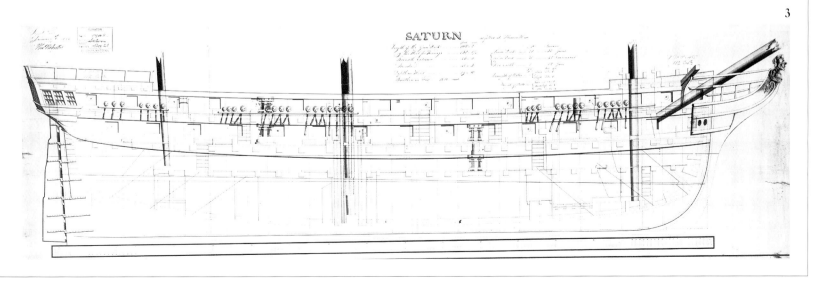

4

5

like conventional frigates, and were referred to officially as 'intermediate between heavy frigates and line of battleships'. Following Hayes' brief, they retained the hull sides of what had been the upper gundeck to full height and scantlings, along with a 'flying forecastle' and a long poop with rails (3). The hatchways were narrowed as much as possible, and the booms and boats carried on crutches just off the deck. The main battery of twenty-eight 32-pounders was retained, while the continuous upper deck was powerfully armed with the same number of 42-pounder carronades, mounted on Congreve's novel principle whereby the gun recoiled on trucks fixed on an axle passing through the loop (it was supposed to speed up the rate of fire by suppressing the recoil). The armament was completed by a 12-pounder bow-chaser on an elevating carriage (although this had become two by the time the ships went to sea) and a complement of 495 men. Although *Saturn* required some repair work, the cutting-down involved no more than about three months in dock for any of them, and *Majestic* was at sea by May 1813.

Captain Hayes, who had instigated the project, was given command of the first to commission, and he was highly pleased with the result. The *Majestic* was, in his opinion, 'superior to any battleship and not inferior to any frigate I have served in'; she was stiff, sailed and handled well, and carried her midships ports 6ft 4in from the waterline. Furthermore, she turned out to be a very fine heavy-weather ship, working off a lee shore by carrying a press of sail for two days while the accompanying frigate remained embayed. While the frigate rolled her quarterdeck ports in the water, Hayes claimed 'it was not even necessary to make a single chair fast in my cabin.' With a black-painted waist cloth to disguise the spar-deck battery, she could also pass for a conventional frigate, as one of her squadron-mates reported:

> her appearance [is] so deceptious [sic] that any one would go down to her for a frigate, having much of the appearance of one of the American frigates; I hope more of the small 74 gun Ships will be equipped in the same way, these seas requiring no other ships, it would be a great saving.

To some extent this was offset by the curious rig, whereby the yards and sails on the fore and main masts were identical. Another of Hayes's ideas, it was an example of the modern concept of 'redundancy', supposed to make the tophamper interchangeable. However, as the captain of the *Goliath* complained, once seen by the enemy they were instantly recognizable forever.

Although they were principally deployed against the American 44s, it is not certain how they would have performed against their intended targets. They carried far more firepower, but they could never had caught one in light airs, the principal advantage of the *rasées* being their power to carry sail, which made them excellent heavy-weather ships. The closest contact was the pursuit of the *President* in January 1815, when *Majestic* led the chase until the wind slackened, when *Endymion* took over. If they could only catch their opponents in heavy weather, they would then have been at a disadvantage in battle given their relatively low gunport freeboard — less than 6 feet in most conditions compared to over 8 feet in the *Constitution*. As the chasing ship it would be more than likely that it would be the *rasée's* lee battery on the engaged side, and it might have proved difficult to fight the main armament in such a seaway.

To prove that it is usually pointless to design any weapons system to meet a single specific opponent, *Majestic's* finest moment came in February 1814, when in pursuit of a Philadelphia privateer Hayes encountered two French 18-pounder frigates and their 20-gun prize. He rapidly dispersed this squadron, capturing one of the frigates, the *Terpsichore*, without any casualties to his own ship (4).

The 40-gun ships were at best an interim reaction, but as further evidence of the success of the American spar-decked frigates came in, there was an increasing desire in the Admiralty to produce an equivalent. Therefore, in April 1813 the Navy Board was instructed to produce a design for 'a 50-gun ship of the frigate class with a spar deck' of about 1500 tons, one draught by the Surveyors

and one by the French *emigré constructeur* J L Barrallier. Assuming that there was no prior discussion of the requirement, the speed with which the draughts were delivered — three days — is a precise indicator of how little time it took to design even a radically new warship type in those days.

Designed to carry thirty 24-pounders on the lower deck and twenty-eight 42-pounder carronades plus two long 24s on the full spar deck, the two ships were similar in size, although, typically, the Frenchman's ship was longer. They were also about the same size as their American opponents, but whereas the American ships, built in the 1790s, were traditional in their appearance with some sheer and tumblehome, the British ships with their wall sides and flat sheerline, looked forward to a more austere, aesthetically brutal age in naval architecture. Christened *Leander* and *Newcastle*, both ships were built by the already heavily committed Wigram yard, and necessarily of softwood to get them into service as quickly as possible. Both ships were launched on the same day, 10 November, command going to two senior captains, Sir George Collier and Lord George Stuart.

When they went to sea, both *Newcastle* and *Leander* proved very fast, both exceeding 13 knots, but they were also leewardly and initially over-stiff. Like the *rasées*, they were better in heavier conditions, although they carried their battery at least 8ft from the waterline at any state of lading (5). After the war they were given poop decks, 'whereby they will be rendered substitutes for 50-gun ships with two decks' (6); and of course they became flag-ships on stations where it was necessary to keep an eye on the Americans.

Once the need for very big frigates had been accepted, the Admiralty had brought the considerable industrial strength of Britain lavishly to bear on the problem. By the middle of 1813 the *rasées* were joining the fleet, followed by the first of the 24-pounder-armed 40s towards the end of the year, and the two 50-gun ships by the spring of 1814.

6

1. 'Glasgow and Cambrian at the Battle of Navarino, 20 Oct 1827', coloured lithograph after an original by George Philip Reinagle, printed by Charles Joseph Hullmandel and published by Colnaghi & Son, 18 Januray 1828.
NMM ref PAF4858

2. 'HM Frigate *Glasgow*', lithograph by L Haghe after an original by Midshipman F Williams, 23 April 1826. One of the *Forth* class; these fir-built ships saw much post-war service being kept in peacetime commission to preserve the long-lasting oak ships for any future war.
NMM neg X88

3. Sheer and profile draught of the *Saturn* as converted, dated Plymouth, January 1814. Unlike the 6ft 4in claimed for *Majestic*, the draught notes the midship gunport freeboard as only 5ft 3ins.
NMM neg DR1748

4. 'This representation of His Majesty's Ship Majestic, 57 guns, John Hayes, Esq. Captain, meeting with two french Frigates — an American Private Ship of war, a Spanish Lima Ship — and a Brig on the 3rd of Feby 1814 . . . and capturing one of the Frigates', coloured aquatint engraved by C Hunt after an original by Gilbert, published by Ackermann & Co, no date.
NMM ref PAH8145

5. '*Leander at sea*', oil painting by Thomas Buttersworth (1768-1842), no date. Although typical of the Surveyors' work of that period, the painting may not be a genuine portrait of *Leander*, since it does not show enough gunports and the waist battery is not evident.
NMM ref BHC3442

6. A sheer and profile draught of Barrallier's *Newcastle*, as refitted with a poop, dated Woolwich, March 1816.
NMM neg DR1446

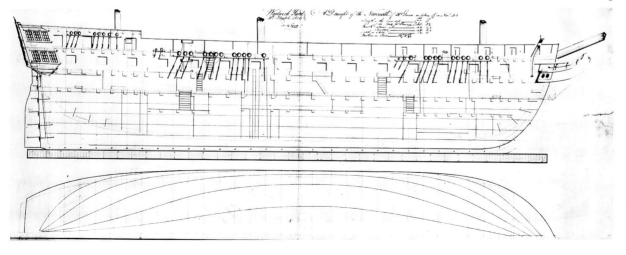

Capture of the *President*

B Y THE end of 1814 the Royal Navy ruled the coastal waters of the United States. Her capital had been burned, trade was at a standstill, all but a few warships had been driven off the seas, and even the privateering menace was being contained. But the one achievement that eluded the British was the capture of one of the big American frigates that had been a thorn in their flesh since the outbreak of war. As a matter of pride and propaganda, it was a consummation devoutly to be

wished. Before his own victory over the *Chesapeake*, Broke had written:

> We must catch one of these great American ships with our squadron, to send her home for a show, that people may *see what a great creature it is*, and that our frigates have fought very well, though unlucky.

When it was finally achieved in January 1815, it was already irrelevant to the outcome of the war, but its importance can be seen in the reaction of the Admiralty to their prize.

For most of the war the American big frigates had enjoyed the fortune which favoured the brave, but *President*'s luck finally ran out in the dying days of the war. Closely blockaded in New York for months, Decatur despaired of getting his squadron safely to sea as a unit, so on 14 January in a fierce snowstorm he left the sloops *Peacock* and *Hornet* with orders for a south Atlantic rendezvous and sailed with *President* and the store brig *Macedonian*. Unfortunately, the frigate was deeply laden for a long-distance raid on the East Indies, and she struck the bar, pounding heavily for an hour and a half before she could get off. Decatur later claimed that the damage spoiled the ship's sailing qualities and that if the weather had permitted he would have put back.

The British blockading squadron was commanded by John Hayes, a consummate seaman known throughout the service as 'Magnificent' Hayes after he saved the ship of that name from almost certain destruction on a lee shore by a brilliant feat of seamanship. Although he had been blown off station, Hayes was able to predict Decatur's likely course, and about dawn on 15 January

President ran into his whole squadron, which comprised the 56-gun *rasée Majestic*, the 24-pounder frigate *Endymion* (Captain Henry Hope), and the standard 38-gun frigates *Pomone* and *Tenedos*. In the strong winds, initially it was *Majestic* which led the field, but by noon with the wind slackening the *Endymion* began to walk away from her consorts (1).

Decatur did everything in his power, lightening the ship by starting his water, and throwing overboard spare gear, boats, anchors and so forth; all canvas was set to studding sails, and kept constantly wet to improve their 'draw'. But he could not throw off the *Endymion*, and by the end of the afternoon she had taken a position on his starboard quarter and began a galling fire; to this *President* could only make reply by yawing to fire partial broadsides, but losing ground at every attempt (2). Decatur had one last weapon in his locker, and it was one that American ships made good use of: dismantling shot. The stores allocation per gun for such ammunition in the US Navy was 25 per cent of all rounds, more than twice that of the French navy and eight times that of the British, whose close-combat doctrine saw little need for it—indeed, so little that in 1811 the Board of Ordnance decided to issue no more double-headed shot (the only kind officially sanctioned), allowing one round per gun until stocks were used up. By comparison the US Navy employed various forms of star and chain shot, elaborate devices that on being fired opened out to form flailing patterns of steel designed to cut rigging and even strip sails from the yards (3).

When *President* finally bore up, therefore, Decatur was

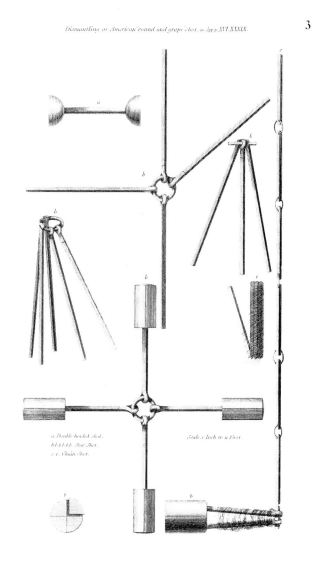

3

Dismantling or American round and grape shot, as per p. XVI.XXXIX.

a. *Double-headed shot.*
b.b.b.b.b.b. *Star Shot.*
c.c. *Chain Shot.*

Scale 1 inch to a Foot.

4

5

prepared. He had to endure two raking broadsides from *Endymion* before she came alongside, but as soon as she did, he let fire with a hail of stars and bars, literally tearing the canvas from the British ship's yards. Unusually, both ships fought under all plain sail plus studding sails, so it took over two hours, but eventually *Endymion* could no longer keep up, and in the winter gloom Decatur must have thought he had escaped. However, about 11pm the *Pomone* arrived on the scene and fired a few broadsides, and with *Tenedos* in the offing (4), Decatur saw no alternative to striking his colours (5). He had suffered by his own admission 24 dead and 55 wounded, while *Endymion* lost 11 and 14 respectively.

Strenuous efforts had to be made by the British to preserve their greatest prize of the war, since the squadron ran into another gale a few days later in which *President* was dismasted. She was seriously damaged by the time she reached Britain, but whether as a result of the grounding, the action, the subsequent dismasting, or simply old age, will never be known. The ship was surveyed and a draught was carefully taken off (6); at first it was estimated that a 'Middling Repair' of about six months' duration would see the ship right, but as she was opened up major weaknesses manifested themselves, and in 1818 a reluctant Admiralty agreed that breaking her up was the only practical course. However, they were not about to lose their greatest propaganda instrument, so they ordered a *precise* copy (most ships 'to the lines of' a foreign prototype were effectively new designs using only the hull shape of the original). This *President* was launched in 1824 and was often flaunted under the noses of the Americans as flagship of one of the transatlantic stations – much as the *Macedonian* was used by the US Navy in response.

6

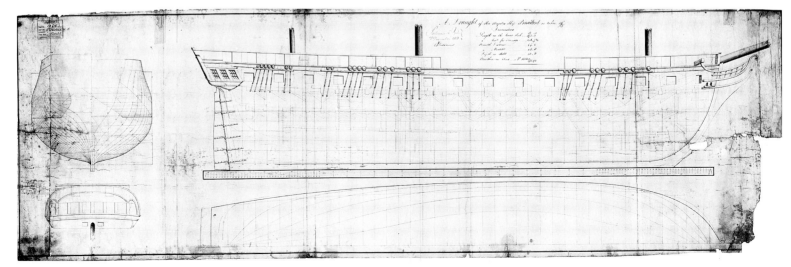

The occupation of Maine

WITH THE satisfactory conclusion of the war in Europe, in the middle of 1814 the British government began to entertain ideas of some serious gains in North America. The northward salient of Maine (1), then a district of Massachusetts, had always formed a serious bar to communication between Halifax and Quebec, the most important British military bases in Canada. The Canadians regarded it as an anomaly of the 1783 peace treaty, the product of ignorance of local geography on the part of the British negotiators, and a permanent rectification would be one useful outcome of the war. Aiming for a conquest that could be retained at the next peace treaty, the Governor of Nova Scotia, Sir John Sherbrooke, was instructed in August to occupy enough of Maine to insure uninterrupted communication between New Brunswick and Lower Canada. How he was to achieve it was left to his own discretion.

Moose Island in Passamaquoddy Bay (2), just on the American side of the line but disputed since 1783, had been seized on 11 July 1814 in an unopposed landing, but on 1 September a major amphibious force of nearly 2000 men arrived off the mouth of the Penobscot, Sherbrooke having decided to make his attack up this river. His original intention had been to capture Machias, but on learning of the presence of a US warship at Castine, switched targets. Castine capitulated quickly, and the large corvette *Adams* (3), seeking shelter after damage by grounding, retreated some thirty miles up to Hampden. A powerful 26-gun ship, cut down and lengthened from a frigate, she was armed with four long 18-pounders, twenty short, or 'Columbiad' 18-pounders and two long 12 pounders. Measuring over 700 tons, she was a commerce-raider worthy of serious attention. Her guns were landed, and the seamen and militia made preparations to defend the ship. However, an amphibious force sent up the river, dispersed the opposition on the 3rd with few casualties to itself, and the Americans were compelled to burn the ship to prevent capture (4). The expedition pressed on to Bangor (5), where it took a large number of merchant ships.

The final act of the military operations was to send a force to occupy Machias. Leaving two regiments at Castine, with transports to evacuate them should they be attacked by superior forces, Sherbrooke then withdrew the majority of his troops to Halifax. The occupation was intended to become permanent so the local population was treated with consideration, and since they were able to benefit from external trade when most of the American coast was tightly blockaded, it was even claimed that the eventual peace was not welcome in

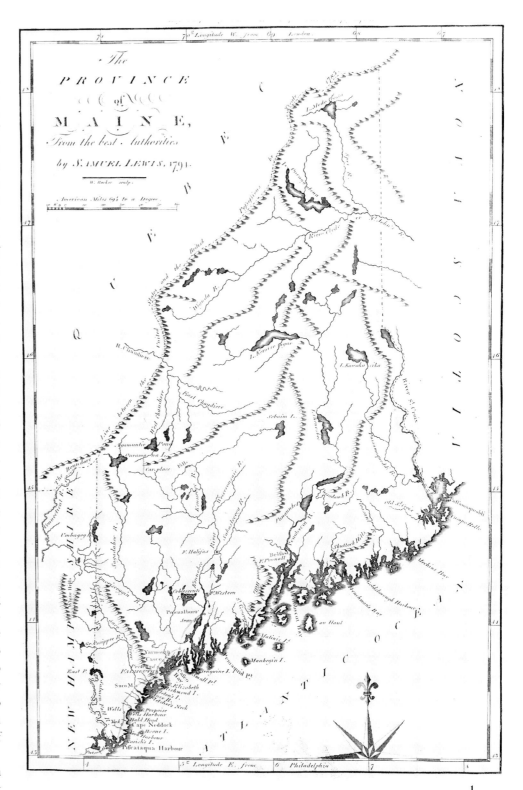

1

Maine. Even without the defeat at Plattsburgh, it is unlikely that such a tenuous hold on the country would have been defensible as 'conquest' at the peace negotiations – even Wellington said an officer might as well claim sovereignty over the ground on which he posted his pickets – and at Ghent Maine came back to America, although the British garrisons were not withdrawn until April 1815.

2

1. 'The Province of Maine . . . by Samuel Lewis, 1794', engraved for Carey's American edition of Guthrie's *Geography Improved*.
NMM neg D9548

2. Passamaquody Bay, as drawn by J F W Des Barres for *The Atlantic Neptune*, 1776. Moose Island is below Deer Island, in the archipelago at the south end of the Bay.
NMM neg D9550-1

3. 'Corvette des Etats-Unis D'Amerique', engraving by J J Baugean, no date. One of the small frigates, but similar in general appearance to the *Adams* before she was cut down and lengthened.
Beverley R Robinson collection ref BRR80.26.9

4. 'Burning the *Adams*, 3 September 1814', watercolour by Irwin Bevan (1852-1940), no date.
Mariners' Museum, Newport News ref QW390

5. 'View of the City of Bangor, Me', lithograph engraved by Pendleton's Lithographers after an original by A H Wallace, published by William A Gilman and Alexander H Wallace, 1835.
NMM ref PA10324

3

4

5

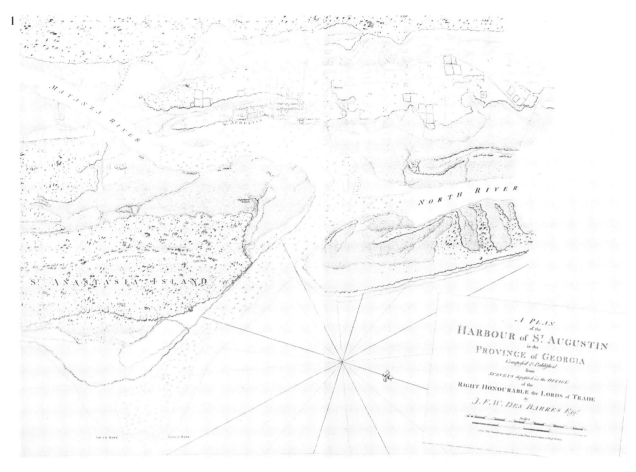

The southern theatre

THE WORST hardships of the blockade were slow in reaching the southern states, although there had been conflict in the region even before the declaration of war against Britain, thanks to the American administration's designs on the Spanish Florida territory. Taking advantage of Spain's preoccupation with the Napoleonic struggle, the USA acquired part of west Florida by bloodless coup in 1810, and in March 1812 an invasion of east Florida by insurgents from Georgia received Madison's clandestine support. Spain was an ally of Britain, and there were many British commercial interests in ports like St Augustine (1), but the numerous islands and inlets of the area also played host to a horde of embargo-breakers, smugglers, and downright pirates.

The suppression of some of these undesirable elements was one inspiration for the insurgents' capture of Fernandina on Amelia Island, but when Congress refused to sanction the operations, American forces had to be withdrawn in the spring of 1813. Nevertheless, in his March 1813 notes on his blockade stations, the British Commander-in-Chief described the area between Savannah and St Augustine as containing 'The most implacable & virulent people in the whole Union'. The British were slow to pay attention to the southern coasts, the commandant of the US Navy base at Charleston, South Carolina (2) noting with surprise that no British cruisers were to be found off the port until October 1812. By August 1813 this had all changed, and there were so many that he could no longer risk sending his small craft to sea to protect the coasting trade, which was a vital contributor to the commerce of the area.

In theory, the coastal trade south of the Chesapeake enjoyed the geographical advantage of long strings of offshore islands and sand banks behind which small craft could creep, but while the British were reluctant to commit deep-draught warships to these restricted waters, they had no such compunction about sending in their boats on cutting-out expeditions – something for which twenty years of similar activity in Europe more than prepared them. What directed the attention of the British to the coastal traffic was the very effectiveness of their blockade of Chesapeake Bay, which diverted trade southwards to North Carolina. The energetic Sir George Cockburn organised the first major attack, on shipping at Ocracoke. A surprise assault at dawn on 12 July 1813,

3

4

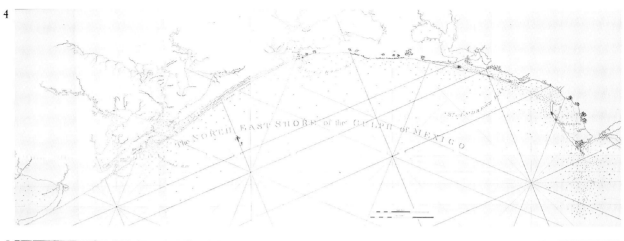

5

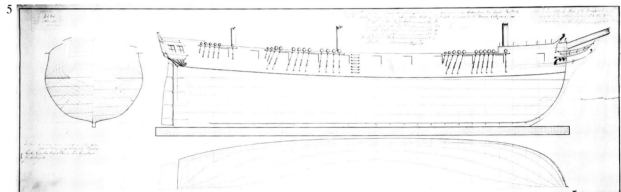

1. 'A Plan of the Harbour of St Augustine . . . Composed & Published . . . by J F W Des Barres, Esq', from *The Atlantic Neptune*, 1776. *NMM neg D9550-3*

2. 'Charleston, South Carolina, 1838'. Coloured aquatint by W J Bennett after an original by G Cooke. *NMM neg A103*

3. 'Capture of the *Anaconda* at Ocracoke, 12 July 1813', watercolour by Irwin Bevan (1852-1940), no date. *Mariners' Museum, Newport News ref QW333*

4. 'The North East Shore of the Gulph of Mexico', by J F W Des Barres, from *The Atlantic Neptune*, 1776. *NMM neg D9550-2*

5. Sheer draught of the *Hermes*, dated February 1810. *NMM neg DR2926*

6. 'Plan Shewing the Attack made by a British Squadron on Fort Bowyer on Mobile Pt', map from Henry Adams, *History of the United States*, Vol 8 (New York 1891), after a contemporary original by Major A Lacarriere Latour, Jackson's chief engineer. *Chatham collection*

7. 'Attack on Fort Bowyer, 15 September 1814', watercolour by Irwin Bevan (1852-1940), no date. *Mariners' Museum, Newport News ref QW393*

8. 'Armide, Seahorse and Sophie off Mobile, 8 December 1815 [sic]', watercolour by Irwin Bevan (1852-1940), no date. *Mariners' Museum, Newport News ref QW418*

6

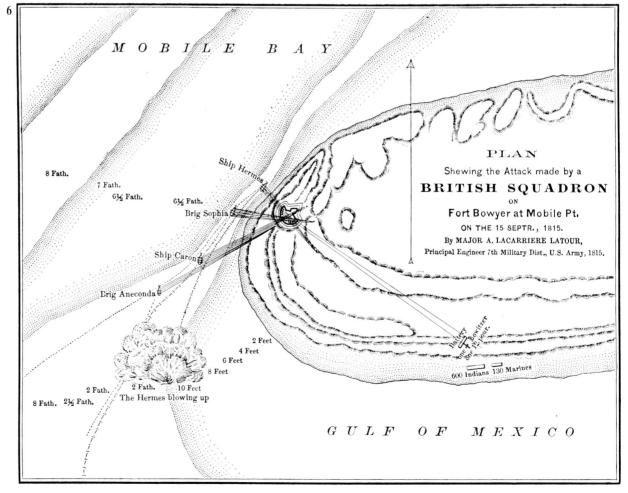

MOBILE BAY

PLAN
Shewing the Attack made by a
BRITISH SQUADRON
ON
Fort Bowyer at Mobile Pt.
ON THE 15 SEPTR., 1815.
By MAJOR A. LACARRIERE LATOUR,
Principal Engineer 7th Military Dist., U.S. Army, 1815.

GULF OF MEXICO

7

under the cover of Congreve rockets, achieved complete surprise, and among the shipping captured were the large privateer brig *Anaconda* and the letter-of-marque schooner *Atlas* (3).

With the arrival of the new British commander, Admiral Cochrane, in March 1814 the emphasis in southern strategy shifted to the Gulf of Mexico, where the British hoped to seize the lower reaches of the Mississippi, and perhaps even drive the Americans out of Louisiana and the Floridas by establishing separate states. Even with the European war drawing to a close, it was beyond their immediate resources, and discussions were opened with the Creek and Choctaw Indians, who might be persuaded to undergo a brief course of European-style military training. The principal target was eventually New Orleans, which the British hoped to hold as a bargaining chip at the peace negotiations.

Between the Spanish port of Pensacola (4), which was open to the British as a base, and New Orleans the only major American force was at Mobile. This had only been taken by the US from Spain in April 1813, and was still poorly prepared for defence. Cochrane favoured Mobile as the starting point for the New Orleans operation, but to gain access to Mobile Bay it was necessary to eliminate Fort Bowyer on the point. A new work of earth and logs, it was not expected to offer much resistance, and Cochrane sent only two small 20-gun ships, *Hermes* (5) and *Carron*, supported by two brigs, *Sophie* and *Childers*.

The attack on 15 September 1814 was one of those fiascos that persuade naval officers that ships should not attack forts (6). Only two vessels could get close enough, and after more than two hours of bombardment at short range – the ships were only armed with carronades – to no visible effect, the *Hermes* had her cable shot away, drifted out of station and ran firm aground. When every effort to free her failed, she was set on fire and abandoned by her crew (7).

The only US Navy forces available in any numbers in the southern theatre were the despised Jeffersonian gunboats, but they possessed nuisance value if nothing stronger. Off Mobile in December 1814, two of them fired on the frigates *Armide* and *Seahorse* and sloop *Sophie*, assembling for the expedition against New Orleans, and had to be chased off by boats of the squadron (8).

8

The New Orleans campaign

THE ATTACK on New Orleans, perhaps the richest city on the American continent (1), had been planned since January 1814, but the unhealthy summer climate and the hurricane season in August and September ruled out any amphibious operations until early December. On 22 November, Vice-Admiral Alexander Cochrane arrived in Negril Bay, Jamaica, aboard his flagship the *Tonnant*, to begin assembling the forces for the campaign. As well as fresh troops from Europe, two black regiments from Jamaica were also to be taken to garrison the city during the summer, making up a total land force of approximately 7500 men.

Although the American commander Andrew Jackson was aware that an attack was imminent, he did not know exactly where the enemy would land. Thinking that the British would prefer to come ashore in Mobile Bay, Jackson had concentrated the bulk of his forces there, leaving smaller detachments to cover other possible sites (2). Of his naval forces, five gunboats commanded by Lieutenant Thomas ap Catesby Jones had been sent to Lake Borgne in the approaches to the Mississippi. On 13 December Cochrane's fleet arrived off Lake Borgne, the admiral being aware of Jackson's concentration at Mobile, and consequently making a direct approach to the city up the bayous.

The British ships could not reach the American gunboats in the shallows, so a boat attack was decided upon. Catesby Jones's gunboats had themselves run aground, and were stuck fast. On 14 December, forty-two boats from the fleet, each armed with a carronade in the bows, carrying 1200 sailors and Royal Marines under Commander Nicholas Lockyer of the *Sophie*, 18, rowed up the lake, against the current, to engage the American squadron. Lockyer halted his boats just out of gunshot from the enemy to allow his men to rest and eat some breakfast after their exertions, before commencing his attack at 11.10am. Despite the considerable armament of the American gunboats (totalling three 32-pounders, two 24-pounders, twenty-two 6-pounders, four 12-pounder carronades, two 5in howitzers and twelve swivels), all five had been captured by 12.30pm, at the cost of 17 British killed and 77 wounded, including Commander Lockyer, whose initial attempt to board ap Catesby Jones's flagship had been beaten off (3). American losses totalled 10 killed, 35 wounded and 86 captured. Jackson's naval forces had been reduced to the single gunboat *Carolina* and the sloop *Louisiana*, and Cochrane was now free to act as he wished. Helped by Spanish fishermen, who were no friends to the Americans, the British made their initial landings in

1. 'New Orleans taken from the opposite side a short distance above the middle or Picayume Ferry', coloured aquatint engraved by W J Bennett after an original by A Mondolli, published by Henry J Megarey, 1841.
NMM ref PA10328

2. 'Map of New Orleans and Adjacent Country', by John Melish, 1815, reproduced in Sir Charles P Lucas, *The Canadian War of 1812* (London 1906). *Chatham collection*

3. 'The Gallant Attack and Capture of the American Gun Boats in Lake Borgne by the Boats of the Squadron under the Command of Captain N Lockyer . . .', coloured lithograph after an original by Lt T M Williams, published by Charles Joseph, no date. *NMM neg 1400*

1

bayou Bienvenue, less than 20 miles from the city of New Orleans, on the night of 22 December, capturing the plantation of General Villeré further upstream.

The shallow waters of the Mississippi delta prevented the ships themselves proceeding up-river, and the entire landing operation and subsequent supply of the forces ashore had to be conducted in boats, with their crews having to row nearly 70 miles upstream. The troops had been initially mustered on Pea Island, an exposed and barren place, where many of the Jamaican troops died due to the unseasonably cold weather. The bad weather, poor living conditions and difficult supply situation took a heavy toll on the British forces. Edward Codrington wrote to his wife from the fishermen's village on 23 December:

> . . . about thirty miles from where the frigates were, we assembled the whole army, as a half-way house; but

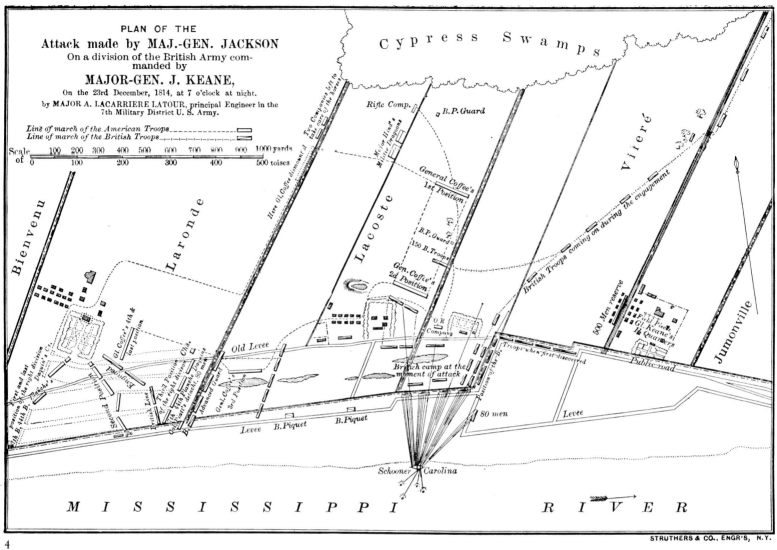

PLAN OF THE
Attack made by MAJ.-GEN. JACKSON
On a division of the British Army com-
manded by
MAJOR-GEN. J. KEANE,
On the 23rd December, 1814, at 7 o'clock at night.
by MAJOR A. LACARRIERE LATOUR, principal Engineer in the
7th Military District U. S. Army.

Line of march of the American Troops
Line of march of the British Troops

STRUTHERS & CO., ENGR'S, N.Y.

4

4. Jackson's counter-attack 23
December 1814, map from Henry
Adams, *History of the United States,* Vol 8
(New York 1891), after a
contemporary original by Major A
Lacarriere Latour, Jackson's chief
engineer.
Chatham collection

5. 'Sketch of the Position of the British
and American Forces, during the
Operations against New Orleans, from
23rd Dec 1814 to 18th Jan 1815', Plate
359 from *Naval Chronicle* 33 (1815).
NMM neg D9544

6. 'Bird's-eye view of the battle near
New Orleans, January 8, 1815 - from a
sketch by Latour, Jackson's chief
engineer', engraving from Benson J
Lossing, *Pictorial Field Book of the War of
1812* (New York 1869).
Chatham collection

the labour of effecting this with our small means (the boats alone), and transporting the necessary ammunition and provisions, is beyond description. To the distance, however, is to be added a severity of weather not characteristic of this latitude.

Alerted to the capture of the Villeré plantation, but still doubting that this was the main landing, given that only 1800 men were ashore, Jackson moved on the afternoon of the 23rd with his Tennesseeans and the 7th US Infantry to attack the British, together with his one remaining gunboat, the *Carolina,* whose commander Daniel T Patterson was ordered to take his ship down-river as quietly as possible until he was opposite the British camp. Jackson's plan, for a three-pronged night attack, was very ambitious for a force consisting largely of untried militia. There had been some skirmishing earlier in the afternoon, but as darkness fell the British were at ease as the *Carolina* slipped slowly down river towards them. The sentries mistook her for a supply ship from the fleet, until she anchored and fired a broadside of grapeshot into the camp, causing great confusion.

This was the signal for Jackson's men to attack (4). There was a confused battle, with both sides advancing, falling back and taking prisoners. The *Carolina* continued to fire into the camp until her crew heard the distinctive reports of American rifles, and then as ordered by Jackson they ceased fire to avoid hitting their own men. As British resistance began to stiffen, with the arrival of men of the 21st Foot who had been on their way from the fleet when the *Carolina's* first broadside had been heard and whose boats' crews had strained every muscle to get them to the field, Jackson decided to break off the action, falling back to the Rodriguez Canal. Casualties were quite heavy on both sides, the Americans losing 24 killed, 115 wounded and 74 missing, while the British lost 46 killed, 167 wounded and 64 missing. However, in the course of the operations, a further 200 British soldiers had died of exposure either on Pea Island or on the way to the landing site.

By nightfall on the 24th, the landings were complete,

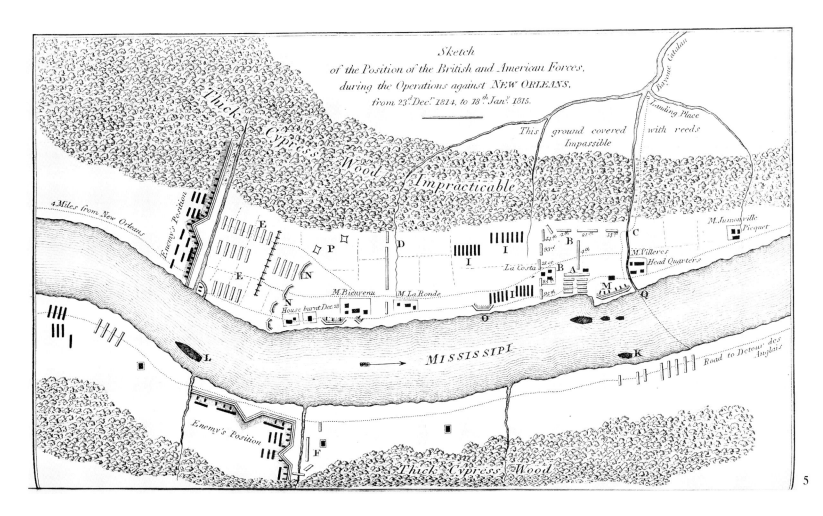

Sketch of the Position of the British and American Forces, during the Operations against NEW ORLEANS, from 23d. Decr. 1814, to 18th. Jany. 1815.

7

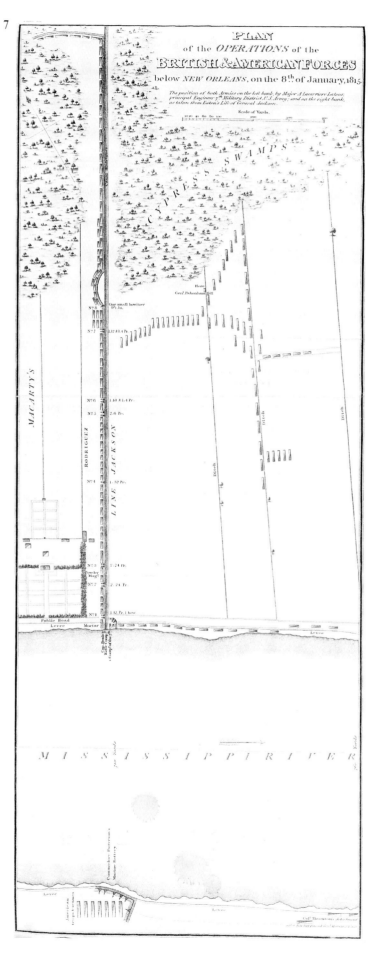

but meanwhile Jackson was busily fortifying the line of the Canal, which would be christened 'Line Jackson', now that he had confirmed this was the main landing. Thanks to an agreement with the Creole pirate and arms-dealer Jean Lafite, Jackson was well-supplied with powder and shot, and was able to equip his position with numerous guns and howitzers. Meanwhile the difficulties the British had in supplying their men, and the losses they had suffered on the night of the 23rd meant they felt themselves unable to take the offensive yet, giving Jackson the time he needed to drawn in his men and strengthen his fortifications.

On Christmas Day the commander of the British army, Major General Sir Edward Pakenham, arrived at the British camp, and it is reported that his first impression was that the force was in a bad position and should re-embark, but that officers who had been at Bladensburg and Baltimore persuaded him that a determined advance with the bayonet would drive the American militia off. His first action was to see to the destruction of the *Carolina*, which had caused such havoc during the night attack, with red-hot shot. Although the gunboat was burnt out, her crew managed to escape, even saving some of her guns, and the sloop *Louisiana* was towed out of danger by her boats. He then conducted a 'reconnaissance in force' against Line Jackson on the 28th, during which the *Louisiana* engaged in an artillery duel with his guns, silencing two 6-pounders and forcing his 9-pounder to withdraw. Despite some of his troops almost breaking the left flank of Jackson's position, Pakenham withdrew, seeing that he needed more artillery to destroy the fortifications.

While the British struggled to get sufficient guns and ammunition up the river and into position, Jackson continued to improve and extend his position, signalling his determination to fight by forcibly closing the State Legislature in the city when he heard that some in it wanted to surrender to the British. By 31 December, Line Jackson was furnished with twelve guns, with a further 24-pounder and two 18-pounders flanking the position from the west bank of the river (5). Jackson had overcome the problem of building positions for his guns on the marshy ground by using 150 requisitioned bales of cotton to build firm bases for them. The popular myth that the ramparts themselves were built of cotton bales is just that, a myth. The British were unable to build good positions for their guns, and when Pakenham attacked the American line again on 1 January 1815, in an artillery bombardment to silence the American guns, the difficulty of working naval 18-pounders on marshy ground, and the shortage of ammunition meant that it too was a failure. The Americans now felt they had seen off two British attacks, and their confidence was growing (as were their ramparts), while the failed attacks and dreadful conditions were sapping the strength and morale of the attackers.

Pakenham's plan for the final assault called for the West Bank battery to be taken first, as suggested by Admiral Cochrane, silencing a threat to the main attack's left, while also turning Line Jackson. However, to get the boats across the river fast enough, the canal had to be extended to cut the levee, but there were problems and the work was not completed on 6 January as planned. The attack was set for the 8th, but the vital attack on the West Bank battery was delayed by the collapse of the dam maintaining the water level in the newly-cut canal, stranding the boats that were to ferry the troops across the river. But the attack could no longer be delayed. Pakenham's men made a frontal attack on a now very strong position, still taking fire from the flank as well (6, 7). Casualties were heavy, and Pakenham was killed (8). Although the West Bank battery was eventually carried at the point of the bayonet, it was too late to affect the outcome of the battle, and Pakenham's successor, General Lambert, ordered the campaign abandoned, although on 12 February 600 British troops did succeed in taking Fort Bowyer at the entrance to Mobile Bay without much serious opposition (9). The next day news arrived that a peace treaty had been signed between the United States and Great Britain on 24 December, making this in some ways the most unnecessary campaign of the 'unnecessary war'.

The logistical problems the bayous of the Mississippi caused the British had given Jackson the time he needed to build the fortifications and site the guns required to

8

support his largely untrained troops, and prevented sufficient guns being brought up to breach those lines, and the delay to the attack on the West Bank battery had made failure almost certain. The example of the Battle of New Orleans, where field fortifications strongly supplied with artillery had allowed militia to defeat British regulars had a considerable influence on American military thinking after the war, an influence that could still be seen in the Civil War nearly 50 years later.

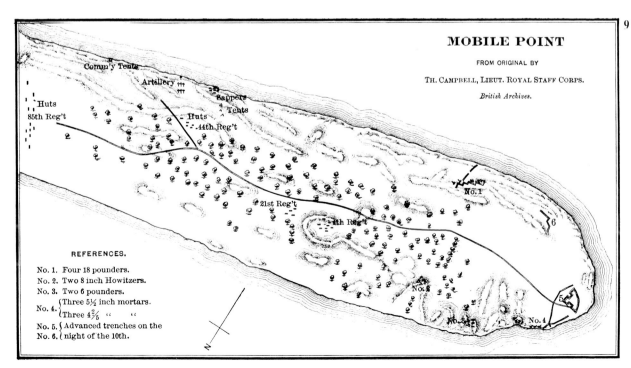

9

7. 'Plan of the Operations of the British & American forces below New Orleans, on the 8th of January, 1815', from William James, *Military Occurrences of the Late War . . .* (London 1818). *Chatham collection*

8. 'Battle of New Orleans and Death of Major General Pakenham', engraving by West published by J Yeager, Philadelphia. *Beverley R Robinson collection ref BRR80.26.20*

9. 'Mobile Point', map from Henry Adams, *History of the United States*, Vol 8 (New York 1891), after a contemporary original by Lt T Campbell, of the British army staff corps showing the operations leading to the capture of Fort Bowyer. *Chatham collection*

1

Prisoners of war

2

SAMUEL JOHNSON famously compared going to sea with being in jail – with the added chance of drowning. But most naval prisoners of war would gladly have accepted the risk of drowning to be out of jail, for no nation of this period seemed capable of looking after their charges properly. Although the treatment of prisoners was hedged about with civilised conventions, in practice crowded conditions, poor diet, little exercise, dirt and disease was the usual lot of those unfortunate enough to fall into the hands of their enemies. Eighteenth-century states were not well equipped, doctrinally or administratively, to provide any form of public welfare, and most criminal codes favoured quick and cheap punishments, whether corporal or capital, rather than incarceration. Therefore, the infrastructure to cope with large numbers of prisoners simply did not exist. Between 1803 and 1814 over 122,000 prisoners passed through Britain, the highest number held at any one time reaching 72,000 in 1814, so the scale of the problem was substantial.

The first thought of every government was to save on expense by exchanging prisoners, and an agreement between Britain and the United States was quickly made in August 1812, when an American agent for prisoners was appointed at Halifax. Exchanges were usually made on a like-for-like basis, but there were tables of equivalents for both navy and army ranks: these ranged from 60 men (seamen or soldiers) per admiral or full general, to 3 for midshipmen, ensigns or commanders of merchant ships. There had always been strains between conservative British governments and the radical rulers of France, and thanks to a victorious Royal Navy the British held far more prisoners than the French, so exchanges became more difficult. Relations with the Americans began well, but were threatened by the British insistence on pressing prisoners they regarded as their subjects and sending suspected deserters to England for investigation; for their part, the Americans were accused of 'persuading' British seamen to join their navy.

There were formal arrangements for the return of prisoners, usually in a ship designated a 'cartel' and given immunity from capture. By an agreement made between the two belligerents in May 1813, these were to be provided by government, and since the US had such a small navy three vessels were specially purchased for the task. However, the British government refused to acknowledge ad hoc agreements made at sea, whether by privateers or regular warships; commerce-raiders, embarrassed by large numbers of prisoners, liked to send them off in one of the prizes with the promise to follow exchange rules, but since the British had no interest in helping raiders stay at sea for longer, they objected to the practice.

At first most American prisoners were kept on Melville Island, a small fort and prison barracks some three miles from Halifax, but growing numbers led the British to ship many of them to England. Here their chances of a quick exchange were greatly reduced and the Americans protested against the practice. Part of the reason for the protest was the likely destination of the prisoners – the dreaded hulks that filled so many of the creeks and harbours of Britain (1). With such a large navy there was no shortage of old, worn-out warships, and such obsolescent vessels were widely used as hospitals, receiving ships and prisons. Dismantled and sprouting ugly shacks and shanties, their appearance was forbidding: one French prisoner described 'the hideous aspect of the old and smoky hulks, which seem the remains of vessels blackened by a recent fire. It is in these floating tombs that are buried alive prisoners of war – Danes, Swedes, Frenchmen, Americans, no matter' (2).

There were prisons on shore, but these were often barely converted medieval castles like Portchester and Edinburgh, although there were a few purpose-built establishments like Norman Cross and Dartmoor. Nevertheless, they were preferable to the hulks, according to one prisoner: 'The difference between the prisons and the hulks is very marked. There is no space for exercise, prisoners are crowded together, no visitors come to see them, and we are forgotten people.' Space was certainly at a premium in the typical hulk (3), even the orlop, barely above the waterline, being inhabited. Short spells of exercise were permitted in the waist, but most of a prisoner's day was spent below. The hulks had small naval crews, often commanded by old passed-over lieutenants, and garrisoned by superannuated soldiers. They were the responsibility of the Transport Board since 1795, which was supposedly one of the more efficient government bodies, but constant complaints about the quality and quantity of food, and above all about dirt and disease suggest otherwise. However, the British rejected the charge of deliberate cruelty and neglect: a survey taken during a specimen month in 1813 among 9227 prisoners in the Portsmouth hulks listed 139 on the sick list (or $1\frac{1}{2}$ per cent), and for the war as a whole the mortality rate averaged about 3 per cent, including the sporadic serious epidemics. Conditions were slightly better in the prisons ashore, but undoubtedly worse in the overseas hulks – Americans were particularly critical of those at Jamaica (4) – so the problem was probably one of resources and organisation rather than policy. There was money to made by the unscrupulous, and prisoners certainly suffered from corruption in the supply chain.

Officers, of course, were better treated. On giving their parole, they were allowed to lodge in towns, and to

3

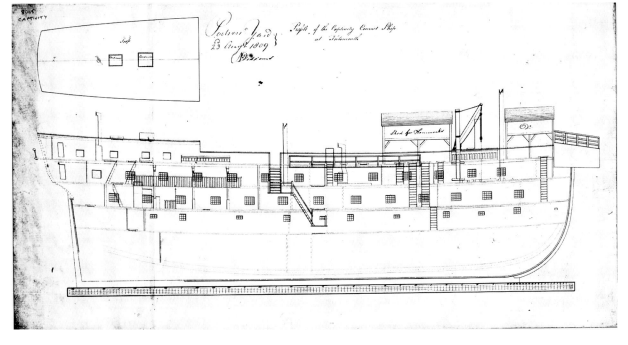

1. '18th century British dockyard and harbour', anonymous watercolour, no date. It is almost certainly Portsmouth, and may be the work of Duclos-Legris, a French prisoner in the *Prothee* from 1806 until 1814. *NMM ref PAH5193*

2. 'Prison Ship York in Portsmouth Harbour', etching by Hunts after an original by Edward William Cooke, no date. It is post-war and shows a convict ship, but it is similar in essential details to the hulks used for prisoners of war. *NMM ref PAG7012*

3. Draught of *Captivity* at Portsmouth, dated 23 August 1809. She was an old 64-gun ship, *Monmouth*, converted in 1796, and shows a typical arrangement. *NMM neg 47472*

4. 'Northern part of Port Royal Harbour, Jamaica', engraved by Baily after an original by 'J E 1806', published by Joyce Gold, London 31 July 1816. *NMM neg D9540*

5. 'Dartmoor Prison & English Barracks', coloured aquatint published by Ackermann Repository of Arts, 1 September 1810. *NMM neg 6498*

4

move with complete freedom within predetermined limits, although there was usually a curfew. They tended to be exchanged more rapidly, certainly between Britain and the United States, and in some cases they might be returned home directly, giving their word not to serve until formally exchanged. However, officers who broke their parole by trying to escape were then sent to join ordinary prisoners of war in the jails or hulks.

Conditions for prisoners of war actually deteriorated during the short duration of the Anglo-American war, and the root cause was political. In response to incidents like Captain Hardy's kidnapping of Joshua Penny (believed involved in a 'torpedo' plot to blow up his ship), President Madison himself ordered a British prisoner to be confined 'in the same state of degradation and suffering'. A round of retaliation and reprisal under-

mined many of the more civilised norms of behaviour towards prisoners for the rest of the war. As far as the British were concerned, the Americans were also rather more troublesome prisoners than other nationalities: as one of their number himself observed, 'The French were always busy in some little mechanical employ, or in gaming, or in playing the fool, but the Americans seemed to be on the rack of invention to escape.'

The lack of personal hygiene, petty crime and chronic gambling among the French was generally deprecated by the Americans, and the customs of democracy made their communities better organised and self-regulating. There was clearly no love lost between these companions in adversity, and there are recorded examples of pitched battles in prisons between the Americans and the French. Unofficially, the British attitude tended to favour the former, one commander of a hulk exclaiming that 'These Americans are the sauciest dogs I ever saw; but damn me if I can help liking them, nor can I ever hate men who are so like ourselves.' Unfortunately for the Americans, their rumbustious behaviour was their undoing, and in 1814 it was decided to concentrate them at Dartmoor, a new prison on what is possibly the bleakest spot in the whole of England (5). By September it housed about 3500 Americans.

Here they continued to plague the authorities for the rest of the war, but the worst incident occurred after the formal conclusion of hostilities. On 6 April 1815, frustrated by the slow pace of their repatriation, a number rioted, and the commandant, determined to teach them a lesson after weeks of unrest, ordered his troops to open fire. Five prisoners were killed and twenty-eight wounded, and although the British government was quick to condemn the action and to offer compensation, it was long remembered in America as a symbol of the tyranny of the whole prison regime.

5

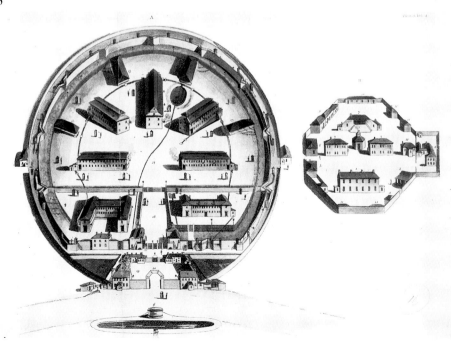

Postscript

1815 — THE HUNDRED DAYS

FOR THE latter half of 1814 Britain was the only European nation still at war, but the Treaty of Ghent bringing peace with the United States was signed on 24 December, and, allowing a few months for the news to reach the more distant quarters of the world, it promised a final end to more than two decades of conflict. Bonaparte had been exiled to rule a tiny kingdom based on the island of Elba, and the Great Powers were in congress to settle the future of post-war Europe. President Madison ratified the Ghent terms on 18 February, but from Britain's perspective this formal peace lasted less than a week. Escaping from Elba on the 24th, Bonaparte made a bold attempt to regain the throne of France, entering Paris to a rapturous welcome from most of the populace on 21 March. A hastily gathered allied army assembled at a little village outside Brussels, and on 18 June the Duke of Wellington fought a long defensive action until the arrival of General Blücher's Prussian army left the allies in possession of the field of Waterloo. Napol-

1

eon's abortive coup is known to history as The Hundred Days, and after the said three months Napoleon was again on the run.

The naval events of this period are necessarily few. In the West Indies, British naval forces supported the Bourbon governor of Martin-

ique and assisted royalist forces in capturing the Bonapartist island of Guadeloupe. Of purely ship-to-ship engagements, the *Rivoli*, 74 ran down and captured the frigate *Melpomène* in April off the Italian island of Ischia, but a more fiercely contended action was that between the

2

3

ships involved were the frigates *Menelaus* and *Havannah*, and the sloops *Fly* and *Ferret* and schooner *Sealark*.

It was fitting that the country, and indeed the military force, that had been his most implacable opponent should finally receive the surrender of Napoleon. After his attempts to reach America were thwarted by the British blockade, Napoleon finally gave himself up on 15 July to HMS *Bellerophon*, 74 lying in Basque Roads off Rochefort (3). The deposed emperor was later to tell a British naval officer that throughout his career wherever there was water to float a ship he had found the Royal Navy to thwart his ambition. *Bellerophon* was one of those ships, a veteran that had fought at the very first fleet battle of the French wars in 1794, that had helped Nelson destroy Napoleon's oriental dream at the Nile in 1798, and finally formed part of the force that annihilated the Franco-Spanish battlefleet at Trafalgar. Napoleon could not have chosen a better symbol of British seapower.

brig sloop *Pilot* and the French corvette *Légère* the day before Waterloo (1). The heavier French ship escaped after suffering considerable damage. A more satisfactory conclusion from a British point of view was achieved by a squadron led by the frigate *Rhin*, Captain Charles Malcolm, in an attack on a coastal convoy in the Breton port of Corigeou. In the kind of small-scale combined operation perfected by the Royal Navy in the preceding wars, the boats of the squadron and a landing party of marines stormed the defending battery, captured the escort of a brig, cutter and gunboat, and took possession of the whole convoy (2). The other

Captain Maitland of the *Bellerophon*, like all officers who might have taken Napoleon, had instructions to return with all possible speed to the nearest English port. Initially he anchored in Torbay, and then sailed to Plymouth Sound, where the man vilified in the British press for over a decade as the 'scourge of humanity' became a major tourist attraction, regularly to be seen pacing the quarterdeck in his characteristic hat and green coat (4). In the meantime, the British Government determined that his place of exile had to be far distant, so that he could not plot with his followers nor attempt another escape, and their choice fell on the remote south Atlantic island of St Helena. The island, a mere ten miles by eight, belonged to the East India Company, by whom it was used as a way-station on the long voyage to and from the Indies, and it was both fortified and settled, although lacking many of the comforts of a more civilised locale (5). One Frenchman described it as 'the most isolate, the most inaccessible, the least attackable, and the most unsocial place in the world.'

Napoleon was shocked and angered to discover his fate, but the convoy to carry him south was already preparing at Plymouth. Sir George Cockburn, fresh from his triumphs in America and newly appointed Commander-in-Chief on the Cape of Good Hope station, was

4

5

deputed to act as jailer, and on 8 August off Berry Head Napoleon was transferred to his flagship, another 74, the *Northumberland* (6). Napoleon considered himself a sovereign who had abdicated and expected those around him to treat him as such, but in Cockburn he met his match. The British had never acknowledged Napoleon as legitimate emperor, and although it piqued him much, he was never addressed as anything except 'General Bonaparte'; Cockburn even banned his officers from removing their hats when they addressed the 'General'. Bonaparte retaliated by drinking vast quantities of Cockburn's claret.

When the convoy arrived off the island on 15 October nothing had been done to prepare for the new resident, but it was soon decided that he and his suite should occupy the lieutenant governor's house, Longwood (7). Here Bonaparte lived out the rest of his exile without again disturbing the peace of Europe until his death in 1821.

In the meantime the victorious allies decided the future relations of Europe at the Congress of Vienna, from which there emerged a concert of major countries dedicated to preserving the status quo and the existing balance of power. Britain, sensitive to the charge of being overly powerful levelled in some capitals, returned to France most of her colonies taken since 1793. The exceptions were Tobago and St Lucia in the West Indies, and Mauritius, the Seychelles and

6

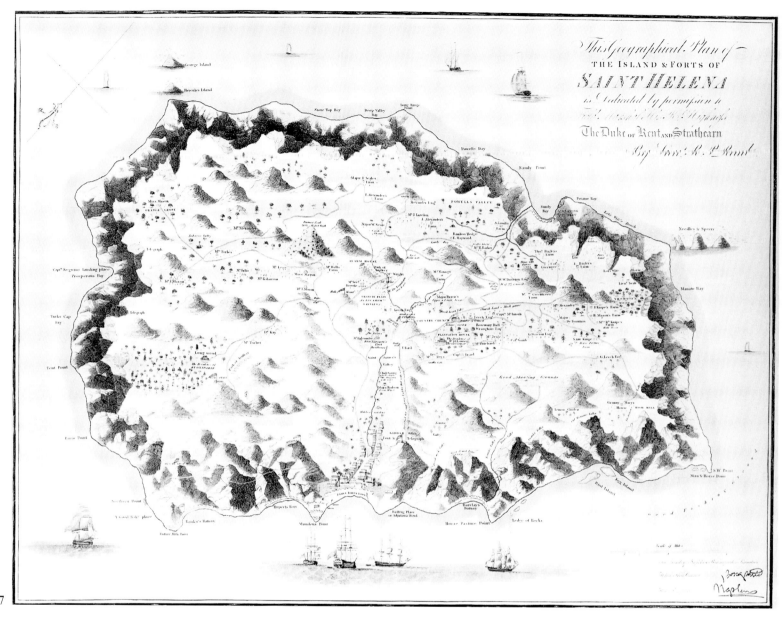

7

the Indian Ocean islands, but she also retained the ex-Dutch colony of the Cape. These reflected the British concern to secure her worldwide trade, denying potential commerce-raiding bases to her enemies and providing a string of bases for her own forces. Unfettered by entanglements on the Continent, Britain was free to develop her commercial wealth, derived from an accelerating industrial revolution and – now that American competition had been temporarily eliminated – domination of world trade. From this developed the Empire on which the sun never set, and the *Pax Britannica* that protected it.

All this was, and had been, achieved by seapower. In the later years of the war against Napoleon it was the 'Spanish ulcer' in the Peninsula and the final act at Waterloo that filled the headlines, but it was only naval and commercial power that had allowed Britain to continue the struggle when France had knocked out all her other opponents, and to subsidise the huge continental armies necessary to defeat the great military genius on the battlefield.

---

1. 'Situation of the Pilot & La Legere, at the close of the action on the 17 June 1815', brown aquatint engraved by Baily, published by Joyce Gold, 31 December 1818.
NMM ref PAD5860

2. 'An attack made by a squadron under the command of Captain Charles Malcolm, of HMS Rhin, on the 18th of July 1815, upon a convoy in the harbour of Corigeou (Bretagne)', coloured aquatint and etching by Charles Rosenberg after an original by William John Huggins, no date.
NMM neg A4890

3. 'Embarquement de Bonaparte a Bord du Bellerophon', aquatint engraved by Jean Pierre Marie Jazet, no date.
NMM ref PAD6031

4. 'The Surrender of Napoleon to Great Britain . . . on board the Bellerophon . . . Supplement to 'Holly Leaves' the Christmas number of The Illustrated Sporting & Dramatic News, December 1910', photogravure after an original by William Quiller Orchardson, December 1910.
NMM ref PAH8156

5. 'A view of the Island of St Helena, to the Honourable the Court of Directors of the East India Company, this engraving by . . . Edward Orme (with inset views of Fairyland and Friars Rock)', coloured aquatint and etching by J Clark and J Hamble after an original by G H Bellasis, published by Edward Orme, 4 June 1806.
NMM neg A1212

6. 'Transfèrement de Bonaparte du Bellérophon à bord du Northumberland, le 8 Âout 1815', coloured engraving by Bovinet after an original by Baugean, no date.
NMM ref PAF7994

7. 'This Geographical Plan of the Island & Forts of St Helena is dedicated . . . to Field Marshal His Royal Highness The Duke of Kent and Strathearn by Lieut R P Read', coloured etching by R Kirkwood after an original by Lt R P Read, published by J & M Rippin, 4 June 1817.
NMM ref PA10413

Notes on Artists, Printmakers and their Techniques

These brief notes cover most of the artists and print-makers who appear in the volume, as well as the principal printing techniques. They are intended only to put the artists in context with the period and readers wanting further information on their art and lives should turn to the sources; in many cases there is little more to tell. This volume contains a number of sketches and paintings by the officers and men who served in the Royal Navy at the time, but details of their lives have been omitted if they did not pursue an artistic career, since little or nothing is known of their work.

Andrews, George Henry *(1816-1898)* English watercolourist of marine subjects who was trained as an engineer. He also did drawings for a number of journals such as the *Illustrated London News* and the *Graphic*.

Aquatint A variety of etching *(qv)* invented in France in the 1760s. It is a tone rather than a line process and is used principally to imitate the appearance of watercolour washes. The process involves the etching of a plate with acid through a porous ground of powdered resin. The acid bites small rings around each resin grain and gradations of tone are achieved by repetition of the biting process and the protection of areas of the plate with varnish.

Barralet, John James *(1747-1815)* Irish water-colour painter and engraver who emigrated to America and settled in Philadelphia where he pro-duced a body of work consisting mainly of land-scapes, portraits and historical subjects.

Baugean, Jean-Jérôme *(1764-1819)* French painter and prolific engraver best known for his collection of shipping prints, *Collection de toutes des Especes de Batiments*, which went through numerous editions in the early nineteenth century. Also well known is his depiction of 'The Embarkation of Napoleon onboard *Bellérophon*'.

Bevan, Irwin John *(1852-1940)* Welsh-born book illustrator, naval historian and painter who depicted scenes from American naval history from the age of sail (see pages 72-73).

Birch, Thomas *(1799-1851)* English marine and landscape painter, particularly of snow scenes, who emigrated to America with his father in 1794. He worked as a portraitist and landscape painter, but he is now best known for his depictions of the naval actions in the War of 1812.

Bowen, Abel *(1790-1850)* American painter, wood engraver, lithographer and publisher. In 1816 he published *The Naval Monument* which contained many War of 1812 scenes engraved by himself.

Burley, David William *(fl early twentieth century)* English watercolour painter of sea- and landscapes, born in Kent.

Cartwright, Joseph *(1789-1829)* English landscape and marine painter and member of the Society of British Artists who was also a naval paymaster. He was made marine painter to the Duke of Clarence and painted a number of naval scenes, particularly of actions in the Mediterranean, including 'The Battle of the Nile' and 'The *Euryalus* Frigate Becalmed in the Channel of Corfu'.

Corné, Michaele-Felice *(1752-1832)* American painter, born in Italy, who lived and painted on the East Coast. From 1807 to 1822 he lived in Boston where he was particularly noted for his paintings of the ships and naval battles of the War of 1812.

Dodd, Robert *(1748-1815)* English marine and landscape painter and successful engraver and pub-lisher, best known for his portrayals of the naval battles of the Revolutionary American and French wars. He is also known for his formal portraits of ships in which three views are included in a single image.

Drypoint Intaglio *(qv)* engraving *(qv)* technique in which the image is scratched into a copper plate with a steel needle, which is held like a pen. Ridges – burr – are created around the lines which give dry-point its characteristic fuzzy effect. The burr is deli-cate and quickly wears away during the printing process so that print runs are short.

Edwards, Joseph *(fl mid-nineteenth century)* English line and mezzotint engraver of portraits and hist-orical subjects after his contemporaries.

Edwin, David *(1776-1841)* Stipple engraver, born in England at Bath, who after studying engraving in England and Holland moved permanently to America in 1797. His engravings of some of the portraits of Gilbert Stuart *(qv)* made his reputation in his chosen country.

Engraving The process of cutting an image into a block or metal plate which is used for printing by using a number of techniques such as aquatint *(qv)*, drypoint *(qv)*, etching *(qv)*, or mezzotint *(qv)*. An engraving is a print made from the engraved plate.

Etching An intaglio *(qv)* process by which the design is made by drawing into a wax ground applied over the metal plate. The plate is then submerged in acid which bites into it where it has been exposed through the wax. An etching is a print made from an etched plate.

Garneray, Ambroise-Louis *(1783-1857)* French marine painter whose early life was spent at sea in the French navy and ashore as a shipwright in Mauritius, before being taken prisoner by the British in 1806. Confined on a prison ship at Portsmouth he made an income painting portraits. Returning to France in 1814 he exhibited his first shipping scenes in 1815. He is probably best known for his work illustrating the ports of France which was published in *Vues des côtes de France dans l'océan et dans le Mediterranée* (1823).

Haghe, Louis *(1806-1895)* Belgian watercolour painter and lithographer who moved to England in 1823 where he founded the firm of Day & Haghe. He produced mainly historical and topographical views after his own designs and those of his con-temporaries, such as his four plates depicting the 'Engagement between the *Shannon* and the *Chesapeake*' after Schetky.

Havell, Robert *(1769-1832)* English aquatint *(qv)* engraver of topographical views as well as transport and military subjects, after his contemporaries and his own designs. He was probably the uncle of Daniel Havell *(fl early nineteenth century)* and the father of Robert Havell (1793-1878), both also prominent engravers of topographical views and historical subjects.

Hayes, Edwin *(1819-1904)* English marine water-colourist, born in Bristol, who spent his early years in Ireland where he developed his skill as a painter of seascapes. He exhibited at the Royal Academy and by the mid-1850s his address was given as Greenwich.

Huggins, John William *(1781-1845)* English marine painter who spent his early years at sea with the East India Company until around 1814 when he established himself as a painter. He produced an enormous number of ship portraits, many of them engraved by his son-in-law, Edward Duncan, as well as a number of large-scale naval battles, in particular the Battle of Trafalgar. In 1836 he was made marine painter to King William IV.

Hullmandel, Charles Joseph *(1789-1850)* English printer and publisher of landscapes and topographical scenes, and one of the first practising lithographers in England. He is credited with a whole range of lithographic developments in the twenty years after his first plate was produced in 1818, and was a central figure in early nineteenth-century lithography.

Intaglio printing The method of printing using metal plates which can be worked as aquatints (*qv*), drypoints (*qv*), engravings (*qv*), etchings (*qv*), or mezzotints (*qv*). Once the lines have been made on the plate, by whatever method, printing is done by pressing damp paper hard enough against the plate so that the ink is lifted out of the incised lines. This explains why prints done by this method have slightly raised lines, a distinct characteristic of the process.

Jazet, Jean-Pierre *(1788-1871)* French line and aquatint engraver who produced historical and military scenes after his contemporaries, popularising many of the depictions of the First Empire.

Lane, Samuel *(1780-1872)* English portrait painter, born in Kings Lynn, who studied under Joseph Farington and Sir Thomas Lawrence. He established a very successful studio and acquired a reputation for the verisimilitude of his portraits.

Lithograph A print made by drawing a design on porous limestone with a greasy material. The stone is then wetted and ink applied to it which adheres only to the drawn surfaces. Paper is then pressed to the stone for the final print. Lithography was discovered only at the very end of the eighteenth century but quickly developed into a highly flexible medium.

Martin, William *(1817-1867)* American marine and landscape painter who spent most of his life in Philadelphia. He painted many of the sailing warships of the US Navy.

Meyer, Henry *(1782-1847)* English aquatint and mezzotint engraver and painter of portraits and decorative subjects.

Mezzotint A type of engraving (*qv*) in which the engraving plate is first roughened with a tool known as a rocker. The rough surface holds the ink and appears as a black background and the design is then burnished onto it by scraping away the rough burr to create lighter tones and by polishing the surface for highlights. Thus the artist works from dark to light, creating a tonal effect which was particularly suited to reproducing paintings and had its heyday in eighteenth-century England.

Monkhouse, W *(fl mid-nineteenth century)* English lithographer of landscapes, based in York.

Neagle, John *(1796-1865)* American portrait painter, born in Boston, who settled in Philadelphia.

Page, William *(1811-1885)* American painter of landscapes, historical subjects and portraits, who worked in Florence and Rome between 1849 and 1860.

Pocock, Nicholas *(1740-1821)* Foremost English marine painter of his day. He was apprenticed in the shipbuilding yard of Richard Champion in Bristol before being appointed to command the barque *Lloyd*, setting sail to Charleston in 1768. This was the first of a number of voyages for which there are illustrated log books, some of which are at the National Maritime Museum. He was present at the West Indies campaign in 1778 or '79, and completed an oil painting in 1780, receiving helpful criticism from Sir Joshua Reynolds. Thereafter he devoted himself to his art and painted numerous depictions of the struggles with Revolutionary France

Pocock, Lt William Innes *(1783-1863)* English marine painter and a son of Nicholas Pocock (*qv*). Like his father he went to sea in the merchant service before spending ten years in the Royal Navy from 1805 to 1814, during which time he recorded incidents in sketch books, many of which are held by the National Maritime Museum. His oil paintings are very much in his father's style and suggest that he spent time as his pupil.

Ropes, George *(1788-1819)* American painter of primitive ship portraits and naval battles. Deaf and dumb, he worked from Salem and his work bears a passing resemblance to that of his teacher, Michaele-Felice Corné (*qv*).

Rosenberg, Charles *(fl late eighteenth to mid-nineteenth centuries)* English aquatint engravers, father and son.

Schetky, John Christian *(1778-1874)* Scottish marine painter from a cultured background whose early interest in the sea led to his joining the frigate *Hind* in 1792. He soon returned to land and in 1801 embarked on a continental tour. He was drawing master at the Royal Military College, Great Marlow, and later Professor of Drawing at the Royal Naval College, Portsmouth, where he remained for 25 years. His painted subjects ranged from ship portraits to reconstructions of naval battles of the Nelsonic era. He continued to paint until his death at the age of 95.

Serres, Dominic the elder *(1722-1793)* French marine painter, born in Gascony, who, after running away to sea, was captured by a British frigate in 1758 and taken to England. He became a pupil of Charles Brooking and was a founder member of the Royal Academy. Though a Frenchman he became one of the most successful marine painters of the Seven Years War and of the American Revolutionary War.

Serres, John Thomas *(1759-1825)* English marine painter and elder son of Dominic Serres, the elder. Though he painted a number of dramatic naval battle scenes in the manner of de Loutherbourg whom he greatly admired, his main activity was drawing the coasts of England, France and Spain in his capacity as Marine Draughtsman to the Admiralty. A selection were subsequently published in *Serres' Little Sea Torch* (1801). He died in a debtors' prison as a result of the pretensions and wild extravagances of his wife, the self-styled 'Princess Olive of Cumberland'.

Seymour, Samuel *(1796-1823)* American landscape painter and engraver from Philadelphia, probably best known for the illustrations of his expeditions to the Rocky Mountains and the upper reaches of the Mississippi.

Smythe, William *(fl mid to late nineteenth century)* British naval officer and topographical artist who accompanied Captain Beechey's expedition to the Bering Strait in 1825. His name is usually rendered without the final 'e'.

Steel, James W *(1799-1879)* American engraver of portraits, landscapes and historical subjects. He later became a banknote engraver.

Strickland, William *(1788-1854)* American architect, painter, engraver and draftsman who supplemented his income during his early years by scene painting, surveying and painting and engraving.

Stuart, Gilbert Charles *(1755-1828)* American portrait painter, son of a Scottish snuff grinder. He was apprenticed to the Scottish painter Cosmo Alexander and accompanied him from Rhode Island to Scotland in 1771. He then worked in London under Benjamin West where he developed his portrait style. After fleeing to Ireland to escape his debts he returned to America in 1793 and his portrait of George Washington was to make him America's leading and most influential portrait painter.

Thresher, George (*fl early to mid-nineteenth century*) American marine painter who established an academy of writing, drawing and painting in Philadelphia, having previously taught in Europe.

Tobin, George (*fl late eighteenth century*) English naval officer and amateur watercolourist.

Walters, Lieutenant Samuel, RN (*1778-1834*) Accomplished amateur painter who trained as a shipwright before joining the Royal Navy in 1796. He retired on half pay in 1815, and little is known of his life after that date. He is not to be confused with his nephew of the same name (*qv*), who was a far more distinguished painter.

Walters, Samuel (*1811-1882*) English marine painter, born at sea, the son of Miles Walters, who had a framing business in Liverpool. Samuel moved to London in 1845 but his lack of success there drove him back to Liverpool where, as a ship painter during Liverpool's swift development as a major port, he at last prospered. As well as his ship portraits he also painted accomplished seascapes and coastal scenes.

Weingaertner, Adam (*fl mid-nineteenth century*) American lithographer of the firm Nagel & Weingaertner of New York.

Whitcombe, Thomas (*born c1752*) English marine painter who, like Pocock (*qv*) and Luny (*qv*), was celebrated for his huge output of paintings depicting the French Revolutionary Wars. He contributed some fifty plates to the *Naval Achievements of Great Britain* and also painted numerous works for engravings. There is no record of his death.

Williams, Henry (*1787-1839*) American portrait painter, miniaturist and engraver, and the author of *The Elements of Drawing*, who lived in Boston all his life.

INDEX

All ships are Royal Navy unless otherwise indicated in brackets after the name.

190